Date Due

Also by Bruce Aidells and Denis Kelly

Hot Links & Country Flavors:
    Sausages in American Regional Cooking

REAL BEER & GOOD EATS

REAL BEER & GOOD EATS

The Rebirth of America's Beer and Food Traditions

BRUCE AIDELLS
& DENIS KELLY

Alfred A. Knopf   New York   1992

This Is a Borzoi Book Published by Alfred A. Knopf, Inc.

Library of Congress Cataloging-in-Publication Data
Aidells, Bruce.
Real beer & good eats: the rebirth of America's beer and food traditions / by
Bruce Aidells and Denis Kelly. — 1st ed. p.   cm. — (The Knopf cooks
American series ; 11)
Includes bibliographical references.
ISBN 0-394-58267-5
1. Beer—United States. 2. Cookery, American. I. Kelly, Denis, [date]. II. Title.
III. Title: Real beer and good eats. IV. Series.
TP577.A37   1992
641.8'73'0973—dc20
91-37159 CIP

Manufactured in the United States of America
First Edition

Acknowledgments

The authors would like to thank the following for their help and encouragement: Alan Eames, author of *A Beer Drinker's Companion;* Vince Cottone, columnist for the Seattle *Post-Intelligencer;* Charles Finkel of Merchant du Vin; Michael Jackson, author of *The New World Guide to Beer;* Will Anderson, author of *Beer USA;* Fritz Maytag and Linda Rowe of Anchor Brewing; Ken Pavichevich of Pavichevich Brewing; Tom Dalldorf of *The Celebrator;* Byron Burch, author of *Quality Brewing;* Jerry Goldstein of Los Angeles Brewing Company; our agent, Martha Casselman; Judith Jones and Kathy Zuckerman at Knopf; William Brand of the Oakland *Tribune;* Nancy Oakes, Kathryn Kelly, and Loni Kuhn, along with other brewers, chefs, and friends—too many to mention—who helped us along the way.

CONTENTS

REAL BEER & GOOD EATS

BEER: THE DRINK THAT GLADDENS THE HEART—FROM NINKASI TO SPUDS MCKENZIE

What makes your heart feel wonderful,
Makes also our heart feel wonderful.
Our liver is happy, our heart is joyful.
May Ninkasi live together with you.

—SUMERIAN "HYMN TO NINKASI,"
GODDESS OF BEER (1800 B.C.)

This Bud's for you!

—BEER AD, MONDAY NIGHT FOOTBALL,
1991

What is it about beer that gladdens the heart and raises up the spirit? It's not just the alcohol—a straight shot of hooch would do that as well. There's something else that makes beer a substance like no other: a golden glass glowing in the afternoon sun, a collar of white foam, the sweet smell of malt and the tang of hops on the palate, hints of dust and the harvest earth in the aftertaste.

Wine is perhaps more complex, somehow more noble, and surrounded with mystery. Fine liqueurs, aged cognacs, and single malt whiskies have more depth and power. But beer is ultimately satisfying and complete, almost restful. Other drinks excite frenzy, contemplation, adoration, awe. Beer relaxes and creates contentment, drawing friends and neighbors together.

Beer is the beverage of celebration, of the shared harvest and communal prosperity. It's what we drink at town festivals and picnics in the park, beach parties and block parties, family reunions and friendly get-togethers. From the Goddess of Beer to Spuds McKenzie, on Oktoberfest or the Fourth of July, at Sunday afternoon baseball or Alderman

Riley's reelection, beer is the drink of parties and holidays, the ritual substance that unites us all.

And beer in America is always tied to food. A hot dog at the stadium or clambake on Cape Cod, a barbecue with the neighbors or the Sheboygan bratwurst festival: all are incomplete without foaming mugs of beer to accompany the feast.

Beer itself is, after all, a form of food. When asked about taxing beer, one of our founding fathers objected, "Sirrah, it is liquid bread!" And indeed it is: The first food purity laws date from the Babylonian law-giver Hammurabi's time and condemn brewers who make bad beer to be thrown into the river. The Bavarian Rheinheitsgebot (Purity Law) of 1516 is still in effect and ensures that only grain, yeast, hops, and pure water be used to brew beer.

Beer is basically fermented grain and is nourishing in and of itself. Early sailors carried it aboard ship to drink in place of foul water and to prevent scurvy. It is said that beer, bread, and onions built Egypt's pyramids. The Vikings brewed a special Portage Ale to give them strength for the great portage around Kiev. Beer was an essential part of the diet of the European peasant from time immemorial. And it was, especially in northern Europe, England, and early America, the beverage of choice at the table.

In colonial America beer was drunk at breakfast, lunch, and dinner, and a ration of beer was part of the everyday wages of the agricultural laborer. Beer accompanied everything from the plowman's simple lunch of bread and cheese to the most elaborate banquet menus in New York, Boston, and Philadelphia.

Most everyday or table beer in England and America in those days was of the small beer category, moderate in alcohol and light in body. Strong ales were served in taverns and at village celebrations, and special brews were often made for weddings (Bride Ale), christenings, funerals, and seasonal festivals (Christmas Ale, Wassail). Sometimes flavorings and spices like nutmeg, cinnamon, and cardamom were added. We even found an old recipe for Cock Ale, which called for a rooster to be beaten in a bag and put into the mash, presumably to add more body and character, perhaps to stiffen the resolve of aging and feeble bridegrooms.

In recent years, beer in America has become an overly carbonated, watered-down version of this once-nourishing beverage. Beers that are so light as to be almost tasteless are the norm. Beers are too often bought because of image, not flavor, and there is virtually no real difference in style or character among most mass-produced brews. Many American beers would have been classified as very small indeed by any honest ale conner—the worthy citizen who inspected alehouses and certified the beer in old England.

But there is hope for American beer. All over the country, small craft breweries, microbreweries, and brew pubs are springing up, producing ales and lagers with real flavor and individual character. Inspired by the wildly successful Campaign for Real Ale (CAMRA) in England—a consumer movement that has resurrected traditional and pub-brewed ales in the British Isles over the past few years—a new generation of American brewers is turning out rich and full-bodied brews that stand up to the heartiest foods. In brew pubs and tiny breweries, in larger regional and craft breweries, and even in the special premium beers made by the huge national breweries, we are seeing a genuine beer renaissance in America.

Great beers can suddenly be found all over America from the hoppy full-bodied ales of the West Coast to the complex and malty lagers of the Midwest and East. And these exciting, hand-crafted beers are being paired with both new and traditional dishes created by the country's finest regional cooks. Some of America's best chefs are talking about a "beer cuisine" and are creating restaurants that explore the fascinating interaction of fine beer and good food. In this book we take you on a beer and food odyssey, seeking out the excellent, individually styled beers being made in America today and describing hearty foods and sumptuous feasts worthy of accompanying them.

A SHORT HISTORY
OF BEER

From the very beginning, human beings have found some way to make drinks with a kick to them, using everything from cactus sap to the morning's porridge. Brillat-Savarin, gourmande and author of *La physiologie du goût* (The physiology of taste), defines mankind as "that animal that fears the future and has a desire for fermented beverages." In fact, some writers have argued recently that the beginnings of agriculture—the growing and gathering of grains and the cultivation of fruit and the vine—were as much for the purpose of making alcoholic beverages as for food.

The process of fermentation, while chemically quite complex, is in practice very simple. All that is needed is some sort of sugar, liquid, and yeast. Yeast acts to break down the sugar into ethyl alcohol and carbon dioxide to produce fermented beverages such as wine, mead, or beer.

The sugar can be derived from various sources: fruit juices, as in wine; the sap of trees and other plants, as in palm toddy, *pulque* (from the maguey cactus), maple or birch beer; honey, as in mead; or starches that are converted to sugar before fermentation, as in beer, ale, *sake,* African *pombe,* Native American *chicha* and *tiswin.* The liquid is either natural juice or sap, or water that is added to honey, dried grains, corn, or rice. Yeast is present just about everywhere on just about everything and will find its way into virtually any sugary solution to begin fermentation spontaneously.

As far as anyone can guess, the first fermented beverages were created by accident some time in the late Stone Age: Berry juice or gruel was left in a jar and later drunk, with seemingly magical results. Soon after, mankind became sophisticated about its drinks, favoring one type of beverage over another and using products that grew successfully in specific areas.

Grapes grew in profusion near the Mediterranean, in Egypt, Greece, and Italy, and they became the main source of wine, although dates and other fruits were also used where grapes didn't thrive. Mead made from wild honey was the drink of Northern European tribes before the spread of cereal agriculture.

Scenes of Egyptian bread and beer making from an Old Kingdom tomb.

Syrian soldier sipping beer in ancient Egypt (top left); Sumerian beer drinkers (bottom left); Egyptian "brewess" (right).

Throughout Asia, rice has always been the basis of fermented beverages from the *tuwak* of the Dayaks and the *tapai* of the Malays to the *badag* of Java and the *zu* of the Nagas, brews whose effects have been described by anthropologists as ranging from soporific to absolutely frenzy-inducing. *Sake* from Japan is the most sophisticated of all the rice-based drinks. Technically a beer, as it is derived from grain, *sake* is noncarbonated, high in alcohol, and generally treated more like wine.

Beers such as *pombe* are made throughout Africa from millet and other grains, and in the Americas beers like *chicha* and *tiswin* are brewed from corn. Oats, rye, wheat, and other grains have also been used in other regions. But it is malted barley that has always been the favored ingredient in beer, and from the beginnings of civilization in Mesopotamia and Egypt it has been the basis of brewing. Barley was originally domesticated in the ancient Near East, and since Neolithic times has been used in both bread-making and brewing. Beer was made by mixing up a thin gruel of grain and water and leaving it to ferment, or by baking loaves of bread and crumbling them into water to referment. The beer was drunk immediately after fermentation or even during it (after only two or three days usually) and was often unstrained. Many scenes of early brewing and beer drinking in ancient Sumeria and

Egypt show brewers baking loaves and making beer, with smiling beer drinkers seated around large jars, happily sipping through long straws.

Beer was an important part of life in the Near East, supplying refreshment and important nutrients to all classes. The builders of the pyramids were supplied with rations of beer to keep their strength and spirits up, and what might be the first recipe ever written was one for beer found on an ancient Sumerian clay tablet. This beer has recently been re-created by Fritz Maytag at Anchor Brewing with his "Sumerian" beer Ninkasi, named after the goddess of brewing (see box, page 9).

Malting, the process by which grain is soaked in water, sprouted, and roasted, was also discovered in the Near East. Barley is the easiest grain to malt, and barley malt is the main ingredient in virtually all beers. Hops were a late addition to beer, although herbs and spices were often added both for flavoring and as a preservative, much as hops are used today.

Beer-making spread throughout the world with the Agricultural Revolution and became especially popular wherever grapes could not be grown successfully. In the colder climates of Northern Europe, for instance, beer became the common drink, and Germanic, Scandinavian, and Anglo-Saxon cultures adopted beer as their national beverage.

Early beers were fermented at relatively warm temperatures using a type of bread yeast, and in the Germanic-speaking tradition were called "ales." They were usually unhopped, but in the Middle Ages ales were often flavored with a mixture of aromatic herbs called *gruit*.

Brewing was usually done in the home as an adjunct to baking and was the province of the woman of the house. In England, early taverns were run by women brewesses, or alewives, who advertised their wares by hanging an "alestake" (most likely a primitive tap or strainer) over

Medieval alewife and the alestake that advertised her wares.

SUMERIAN BEER

In August of 1989 Fritz Maytag of Anchor Brewing Company and Solomon Katz of the Anthropology Department at the University of Pennsylvania brewed a beer that had not been brewed for almost 3,000 years. Named after the Sumerian goddess of brewing and based on "The Hymn to Ninkasi," dating from 1800 B.C., the beer was an attempt, what Maytag calls "an essay," to re-create a Sumerian beer made from *bappir*–bread made from barley, honey, and dates.

Katz, an expert on early food and fermented beverages, maintains that the Neolithic Agricultural Revolution came about because Middle Eastern hunter-gatherers needed a source of grain for beer. He and Maytag found in "The Hymn to Ninkasi" the earliest recipe for beer, and perhaps one of the earliest recipes ever written.

Maytag and his staff rented a San Francisco bakery and baked 1,000 loaves of barley bread for the special brew. They made 286 cases of Sumerian Beer based on the recipe using the bread, barley malt, honey, and dates. No hops were used since this aromatic preservative herb was probably not added to beer until the Middle Ages in Europe.

The result was Ninkasi—a straw-colored, yeasty beer that is sweet and full-flavored, with bready flavors and a sweet, fruity finish. The beer was first served at the Micro-Brewery Convention in 1989 and drunk through straws in the Sumerian manner by the brewers.

Maytag presented the beer to the audience with these words: "Ladies and gentlemen, I would like to propose a toast. Here's to Ninkasi, the goddess of our trade." And then, he commented later, "Everyone sucked on those tubes, and I was overwhelmed by the sense that we had summoned her for the first time in three thousand years."

In the Middle Ages, monks brewed the finest beers, and enjoyed the product.

their doors. These "nut-brown ales" were probably slightly sweet, amber to brown in color, lightly carbonated, and served from the barrel a few days after fermentation was complete.

Modern beer-making originated in European monasteries, where the monks developed a new brewing technology, producing beers that were biologically more stable and decidedly more palatable than the earlier cruder ales. Bohemian and German monks discovered that the addition of a bitter herb—hops—grown in monastery gardens helped to preserve and flavor beer. Bitter resins in hops stabilized beers that ordinarily spoiled in just a few days and also provided a pleasantly astringent undertone to balance the sweetness of the malt. These brewer-monks also found that fermenting beers in cool cellars provided cleaner and lighter brews. The monks eventually developed a special yeast that worked well at cool temperatures and enabled them to store or lager their beers over the winter months. To distinguish this new and sophisticated brew from the older style "ale," they called it "beer"—most likely derived from the Latin verb *bibere*—to drink—although possibly from the Anglo-Saxon root *beor*—to brew.

Hops spread from the Continent to England some time in the sixteenth century, planted by Flemish immigrants in Kent in the south of England, still today the home of England's finest hops. And with hops came this new style beer, lighter and fresher than the heavier English ale. As a popular song of the time puts it:

> *Hops, Reformation, bays, and beer*
> *Came into England all in one year.*

The distinction between ale and beer was clear to most Englishmen in those days. Ale was the old-fashioned English brew, strong, dark,

Ale drinking in Merrie Old England.

and sweet, drunk after only a few days fermentation. Beer was the sophisticated European-style brew, lighter in color, alcohol, and body, with the bitter tang of hops, and often aged for some time before drinking. A controversy raged: While some drinkers defended the old English ale, others preferred the new-fangled drink called beer. Petitions were signed against "the wicked weed called hops," but after some years hops prevailed, and came to be added both to strong ale (high in alcohol and full bodied) and small beer (made with less malt and usually lighter in color, alcohol, and body).

Today, ale is a robust, full-bodied, high-hopped brew made with the older-style yeast that ferments at warm temperatures. Beer is the more general term, but usually refers to the lighter, more delicate lagers made with the cold-fermenting yeast originally developed by the German monks.

During the nineteenth century in Germany, lager yeast was isolated and propagated by a new generation of scientific brewers, and lager-making spread all over the world, becoming the main technique of modern brewing. Almost all beers today, whether they are made in Manila or Mexico City, St. Louis or Dusseldorf, are lagers. The exceptions are English and Scottish ales and stouts, a few specialty beers made in Germany and Belgium (Altbier, Lambic), and the rapidly growing group of American ales made by craft breweries.

STYLES OF BEER

For most Americans, beer is a pale, light-bodied, fizzy, and slightly sweet malt beverage. You drink it as cold as possible straight from the can, or in frosty mugs if you want to impress your friends. Many of us are realizing, however, that this is just one style of beer, American Pilsner, a highly carbonated light lager modeled on one of Europe's great beer styles.

Through travel and tasting, lovers of beer are now discovering the immense variety of beers made all over the world. Adventurous importers and creative microbrewers in virtually every state and province of the United States and Canada are offering North American beer lovers the chance to experience an amazing range of beers from the the lightest Weizenbiers to the darkest Stouts, from Fruit Ales to Barley Wines.

Alan Eames, an erudite and influential beer enthusiast and author of *A Beer Drinker's Companion* (Ayers Rock Press, 1986), maintains that there are over 117 separate and distinct beer styles made in the world today. Michael Jackson, the dean of beer writers, lists over 1,000 beers worldwide in his invaluable *Pocket Guide to Beer* (Simon & Schuster, 1988) and *The New World Guide to Beer* (Running Press, 1988). This rich diversity of beer and beer styles seems inexhaustible, and an exploration of the great variety of ways that grain, hops, yeast, and water (along with other more exotic ingredients like fruits, herbs, and spices) can be combined is a rewarding and enjoyable task.

To understand what is happening in North America's exciting new brewing scene today, we should become familiar with the major styles of beer found throughout the world. These individually styled brews are constantly inspiring our artisan brewers and are transforming American beer. (For a full discussion, see Appendix II, World Beer Styles).

The three main elements of style in beer are the type of yeast and temperature of fermentation; the color resulting from the malt used in the mash; and the body, malt flavor, and alcohol of the final brew. Other factors such as hop flavors and aromas and the amount of carbonation and head retention are also important.

Ale and Lager:
Yeast and Temperature Make the Difference

Ale yeast, which works at warm temperatures, has been the traditional yeast used for beer-making through the ages, and is still used in most English and some Continental and American brews. Ale's warm, quick fermentation creates aromas and flavors (esters) that are often described as "fruity," and most ales are highly hopped, robust, and strongly flavored.

Lager yeast is a later development. First recognized in Bavaria in the early 1800's, it probably had been in use earlier in Pilsen and Munich. Lager yeast ferments at cool temperatures and creates beers that are generally smoother and more subtle than ales, without the "estery" fruitiness and robust character caused by warm fermentation. German lager brewers created a new beer style that virtually took over European and American brewing in the nineteenth and twentieth centuries.

Many of America's microbrewers, especially on the West Coast, have reacted against the domination of lager as the main American beer style and are making full-bodied and robust ales. Other new brewers, particularly in the German-influenced Midwest, are refining the lager tradition and are making rich, malty lagers modeled on classic German and Czech styles.

Color: It's All in the Roasting

Color in beer can range from the light straw-gold of American Pilsner to the deep brown-black of Irish Stout. Color depends on how the malt is roasted. Pale or standard malt is the lightest and is dried at relatively low temperatures. Specialty malts—crystal or caramel, chocolate or black roasted—are roasted at increasingly higher temperatures for longer periods; caramelized malt sugars give color and flavor. Most beers are made largely from pale malt, which generally has the highest sugar level, with specialty malts blended in to create the color and flavor typical of the beer style.

Other grains added to beer can have an influence on color: Wheat malt, corn, and rice are used in lighter beers; oats and roasted unmalted barley help to color dark beers and Stouts.

Body, Flavor, and Alcohol: From Light to Wee Heavy

The amount of malt used in brewing beer determines the body, malt flavor, and alcohol of the final brew. Since beer is mostly water, the proportion of malt to water used in mashing and brewing is a key factor in beer quality. In general, the principle is the more malt, the heavier and stronger the beer. Thus beers that use very little malt and add adjuncts like rice and/or corn (e.g., American Pilsner) will be generally low in alcohol, body, and flavor. Beers that use more malt will generally be stronger and heavier, with more character and depth.

Alcohol levels in beers vary from light Weissbiers, Mild Ales, and American Light (3 to 4 percent) to powerful Maibocks, Scotch Wee Heavy Ales, and Barley Wines (8 to 12 percent). Body and malt flavor vary from the virtually tasteless American Light to thick and viscous Stouts and Dopplebocks.

Hops: Is Bitter Better?

Hops add two elements to beer: bitter flavors derived from the resins in the hop flower, and fragrant oils that create floral aromas in ales and lagers. Brewers use the characteristic bitterness and pungency of hops to balance sweet malt flavors and aromas.

Ale brewers tend to emphasize the bittering function of hops, and often use powerfully flavored varieties such as Bullion, Northern Brewer, or Styrian Goldings to balance the estery fruitiness of their brews. Lager brewers often look for milder flavors and prefer the aromatic, floral notes of more fragrant European hop varieties like Saaz, Hallertau, or Tettnanger. Many American brewers opt for domestic varieties grown in areas like the Yakima Valley, such as Cascades or Clusters.

Hop levels are often used by brewers to balance malt levels. In American Pilsners, which have very little malt character, small amounts of mild hops, such as Clusters, are the norm. Full-bodied ales and malty lagers generally have larger proportions of the more powerfully flavored and fragrant hops, such as Cascades or Saaz.

Malt sweetness and hop bitterness are two considerations in the matching of beer with food, and in the pages that follow we will often use these elements in pairing individual beers with special dishes.

Bubbles in the Beer: Or, How to Get a Head

Carbon dioxide is a by-product of fermentation, and quality beers are most often naturally carbonated. Some brewers depend on the CO_2 dissolved in the beer during brewing and aging, while others add priming sugar or partially fermented beer (*kräusening*) before kegging or bottling. Many large producers simply inject carbon dioxide into the beer at bottling.

The way CO_2 is introduced and the level of carbonation are important elements in the mouth feel and overall character of the beer. English-style ales are only lightly carbonated; European-style lagers usually have higher amounts of CO_2; and the American Pilsner style is often described as "fizzy," or overly carbonated.

Most mass-produced American beers are carbonated at bottling, by the addition of sterilized CO_2 recovered and stored from earlier fermentations. The high levels of carbonation in beer reflect the American penchant for cold and fizzy drinks—one of the rationales for the predominant style of American Pilsner.

The method of carbonation along with the amount and type of malt has much to do with the quality and duration of the beer's head, or collar of foam in the glass. Beer lovers give points for the appearance and lasting quality of a beer's head even before taking the first sip (see How to Taste Beer, page 17).

One of the complaints beer lovers have about standard American Pilsners is that the combination of high carbonation and low malt levels makes the beers foam up when poured, but leaves no lasting head on the beer. A good Dublin bartender takes great care in sculpting the creamy head on pints of draft Guinness for discriminating patrons. New American brewers, who use large amounts of malt and natural carbonation, are rightly proud of the long-lasting head and the rich mouth feel of their brews. (See Appendix I, How Beer Is Made, for more information.)

American Beer Styles: A Short List

Here is a short list of the styles of beer being made in the United States today. A full discussion of these beers can be found in the chapters that follow and in Appendix II, World Beer Styles.

Ales

Cream Ale Light-bodied, mildly hopped ale popular in the Eastern U.S. Example: Genesee Cream Ale.

American Ale Medium-bodied pale ale, moderately hopped with fruity flavors. Example: Rainier.

India Pale Ale Full-bodied pale ale, pleasantly bitter with full malt flavors. Example: Ballantine India Pale Ale.

Weiss Beer Pale, tart, German-style ale, made with wheat malt. Example: Schell Weizen.

Alt Beer Old-style German ale; color and flavors vary. Examples: St. Stan's Alt, Widmer Alt.

Amber Ale   Coppery amber color, full body, generally high hop level, malty flavors. Example: Boulder Amber Ale.

Bitter   English-style amber ale, pronounced hop bitterness, full malt flavors. Example: Redhook ESB.

Scotch Ale   Strong amber ale, quite hoppy, with full-bodied, malty flavors. Example: Grant's Scottish Ale.

California Ale   Pale to amber ale, very hoppy with strong malty flavors. Example: Sierra Nevada Pale Ale.

Dark Ale   Amber to brown ale, medium hop levels, often quite malty. Example: Pete's Wicked Ale.

Porter   Dark brown to black ale, full body, high hops and malt levels. Example: Anchor Porter.

Stout   Dark brown to black ale, very full body, high hops and roasted grain flavors. Example: Hart's Sphinx Stout.

Barley Wine   Amber to brown ale, very malty, strong and sweet. Example: Anchor Old Foghorn.

Fruit Ale   Specialty ale that mixes fruit with malt. Example: Buffalo Bill's Pumpkin Ale.

Holiday/Winter Ale   Specialty ale, amber to dark, full bodied, and often spiced. Example: Anchor Christmas Ale.

Lagers

American Light   Very pale, thin lager, low hops, low malt, not much character. Examples abound, unfortunately.

American Dry   Same as above. Examples: ditto.

American Pilsner   Pale lager, light body, low hop and malt levels, high CO_2. Example: standard U.S. lagers.

Continental Pilsner   Gold lager, medium body, medium malt and hops. Example: Augsburger, Schell Pilsner.

Pilsner   Gold lager, full body, high hops, lots of malt flavor. Example: Baderbrau, Gartenbrau Special.

American Dark   Amber lager, low hops, medium malt, sometimes slightly sweet. Example: Berghoff Dark.

American Bock   Amber to brown lager; varies from light to full hop/malt flavors. Example: Schell Bock.

Märzen/Maibock Pale to amber lager, full malt flavors, medium hops, strong. Example: Sprecher Maibock.

Dopplebock Amber to brown lager, full body, malty, hoppy, high alcohol. Example: Gordon Biersch Dopplebock.

Oktoberfest Amber to brown lager. Full body, malty, sometimes slightly sweet. Example: Sprecher Oktoberfest.

Rauchbier Smoky lager made from smoked malt; unusual taste. Example: Buffalo Bill's Rauchbeer.

Winter Lager Specialty beer, often amber to brown, sometimes spiced. Example: Coors Winterfest.

OKTOBERFEST
"Brewed according to Reinheitsgebot: Only Water, Malt, Hops, and Yeast Culture."

HOW TO TASTE BEER

The appearance of the beer is the first thing you notice. Color can vary from the pale gold of a Pilsner to the deep amber brown of a Porter or Stout, and should be characteristic of the style of beer being tasted. (See Appendix II, World Beer Styles, for more information.)

The head should be substantial and firm, a collar of foam around the top of the glass. How long the head lasts is often an indication of quality—a long-lasting head generally indicates good body and malt character. As you drink the beer, notice the foam that clings to the glass. This "Belgian lace" is another quality indicator.

Carbonation levels will vary as to the type of beer: English ales tend to be low in CO_2, while European-style lagers will be livelier in the mouth. Standard American Pilsners often have a "fizzy," overly carbonated feel from high levels of CO_2 injected just before bottling.

The aroma should be pleasant and usual for the style: Ales will often exhibit powerful hop aromas with fruity,

"estery" undertones; lagers usually provide malty aromas, with lighter hints of hops. But this will vary with the style: a Pilsner, for example, will usually be hoppier than a Munich-style lager, a Mild Ale less assertive than an India Pale Ale. Flavors should balance hop bitterness and malt sweetness, with some styles emphasizing one element or the other. The finish, or aftertaste, should be smooth and balanced.

The overall pleasure is finally the most important factor in tasting beer. Enjoyment is, after all, what drinking beer is all about.

HOW TO SERVE BEER

Beer glasses vary from the elaborate German beer stein to the straight-sided English pint glass to the sloping Pilsner flute. Whatever the glass, it should be perfectly clear so you can see the beer and large enough to hold a twelve-ounce bottle at one pour. The glass should also be absolutely clean, with no residue of soap or grease, which will make the beer go flat as it is poured.

The best way to pour most beers is to begin with the glass at a slight tilt, then gradually straighten the glass to upright as you

pour, carefully building the head. An inch to an inch and a half is a good size for the collar of foam on most beers.

Pilsners, Wheat Beers, and light lagers are usually served quite cold, about 45° to 48° F. Darker, full-bodied lagers and most ales are best appreciated a little warmer, 48° to 50° F. Ales and Stouts in the British style taste best at cellar temperature, about 55° F. Some barley wines and strong ales do best at room temperature, around 60° F.

THE AMERICAN BEER RENAISSANCE

It is no surprise that two of the more dubious achievements of American culture are white bread and Light Beer. The two products are intimately connected, and are part of the same tendency to create mass-produced, standardized foods with little flavor or individual character.

With all the rich diversity of beer styles available, why did only one type of lager, American Pilsner, become the dominant American beer? The answer lies in the mechanization of American agriculture and the industrialization of American food, historical developments described in Chapter 5, The Lager Revolution.

One of the great successes of American technology in the twentieth century has been the ability to produce and deliver at low cost massive amounts of safe, consistent, and nourishing food. From the great processing centers of the Midwest, immense quantities of grain-based foods and beverages flow to one of the best-fed populations in human history. But at what cost? We are increasingly besieged by studies and reports about the environmental, social, and cultural consequences of this technology. Canned and frozen meats and vegetables, packaged cereals, battery-fed chickens, and hormone-stuffed cattle may make economic sense, at least to the producers, but the whole idea of a cuisine based on processed foods is being challenged today.

All over America we see small artisan producers of bread, cheese, poultry, sausages, wine, and beer reacting against these mass-produced foods and beverages. Small farmers sell free-range chickens; tiny wineries make a few barrels of homegrown Zinfandel; goat farmers produce farmhouse cheese; bakers make chewy loaves of dark bread:

Americans are once again producing—and demanding—good, hand-made food.

Just as small wine-makers started a wine revolution a few years ago, hundreds of craft brewers all over the United States these days are making flavorful ales and lagers that bear little resemblance to the beers from the huge national breweries. These new brewers are part of a revolt against the bland and standardized products that have dominated our national life for much of this century.

It is hard to keep track of the many brew pubs and micro-breweries springing up in every region of the United States and Canada (the best source for statistics is *The Brewer's Resource Directory*, published by the Institute for Brewing Studies in Boulder, Colorado; see Appendix IV, Mail Order Sources). At this writing, microbreweries (defined as breweries producing fewer than 20,000 30-gallon barrels of beer annually) number over 100 in

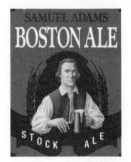

the United States and Canada; brew pubs, which make the beer that is served on their premises, are nudging the 200 mark, with more opening every day. In addition, many contract breweries are marketing beers that are made to their individual specifications at microbreweries and regional breweries.

Some regional breweries have survived the almost universal amalgamation of U.S. brewing into only a few national breweries—August Schell of New Ulm, Minnesota, and D. G. Yuengling & Son of Pottsville, Pennsylvania, are two examples. And successful small breweries, Anchor, for one, and rapidly expanding contract brewers, such as the Boston Beer Company, are on the verge of becoming national brands.

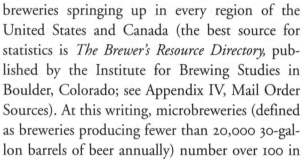

In an article by William Brand, the beer columnist for the Oakland (California) *Tribune,* we find that the largest beer maker in the United States, Anheuser-Busch, producer of Budweiser, makes 36 million barrels of beer at 12 different regional facilities. The total annual production of all the microbreweries in the U.S. last year was 350,000 barrels. That's still a pretty good amount, a little under 5 million cases, but it represents only a small fraction of our total beer consumption.

What is impressive, though, is the *rate* of increase. Most microbreweries have been around for only a few years, many dating from the late 1970's and early 1980's. The 1991 figures show a jump of 40 percent over the previous year, while national beer consumption is climbing at only 3 percent per year. This gain in market share by the small breweries is impressive, and the national breweries are beginning to notice that more and more Americans prefer the artisan beers to their own.

In fact, the large breweries are increasingly offering specialty and "super-premium" beers modeled on European and microbrewery styles. Malty lagers like Augusburger, Erlanger, Stroh's Signature, and Coors Winterfest, and hearty ales such as Coors Killian's Red, Ballantine India Pale Ale, and Rainer Ale are available nationally, and they are more and more in demand.

In the chapters that follow, we will range over this exciting American beer scene, describing many of these new beers, and linking them with regional and ethnic dishes with which they have an affinity. Many of our recipes will use beer as an ingredient, but we are more interested in

matching fine beer with good food than in writing a beer cookbook that uses beer in every recipe.

We will usually suggest a couple of beers to go with each dish, most of the time from the region or tradition that is being described in the chapter. Many of the beers we'll write about are available only locally, however, so take our suggestions as guidelines only. We will always describe the *type* of beer being recommended, a light ale or an amber lager, for example, so you can seek out the regional or national equivalent in your area.

Note also that we are not able to mention every beer from every microbrewery and/or brew pub in the country. This is a book about American beer and food, and we just don't have the space or the resources to provide an exhaustive list of all the new American brews. We'll try to describe the major styles and types of beers found in most regions of the country, but we have had to select representative breweries and brew pubs from among many. The fact that we don't list a brewery or specific beer shouldn't be taken for either scorn or neglect. There is so much going on in American beer these days that we just couldn't get all those wonderful brewers and their beers in this book.

3
BEER AND FOOD

You hear a lot of discussion these days about matching *wine* and food, but creative American chefs and home cooks are looking for more ways to pair beer and food. With growing interest in artisan beers from all over the world, and particularly in the products of new American brewers, beer is now being seen as a beverage that can enhance fine food.

Perhaps it's time to see if we can work out some general guidelines for matching beer and food, realizing, of course, that we are just beginning to tap into the rich barm of a tradition of good beer and hearty food that dates back over 3,000 years.

First of all, it's important to remember that beer *is* food and has been an important source of healthful nourishment through the ages.

There's a wonderful illustration in Michael Jackson's *The New World Guide to Beer* (pages 150–151), "Lads of the Village," that shows a group of old geezers sitting over their pints at the local pub. Their average age is, say, eighty-nine or so, a testimonial to the healthful results of the steady consumption of good ale.

Drummond and Wilbraham in *The Englishman's Food* (Jonathan Cape, 1959) estimate that in the eighteenth century a "young boy drinking about 3 pints a day would get some 500–600

Cal. towards his daily needs of about 2500." Beer also supplied calcium, riboflavin, vitamin B1, and other essential minerals and vitamins.

From its earliest origins, beer has been closely connected to baking, and those who described beer as "liquid bread" were not speaking metaphorically. Brewing and baking have always been intimately linked, since the ingredients (ground grain, yeast, and water) are virtually identical and the brewhouse and bakery often shared the same premises.

"Lads of the Village"—a testimony to the healthful qualities of good ale.

Beer and bread were staples in cultures as diverse as those of ancient Egypt, medieval Europe, and nineteenth-century Germany. The combination is still delicious and healthful today. It's hard to think of eating pizza without a cold glass of beer; the traditional plowman's lunch of ale, bread, and cheese is the favorite of English pub-goers; and a freshly baked pretzel with horseradish mustard is the preferred accompaniment to a malty Munich *dunkel* at Oktoberfest.

Beer has a special affinity to hearty, powerfully flavored foods. The sweet earthiness of malt, bitter undertones of hops, and bready flavors of the yeast all combine to provide a rich matrix that absorbs and plays against spices, herbs, hot peppers, and intense tastes. Where a delicate wine would be overwhelmed by a spicy dish, beer digs in and fights back. Thus highly flavored foods from cultures with a healthy respect for chiles, garlic, and spices go particularly well with beer: Mexican, Thai, Szechuan, Indian, and Southern Italian dishes all seem to taste better with beer.

Cheeses, especially the more pungent types that have developed some zest with aging, are delicious with beer. An aged Cheddar, double Gloucester, or Wensleydale is the perfect match for a hoppy Brown Ale like Pete's Wicked Ale; Muenster and thinly sliced onions on dark

German pumpernickel combine beautifully with a silky Amber Lager such as Gartenbrau Oktoberfest; and a powerfully ripe Liederkranz on dark rye with hot mustard is a natural with a full-bodied Midwestern lager like Berghoff Bock. Great snacks and lunches can be put together by pairing beer and cheese, and some classic dishes—for example, Welsh Rarebit* or Wisconsin Cheddar and Beer Soup*—combine full-flavored beers with pungent cheeses.

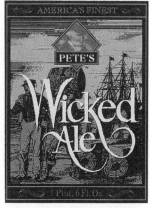

Smoked foods—meats, poultry, fish, cheese—go particularly well with beer (see Smoking Fish and Seafood, page 121). The salty, smoky flavors of ham or kielbasa, smoked chicken or turkey, smoked salmon or black cod, smoked Gouda or Cheddar, all tie in beautifully with the refreshing hoppy tang of a full-bodied ale or malty lager.

Certain cuisines that use smoked ingredients extensively—German food is probably the best example—seem destined to go with beer. It's hard to imagine what would go better with a platter of sauerkraut and smoked ham hocks than a foaming seidel of malty lager like Olde Heurich Maerzen. What else would one have with Bainbridge Island Smoked Fish Chowder* than a full-bodied, high-hopped ale like Grant's India Pale?

Beer is particularly suited to vinegary and piquant dishes. The sweetness of the malt balances vinegar's natural acidity, while the bitter hops provide a pleasant liason between the sweet and the sour. Vinegar in a dish will usually ruin a wine, but beer's sweet and astringent flavors are often enhanced.

Malt vinegar made from beer is exceptionally good with beer, as in the classic fish-and-chips with malt vinegar. But other vinegars made from red or white wine, from fruits such as raspberries and pears, and various herbs and spices, also work well. Salads, made with beets (see Beet and Apple Salad with Horseradish Vinaigrette*), marinated fish (see Alice's Ceviche,* Marlene's Three Herring Salads*), sauerkraut (see Sauerkraut and Apple Salad*), or pickled onions (see Tavern Pickled Onions,* Red Onions Pickled in

*See Index.

Lime Juice*) almost ask for beer. These piquant salads make delicious and easy-to-make appetizers, first courses, or light luncheons that are complemented by Pale Ales like Ballantine India Pale Ale and light lagers such as Augsburger.

Fried foods need the gusto of beer, especially if you use a crunchy beer-based batter (see Deep Frying Seafood and Vegetables, page 240). Certain cuisines have a light hand with deep-fried dishes—Japanese tempura and English fish-and-chips are two examples—and beer is the beverage of choice with them. Fried foods are often accompanied by spicy sauces and condiments (see Rémoulade Sauce* and Spicy Tartar Sauce*), still more reason to match them with beer.

Seafood and beer are traditionally joined in many regions in Amer-

ica. A crab boil near Chesapeake Bay, Cajun-style Shrimp Boiled in Beer and Spices,* a clambake on Cape Cod, alderwood-smoked salmon in Seattle, fish tacos on the beach in San Diego, ceviche in an L.A. restaurant—all taste immeasurably better with a cold glass of light lager like Los Angeles Brewing's Eureka.

The American Pilsner style, when transformed by a new generation of Midwestern brewers into a high-hopped and malty beer like Gartenbrau Special, seems to go particularly well with fish. And the tart, light Wheat Beers based on the German *weizenbiers* made by small American breweries such as Widmer Weizenbier or Schell Weizen Beer are delightful with many fish and seafood dishes. A slice of lemon in Wheat Beer or a light lager increases the acidity of the beer and helps to cut any strong fishy flavors.

One of our favorite places to enjoy seafood and beer is along the beachfront and piers in Southern California. Here whole families of Mexican and Asian seafood lovers cluster around vendors of smoked fish and fresh seafood. They put together mammoth picnics of cracked crab and raw clams, smoked shark and bonito, boiled and fried prawns, marinated octopus and calamari. Family and friends gather at big cement tables or benches along the piers, dip the seafood into spicy sauces like salsa and *nuoc mam* and condiments like *sambal,* and wash down the savory combinations with cold beers.

The tremendous range of styles of beers made by today's brewers

*See Index.

offers a great opportunity to experiment with flavor combinations. The array of widely different beers available these days provides us with a palette of flavors that can match up with any type of food from powerfully flavored Mexican or Indian dishes to mild and subtle foods from cuisines as various as Belgian, Chinese, and American regional cooking.

While the art of matching beer and food is still in its infancy, a couple of general principles seem to work. First of all, just as with wine, it's a good idea to match like with like: milder lagers and Pale Ales with light and subtle dishes, more powerfully flavored Amber Ales and Dark Lagers with aggressively seasoned, intense foods.

Lagers in the American Pilsner style, Pale Ales, and tart Wheat Beers usually complement lighter dishes—Lobster Boiled in Light Ale,* Sole Stuffed with Crab in Light Lager Sauce,* or Grilled Chicken in Lemon/Lager Marinade.*

Robust ales and dark, sweet lagers are often paired with more strongly flavored foods. Thus a spicy goulash (Great Goulash*) might be matched with a high-hopped Amber Ale like Boulder Amber or a malty lager such as Schell Oktoberfest. Chestnut-stuffed Quail with Sweet Stout Gravy* is a natural match for a deeply flavored Stout such as Pike's Place XXXX Stout, and Porter Pot Roast* is delicious with Yuengling Porter.

Eastern European cooking has a long tradition of highly flavored dishes that go well with dark beers. Sauerkraut (see Making Sauerkraut, page 215) and savory spiced meats like Corned Beef and Pastrami* are all beautifully balanced by full Dark Lagers such as Kemper Dunkel or Sprecher Black Bavarian.

The idea is not to let either the beer or the food overwhelm the other, balancing intensity with intensity, lighter flavors with lighter beers. What we look for is a kind of synergy; both the beer and the food should taste better together than either would separately.

There is another approach, sometimes noted with wine, but especially apropos for beer that can be called the "refreshment factor." Here, particularly with *very*

*See Index.

hot and spicy food that would overwhelm even the most powerful beer or wine, we look to the beverage for relief, coolness, and an unobtrusive undertone of flavor. With the spiciest dishes—a mouth-blistering Southern Indian curry, serious Tex-Mex chile, or incandescent Cajun blackened anything-that-walks-swims-flies-or-crawls—a light beer spells relief. Try an American Pilsner—Dixie Beer, for example, from New Orleans—a light lager like Pacific Pils, or a mild Wheat Beer like Widmer Weizen.

With these two general principles in mind (like with like, and bail out if the going gets too hot), you can have a lot of fun experimenting with more subtle aspects of color, body, aroma, and flavor. Try pairing a full-bodied Amber Lager like Hubsch Märzen with a Szechuan Chicken Salad* to play with sweet/sour, mild/spicy combinations. Or match up a hoppy Pale Ale such as Sierra Nevada Pale Ale with Pheasant Braised with Ale and Stuffed with Wild Rice and Mushrooms* to taste the interplay of bitter hops and earthy wild rice and mushrooms. Or combine the robust and spicy flavors of Adobo Chicken Wings* with a big and brawny Boont Amber Ale from Anderson Valley Brewing.

But above all, feel free to experiment. Any writer on beer and food is just giving you his or her educated guess based on individual tasting experiences. You might prefer something entirely different. Have a potluck beer and food party with your friends: Line up a bunch of different beers, set out some delicious foods, and taste away. Experiment, enjoy, and put together your own favorite combinations. As the bishop said to the actress, it's an intrinsically pleasant experience any way you choose to do it.

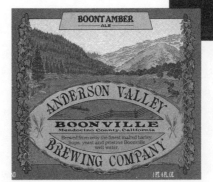

*See Index.

BEER AND BREWING IN EARLY AMERICA

Pickled Oysters

Smoked Trout Pâté

Creamy Horseradish Cocktail Sauce

Lobster Boiled in Light Ale

Cod and Potato Gratin

Welsh Rarebit

Cheese Corn Cakes

Chestnut-Stuffed Quail with Sweet Stout Gravy

Stuffed Duck Legs in Ale and Bourbon Gravy

Pheasant or Chicken and Wild Rice Braised in Ale

Veal Shanks and Winter Vegetables in Ale

Onions Braised in Porter

Turnips and Greens

Kathy's Strong Ale Spice Cake

Pumpkin Cookies

Our victuals being much spent, especially our Beere. . . .

On the nineteenth of December, 1620, the Pilgrims on the *Mayflower* were in trouble. After a difficult journey across the stormy Atlantic, they had finally made landfall near Cape Cod, far to the north of their intended destination of "Hudson's River." The season was far advanced

Lack of beer was one of the reasons the Pilgrims landed in New England rather than farther south. In early America, beer was made from native ingredients, like corn and pumpkins, or imported in barrels from England (left).

and winter setting in; there were shoals and rough water to the south; supplies were running low. An early chronicler reports:

> So in the morning, after we had called on God for direction, we came to this resolution—to go presently ashore again . . . for we could not now take time for further search or consideration, our victuals being much spent, especially our Beere. . . .

Notice the emphasis here: "especially our Beere." These Puritans weren't a band of jolly topers suddenly gone dry—far from it. They were English men and women for whom beer was a necessary and essential part of their diet.

So they abandoned hope of continuing south to warmer climes, and settled out of necessity in what came to be the Massachusetts Bay Colony. Beer and American life were intertwined from the beginnings of European settlement here, and beer was the everyday beverage of early America.

One of the great hardships noted by early New England and Virginia settlers in letters and journals was the shortage of beer and the dangerous necessity of having to drink water. Due to unsanitary conditions, water was often unsafe in England and early America, and beer was rightly considered to be a much healthier beverage. Water is boiled during the beer-making process, thus eliminating bacteria and dangerous microbes, and alcohol and hops both have an antiseptic effect. To be without beer was a serious health hazard, and this led to the rapid growth of American brewing, both in the home and in the emerging commercial breweries.

Beer from Corn, Pumpkins, and Parsnips

Settlers in the early colonies quickly set about making beer, from whatever ingredients they could. Barley was planted and harvested early, even by the ill-fated Roanoke colonists in the 1580's. But corn, the staple that sustained Native Americans and saved early European settlers

THE DANGERS OF WATER DRINKING

An early visitor describes Jamestown, Virginia, in 1613:

> There are about three hundred men there more or less; and the majority sick and badly treated, because they have nothing but bread of maize, with fish; nor do they drink anything but water—all of which is contrary to the nature of the English.

Some colonists made do with water, even boasting that they could actually thrive on the dank and dangerous drink. Reverend Higginson, a staid Salem minister, wrote home in 1629 that "whereas before my stomach could only digest and did require such strong drink as was both strong and stale, I can and of times do drink New England water very well." Admirable sentiments indeed, but misguided. Higginson died shortly after he wrote the letter, of what we are not told, but his is certainly not a convincing testimonial to the safety of drinking water in early America.

from starvation, was used to make beer from the beginning. Corn was readily available, even to the earliest settlers, and always cheaper and more plentiful than barley.

Thomas Hariot, one of the lucky few who returned from Roanoke, wrote in his *Narrative of the First English Plantation of Virginia* published in London in 1588:

> Pagatown is a kind of graine, so called by the inhabitants; the same in the West Indies is called Mayze. . . . Wee made of this same in the countrey some mault, whereof was brued as good ale as was to be desired. So, likewise by the help of hops, thereof may bee made as good beere.*

Beer made from corn was quickly accepted in the early colonies, although barley malt, either homegrown or imported from England, was thought to make the best, and strongest, ale. But thirsty settlers also made do with other ingredients for their daily brew—from molasses and wheat bran to pumpkins and persimmons. A popular New England song testifies to the improvisations (and good spirits) of the early Puritans:

> *If barley be wanting to make into malt,*
> *We must be content and think it no fault,*
> *For we can make liquor to sweeten our lips*
> *Of pumpkins, and parsnips, and walnut tree chips.*

An early governor of Virginia wrote that the richer colonists brewed beer with malt, but "the poorer sort brew their beer from molasses and bran, with Indian corn malted and drying in a stove; with persimmons dried in cakes and baked; with potatoes; with the green stalks of Indian corn cut small and bruised; with pompions [squash and pumpkins] and with 'batates Canadensis' or Jerusalem artichokes, which some people plant purposely for that use, but this is the least esteemed of all such before mentioned."

Other ingredients used in brewing and found in early recipes include spruce, roxberry, fever-bush, sweet fern, horseradish, oil of lemon, gingerroot, sassafras roots and bark, checkerberry, rye, oats and

*This and other references to early American brewing can be found in Stanley Baron, *Brewed in America: A History of Beer and Ale in the United States* (Little Brown, 1962).

wheat grain and bran, corn bread and brown bread, honey, brown sugar, and molasses. The various aromatics (including the "walnut chips" of the song) added flavors and bitterness to the brews; the grains, body and color; the sweeteners, alcohol, carbonation, and flavor. From this admittedly random list we can see that the addition of corn and other adjuncts to beer is a longstanding American tradition, and that some of the beers our forefathers drank must have tasted very strange indeed.

Strong Ale, Small Beer, and the Common Brewer

Most of these makeshift and odd ingredients, however, were used by home brewers to make table or small beer for daily consumption. As more and more barley and hops were planted, a brewing industry quickly grew up in the colonies, producing beers and ales in the English style. Just as in England, a distinction was made between "strong ale," brewed from barley malt, and "small beer," made from a second rinsing of the malt in the breweries or by home brewers who would use molasses, wheat bran, corn, and other ingredients. Public or "common" brewers in New England set up professional brewhouses to supply the gentry and tavern-goers with the full-bodied ales and beers they had been used to in England.

AN EARLY RECIPE FOR COMMON BEER

Two gallons of water to a large handful of hops is the rule. A little fresh-gathered spruce or sweet fern makes the beer more agreeable, and you may allow a quart of wheat bran to the mixture; then boil it two or three hours. Strain it through a sieve, and stir in, while the liquor is hot, a teacup of molasses to every gallon. Let it stand till lukewarm, pour it into a clean barrel and add good yeast, a pint if the barrel is nearly full; shake it well together; it will be fit for use the next day.

Sarah Hale, *The Way to Live Well* (1849), quoted in John Hull Brown's *Early American Beverages* (Charles Tuttle, 1966)

CORN BEER, WITHOUT YEAST

Cold water 5 gals.; sound nice corn 1 qt.; molasses 2 qts.; put all into a keg of this size; shake well, and in 2 or 3 days a fermentation will have been brought on as nicely as with yeast. Keep it bunged tight.

It may be flavored with oils of spruce or lemon, if desired, by pouring on to the oils one or two quarts of the water, boiling hot. The corn will last five or six makings. If it gets too sour add more molases and water in the same proportions. It is cheap, healthy, and no bother with yeast.

A. W. Chase, *Dr. Chase's Recipes* (1869), in *Early American Beverages*

One of the first acts of the Dutch settlers in New Amsterdam was to establish a public brewhouse on Brouwers Straet (Brewers Street) on lower Manhattan island; quickly beer became an important item of commerce in the thriving port.

The Puritan Fathers of Massachusetts Bay encouraged brewing and required professional brewers to prove that they possessed "sufficient skill and knowledge in the art and mystery of a brewer and could brew a good and wholesome beer." In 1635 they licensed a Captain Sedgwick as the first common brewer in the colony at Charlestown near Boston who "set up a brew house at his great charge and very commodious for this part of the countrey."

Beer Laws

Soon laws were passed regulating the strength, purity, and price of beer and ale. In 1637 in Massachusetts brewers were required to use two bushels of malt per hogshead of ale for the lowest grade, three bushels for the second grade, and four

William Penn, brewer and statesman.

New Amsterdam Dutch brewed beer from the start—one of the first buildings in Manhattan was a brew house and tavern.

for the first grade. In 1677 in Virginia laws ensured that beer selling at threepence a quart would be made from three bushels of malt to a barrel, beer at fourpence a quart would be made from four bushels. In general, throughout the colonies, authorities linked quality with price: More malt in a brew gave the beer more body and alcohol and also made it more expensive to produce. As in England, strong ale was more esteemed; small beer was cheaper and for everyday use. A price list from Rensellaerwyck (Albany) on the Hudson River in 1658 gives us an idea of the relative value of strong and small beer (and the colorful currency of the times):

> A tun of strong beer when sold by the brewer: ten guilders in silver, twenty-two guilders in wampum. . . . A tun of small beer, three guilders in silver; four and a half in beaver, and six guilders in wampum.

Early Brewers: Founding Fathers, Substantial Citizens

While beer, malt, and hops were still brought in from England, increasingly throughout the seventeenth and eighteenth centuries in the colonies we find more barley and hops planted, malt manufactured, and

Samuel Adams (left) and Matthew Vassar (right) were prominent early American brewers.

a wide variety of beers and ales made. Members of influential families in New England, New Amsterdam, and Virginia took up malting and brewing, and some of America's greatest fortunes were founded on ale and beer. New Amsterdam patroons like Van Rensellaer, Beekman, and Rutgers, upstanding New England burghers like John Winthrop the Younger and Samuel Adams, William Penn and Anthony Morris in Pennsylvania, Matthew Vassar in upstate New York, and George Washington, Thomas Jefferson, and James Madison in Virginia, all were part of a cultivated elite of brewers, amateur and professional, who recognized beer as a valuable and salutary addition to American life.

By the Revolution, brewing was an established industry in cities like New York, Boston, and Philadelphia, with a good portion of the malt and hops being produced by local farmers. Some areas—Esopus on the Hudson with its famous Sopus Ale, the Dutch brewery-estates in upstate New York, and the Swedish settlements in New Jersey and Delaware that brewed "strong and remarkably clear beer" from maize—became well known for their fine beers.

But Philadelphia soon became the most famous brewing center in America and its beer gained a reputation that rivaled that of the finest English products. Gabriel Thomas, an early traveler, writes in his *Account of Philadelphia* (1696):

> There are also three or four spacious malt-houses, as many large brew-houses and many handsome bake-houses for public use. . . . The brewers sell such beer as is equal in strength to that in

London, half ale and half stout, for fifteen shillings per barrel, and their beer has a better name, that is, is in more esteem than English beer.

Porter: A New and Popular Style

This mix of "half ale and half stout" prefigures the new style of ale called Porter that revolutionized English (and American) brewing in the eighteenth century. Both English and American beer drinkers were in the habit of asking for different types to be mixed in their mugs and tankards, ale and beer, for example, or even more commonly "three threads": strong ale, common beer, and twopenny (small beer). This became a problem for tapsters who had to go to three different casks to draw a pint.

So, in 1722, Ralph Harwood of the Bell Brewhouse in Shoreditch near London created a richly flavored, strong dark ale he named "entire butt" or "intire" that combined the virtues of all three types. The new ale was an instant success with London's manual workers, especially the porters of Covent Garden, and soon became famous as "Porter." It was seen as a particularly nourishing brew, "a wholesome liquor which enables the London porter-drinkers to undergo tasks that ten gin-drinkers would sink under" (John Bickerdyke, *The Curiosities of Ale and Beer,* London, 1889).

A craze for the new ale swept England, and consumption and production soared, at the expense of the noxious and dangerous gin, the scourge of the lower classes in eighteenth-century England. Porter was more suited to large-scale production than paler ales and beers were, and new techniques of mashing and brewing made the flavorful brown ale widely available. London's soft water and a higher level of extract in the mash gave the new brew a round, full feel in the mouth, and when brewed to a stronger alcohol level and higher hop level, the ale was called "Stout."

George Washington's Favorite Ale

The popular ale soon migrated to America, and we first hear of it produced in Philadelphia by Robert Hare in the 1770's. It became the favorite brew of many Americans, including the new country's first citizen, George Washington. Brewing in the newly United States got a big boost from a "Buy American" campaign launched by Washington and others ("I use no porter or cheese in my family, but such as is made in America," he writes Lafayette). Brewers like Hare and Anthony Morris

George Washington (left) was an enthusiastic home brewer and lover of Porter. Above, Anthony Morris's brewery in Philadelphia.

in Philadelphia became rich shipping their fine Porters to all of the thirteen new states, especially in the South, where the warmer, humid climate made brewing difficult.

In 1789, Washington wrote Philadelphia merchant Clement Biddle after a Fourth of July procession: "I beg you will send me a gross of Mr. Hairs best bottled Porter if the price is not much enhanced by the copious draughts you took of it at the last Procession." Washington's fondness for the new brew is further seen in a letter from his secretary Tobias Lear in 1790: "Will you be so good as to desire Mr. Hare to have if he continues to make the best Porter in Philadelphia 3 gross of his best put up for Mount Vernon? as the President means to visit that place in the recess of Congress and it is probable there will be a large demand for Porter at that time." In addition to buying Porter from Mr. Hare, Washington, like most landowners and small farmers, brewed his own beer at home.

Thomas Jefferson: Gentleman Brewer

Another lover of fine beer was Thomas Jefferson, who brewed excellent beers from wheat grown and malted on his plantation. During the War of 1812 he procured the services of a Captain Miller, an English citizen and former brewer interned as a hostile alien. Miller taught Jefferson and his slave/foreman John Hemings the latest English brewing techniques.

Thorough and meticulous as ever, Jefferson kept careful notes on the process in his *Garden and Farm Books* (Fulcrum, 1987): "1814, Sep-

GEORGE WASHINGTON'S
HOME BREW RECIPE

To Make Small Beer

Take a large Sifter full of Bran, Hops to your Taste. – Boil these 3 hours then strain out 30 Gallons into a Cooler, put in 3 Gallons Molasses while the Beer is Scalding hot . . . let this stand till it is little more than Blood warm then put in a quart of Yeast – if the Weather is very Cold cover it over with a Blanket & let it Work in the Cooler 24 hours, then put it into the Cask – leave the Bung open till it is almost done Working – Bottle it that day a Week it was Brewed.

Stanley Baron, *Brewed in America: A History of Beer and Ale in the United States* (Little Brown, 1962)

tember 3. began to malt wheat. a bushel will make 8. or 10. gallons of strong beer such as will keep for years, taking ¾ lb of hops for every bushel of wheat."

Jefferson, Hemings, and Miller brewed more than enough beer for the estate's consumption, and Jefferson's beer gained an estimable reputation among his friends and neighbors. He wrote James Madison, another beer lover and hopeful amateur brewer, in 1820, "About the last of Oct. or beginning of Nov. we begin for the ensuing year, and malt and brew three sixty gallon casks." And later to another friend desirous of setting up as a brewer, "We brew 100 gallons of ale in the fall & 100 gallons in the spring, taking 8. gallons only from the bushel of wheat. the public brewers take 15. which makes their liquor meagre and often vapid."

Beer: A Temperance Beverage

"Cheap beer is the only means to keep rum out!"

Prominent citizens like Washington, Jefferson, and Madison encouraged brewing not simply because they had a preference for the suds, but also because they viewed beer as a healthful and temperate beverage. Early Americans were heavy drinkers of hard liquors, in amounts that would (literally) stagger American consumers these days. Home-

distilled whiskey and apple-jack, and rum imported from the West Indies or produced in New England, were common drinks in the colonies, and spirits were consumed on virtually any occasion.

Beer drinking was seen as a solution to excessive drinking of spirits, and brewing was looked upon as a noble and socially useful profession. Beer was esteemed because of its nourishing qualities, and in the late eighteenth century state legislatures passed many laws favoring beer over distilled spirits. Taxation was the means used throughout the emerging republic to make hard liquor more expensive and difficult to procure, and beer cheap, wholesome, and available. As General Ogelthorpe, governor of Georgia, exclaimed, "Cheap beer is the only means to keep rum out."

TAVERNS, INNS, AND ORDINARIES IN COLONIAL DAYS

I William McDermott lives here,
I sells good porter, ale, and beer,
I've made my sign a little wider
To let you know I sell good cider.

COLONIAL TAVERN SIGN

Daniel Webster, looking back at the heady days just before the American Revolution, called taverns "the headquarters of the Revolution," and he wasn't exaggerating. Alice Morse Earle in her warm evocation of the taverns and inns of colonial times, *Stagecoach and Tavern Days* (Benjamin Blom, 1900), tells us that "Sons of Liberty drank and toasted and schemed within the walls of the Province Arms," the famous tavern on early New York's Broad Way. The Province Arms was also the scene of the first mass protest against the infamous Stamp Act, where two hundred prosperous New York merchants met in the Long Room to sign the Non-Importation Agreement to boycott British goods.

Plotters met at Providence's Red Sabin Tavern to plan the seizure of the British naval schooner, *Gaspee,* and also to fortify themselves for the task. The Boston Tea Party really began, and probably ended, at the famous Green Dragon Tavern, where Boston burghers and artisans, Sons of Liberty all, stoked up on strong ale and rum before venturing out to turn Boston Harbor into a giant teacup. Thomas Jefferson penned the immortal words of the Declaration of Independence at the Indian Queen Tavern in Philadelphia, most likely with a mug of Mr. Hare's good porter at his elbow.

Taverns: Centers of Village Life

Taverns were the centers of social and political life in the villages and neighborhoods of early America. Every traveler who entered the tap-

The Green Dragon Tavern, Boston.

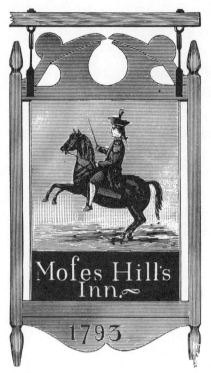

Inns and taverns were centers of social life in the early colonies.

room was relentlessly quizzed about his business, destination, religion, politics, and, especially, news of the outside world. Strangers brought that wonderful commodity, news, to isolated villages, and inns and taverns purveyed information along with their mugs of ale.

In *Stagecoach and Tavern Days,* Alice Morse Earle tells the story of one Virginia traveler who became so exasperated at having to answer so many questions before he could get a mug of ale that he simply exclaimed loudly every time he entered a tavern: "Worthy people, I am Mr. _____ of Virginia; by trade, a tobacco planter and a bachelor; have some friends in Boston whom I am going to visit: my stay will be short, when I shall return and follow my business as a prudent man ought to. This is all I know of myself and all I can possibly inform you. I have no news. And now, having told you everything, have compassion upon me and my horse and give us some refreshment."

The tavern, with its spacious taproom, was the logical and preferred venue for town meetings, assemblies, dances, auctions, lodge meetings, theatricals, lotteries, caucuses, and just about any other gathering. It was often situated next to the church, that other center of village life. Town councils, especially in Puritanical New England, were constantly passing laws that attempted, unsuccessfully it seems, to prohibit tapsters from offering their wares while services were in progress. The village tavern, with its warmth, jollity, and ample opportunities for refreshment offered a tempting alternative to the chill and austere chapels and meeting halls of early New England.

Strong Ale, Flip, and Whistle-Belly-Vengeance

Strong ale, small beer, and Porter were universal favorites and were the mainstay of any tavern, inn, or ordinary from Cape Cod to Charleston. Almost all beer was drunk from the cask, drawn from barrels behind the bar into huge black jacks—leather tankards chased with brass or silver—or pewter or silver mugs, some elaborately crafted by American artisans like Paul Revere. Bottles were expensive and difficult to come

BEER: A MORAL BEVERAGE

The moralizing tendency and salubrious nature of fermented liquors—beer, ale, porter and cider—recommend them to a serious consideration and particularly in our country.

Alexander Hamilton, *Report on the Subject of Manufactures, Made the 5th of December 1791* (Philadelphia, 1827)

READ MY LIPS: NO TAXES ON BEER

Whereas, The wholesome qualities of malt liquors greatly recommend them to general use as an important means of preserving the health of the citizens of this commonwealth, and of preventing the pernicious effects of spiritous liquors . . .

Bee it therefore enacted that by this act brewers are exempted from all taxes and duties of every kind for the term of five years.

Decree of the Massachusetts Legislature, 1787

by, and it wasn't until the lager revolution of the mid-nineteenth century that bottled beer began to rival beer on draft.

Drinks made from beer were often favored by tavern regulars, and the most popular was flip, a lively mixture of strong ale, rum, molasses, dried pumpkins, cream, and eggs. Flip was mixed in a large glass tumbler and heated by plunging into it a red-hot poker or loggerhead. Taverns became famous for their flip, and creative landlords came up with endless variations on the original recipe. One tapster in Massachusetts, for example, gained a great reputation for his flip by adding, at the last minute, eggs, cream, and sugar whipped together. When fresh eggs were beaten into the flip just before heating so that froth billowed over the glass, it was called a bellow's-top, a drink highly regarded by connoisseurs.

Perhaps the strangest beer-based drink of our forefathers was whistle-belly-vengeance or whip-belly-vengeance, described by Alice Morse Earle as "a terrible drink . . . said to have been popular in Salem. It is difficult to decide which was worse, the drink or its name. It was sour household beer simmered in a kettle, sweetened with molasses, filled with crumbs of 'ryeinjun' bread, and drunk piping hot." The name, we are told, was "not a Yankee vulgarism, but well-known old English term," used to describe small beer a bit past its (always debatable) prime.

A COLONIAL RECIPE FOR FLIP

To make a quart of Flip: Put the Ale on the fire to warm, and beat up three or four eggs with four ounces of moist sugar, a teaspoonful of grated Nutmeg or Ginger, and a Quartern of good old Rum or Brandy. When the Ale is near to a boil, put it into one pitcher and the Rum and Eggs, etc., into another; turn it from one Pitcher to another till it is as smooth as cream. To heat, plunge in the red-hot Logger-head or Poker. This quantity is styled One Yard of Flannel.

> Quoted in Richardson Wright's *Grandfather Was Queer*. Wright was the author of many colorful books on early America.

COLONIAL FOOD AND FEASTS

After the "Starving Times" of the first few years, colonists in America found an abundance of food in the forests, bays, and fertile earth of the New World. Game was everywhere, and early colonists hunted extensively; they also traded for game with Native American hunters. In Georgia in the early 1700's, deer were sold for sixpence; in Albany, for a jackknife or a few iron nails. At the first Thanksgiving in the Massachusetts Bay Colony in 1621, Indians brought five deer to the feast along with a "great store of wild turkies." Flocks of the huge birds, weighing 30 pounds and more, were everywhere from New England to the Chesapeake, and they sold for a shilling each, William Penn tells us, in the Philadelphia markets. Pigeons sold in Boston for a penny a dozen and we are told that "flights of pigeons darkened the sky, and broke down the limbs of trees on which they lighted."*

Not only was game found in the forest, but also wild honey, sap from maple trees for sugar and syrup, herbs and greens, wild onions, garlic, fruits, berries, and nuts.

The seas that bordered the new colonies and its bays, rivers, and lakes teemed with fish and seafood. One early explorer complains that the ships were "pestered with cod," and John Smith boasts that he caught upwards of 60,000 in one month. Colonists learned from the Indians how to harvest the bounty of the coasts and inland streams: clams and oysters from the tide pools, eels and sea trout from the tidal streams, deepwater crabs and lobsters in fantastic abundance. That ill-fated water-drinker Reverend Higginson of Salem wrote that he had seen lobsters weighing 25 pounds or more and that "the least boy in the plantation may catch and eat what he will of them." Lobsters five and six feet long were caught in Long Island Sound, although the Dutch traveler Van der Donck comments that "those a foot long are better for serving at table."

Oysters, especially those of Brooklyn's Sheepshead Bay, were much esteemed as an early description (1697) of an oyster roast attests: "Then was thrown on the fire, to be roasted, a pail full of Gowanes oysters which are the best in the country. They are fully as good as those of England, better than those we eat at Falmouth."

In early years, new colonists survived on Native American plants such as corn, squash, and beans, and these soon became staples for all the settlers. Corn or maize was the most important crop, and Europeans quickly learned the methods of growing, preparing, and cooking this versatile and nutritious grain. Powhatan, father of Pocahontas, sent "some of his People" to Jamestown "that they may teach the English how to sow the Grain of his Country."

By blending European foods with the bounty of forest, sea, and land, Americans soon developed a distinctive, nutritious, and richly varied cuisine. In the old country only the upper classes ate meat and wild game, and the peasantry subsisted on a diet limited in protein and

*This and other references are from Alice Morse Earle, *Home Life in Colonial Times* (Macmillan, 1898).

"STREAMS TEEMED WITH FISH"

Fish abounded in the waters all along the coast from Cape Cod to Cape Hatteras. We are told by Alice Morse Earle in *Home Life in Colonial Times* that "the arms of the sea and fresh water streams . . . teemed with fish. The Indians killed them in the brooks by striking them with sticks, and it is said the colonists scooped them up in frying-pans. Horses ridden into the rivers stepped on the fish and killed them. In one cast of a seine the governor, Sir Thomas Dale, caught five thousand sturgeon as large as cod."

essential vitamins. In America, all you needed was a length of line and a hook, a Pennsylvania rifle, a plow and a mule, to create a nutritious and healthy diet for yourself and your family, all washed down by home-brewed ale or homegrown cider.*

The American Table

American food, however, showed distinct local variations caused by regional attitudes, climate, and crops. New England, with its cold climate and unyielding soils, was populated by Puritans who tended toward the plain and simple—boiled fish and seafood, cornmeal mush with molasses, and small beer. The warm and fertile South was peopled by landed gentry from Southern England and hardscrabble folk from the Scottish and Irish borders who enjoyed life to the full with smoked

*Apple cider, especially in New England and northern New York State, was a popular drink in early America. For a discussion of cider and its role in American life, see Vrest Orton's *The American Cider Book* (Tuttle, 1973).

hams and terrapin stew, Porter and aged Madeira. The prosperous Quakers, comfortable Dutch burghers, and German farmers of Pennsylvania and the Middle Colonies set ample tables rich with butter and cheese, roast beef, and strong ale.

John Adams, a brewer by profession, a highly respected citizen of New England, and the second American president, offered an honored visitor the following meal at his frugal table: "The first course was a pudding of Indian [corn] meal, molasses, and butter; then came a course of veal and bacon, neck of mutton and vegetables." When Adams visited Philadelphia during the framing of the Constitution he was shocked (and we hope secretly delighted) by the sumptuous table set by Miers Fisher, a young Quaker lawyer:

> This plain Friend, with his plain but pretty wife with her Thees and Thous, had provided us a costly entertainment: ducks, hams, chickens, beef, pig, tarts, creams, custards, jellies, fools, trifles, floatings islands, beer, Porter, punch, wine and a long, etc.

Tavern Fare

Tavern fare in early America was ample and tasty. An English traveler writes in 1807:

> At the better sort of American taverns very excellent dinners are provided, consisting of almost everything in season. The hour is from two to three o'clock, and there are three meals in the day. They breakfast at eight o'clock upon rump steaks, fish, eggs, and a variety of cakes with tea or coffee. The last meal is at seven in the evening, and consists of as substantial fare as the breakfast, with the addition of cold fowl, ham, etc.

Taverns became famous for their specialties, and guests would often ride miles to taste the broiled trout in one, the planked shad in another. Some were known for their johnnycakes and waffles, others for special delicacies such as locally caught salmon, freshly gathered oysters, turtle soup, or catfish suppers.

Americans cared about quality, and were willing to seek out those who provided it. Cooking styles ranged from the elaborate banquets and effusive hospitality of Tidewater planters to the simple fare of New England farmers, but the food was generally hearty, locally grown, and plentiful.

And most often, in the early years, it was accompanied by home-grown, and usually homemade, ale. While Madeira or claret often graced the tables of the affluent, ale or Porter would also be offered to guests. The everyday drink of most Americans, rich or poor, was robust and flavorful ale.

Ale was the Englishman's drink and became the American's drink as well. It remained the country's most popular beverage until the mid-nineteenth century, when the arrival of German immigrants with different traditions and new technologies would revolutionize American life and attitudes toward beer and food.

CATO'S TAVERN

One of the most popular taverns of old New York was Cato's Road House, built in 1712 at the junction of Fifty-first and Fifty-second streets and the Post Road. Here Cato, a Negro slave who had bought his freedom through plying his culinary skills, kept an inn for forty-eight years. "Knickbocker braves and belles" drove out to Cato's to dine and dance, and we are told by Alice Morse Earle in *Stagecoach and Tavern Days* that "those who tasted

his okra soup, his terrapin, fried chicken, curried oysters, roast duck . . . wondered how any one who owned him ever could sell him even to himself."

Pickled Oysters

Pickled oysters were a favorite snack of English and colonial American tavern-goers. The oysters were usually accompanied by tankards of strong ale and freshly baked crackers. Try them with traditional ales like Massachusetts Bay Brewing's Harpoon Ale or Samuel Adams Boston Stock Ale.

For this piquant dish, the oysters should be impeccably fresh and fairly small, 1 to 2 inches shucked length. We've used small West Coast varieties like Olympias, Hama Hamas, and Kumamotos, but ask your local fishmonger what small varieties are available in your area.

Once the oysters are pickled, they will keep up to 5 days refrigerated. They can be served as is, or with some finely chopped mild red onion and Tabasco. They are also excellent with our Creamy Horseradish Cocktail Sauce (recipe follows).

2 pints freshly shucked oysters (about 25–30), with any juices	16 whole black peppercorns
	10 whole coriander seeds
1 cup tarragon vinegar	½ teaspoon dillseed
6 whole allspice	Finely chopped red onion as an accompaniment
4 whole cloves	Tabasco to taste
2 bay leaves	

In a saucepan over medium heat cook the oysters in their own juices until the edges just begin to curl, about 3–5 minutes. Strain the oyster liquid and save. Plunge the oysters into a large bowl of cold water and ice cubes, and chill for 10 minutes.

Put the vinegar and spices into a 2-quart nonaluminum saucepan. To remove any grit strain the reserved oyster liquid through a coffee filter or fine cheesecloth into the pan. Gently boil the mixture for 5 minutes. Add the oysters and immediately shut off the heat. Let the oysters cool gradually in the marinade until they are completely cool, about 45 minutes. Pour the oysters and marinade into glass jars or plastic storage containers and refrigerate.

SERVES 4–6 AS AN APPETIZER OR FIRST COURSE. MAKES 1 QUART.

Smoked Trout Pâté

In colonial times, when trout were in abundance in the streams and lakes, smoking was a common way to preserve the fish (see Smoking Fish and Seafood, page 120). Later the smoked fish could be used in salads, soups, or spreads to be served with ale in the home or in taverns. Serve this easy-to-make pâté with crisp toast points or Melba toast and a light ale like Geary's Pale Ale from Portland, Maine, or New Haven Brewing's Elm City Connecticut Ale.

3 tablespoons olive oil
2 slices day-old French bread
½ pound smoked trout, whitefish, or other white-fleshed smoked fish, all skin and bones removed
½ pound butter, softened
2 tablespoons finely chopped green onions or scallions
2 teaspoons lemon juice, or to taste
½ cup sour cream
Salt and pepper

Sprinkle the olive oil over the bread. Break the bread into pieces and put them in a food processor along with the trout, butter, green onions or scallions, and lemon juice. With the motor running, spoon in the sour cream. Taste for salt and pepper and lemon juice. Pack the pâté into a small bowl and chill thoroughly.

SERVES 4–6 AS A BAR SNACK OR APPETIZER.

Creamy Horseradish Cocktail Sauce

This creamy cocktail sauce is good with any cooked or raw seafood, such as shrimp, crab, clams, or oysters. It is also a zesty condiment for cold roast beef sandwiches when mixed with an equal part of mayonnaise. The recipe was adapted from The Gold Cook Book, *an excellent and comprehensive book on American cooking by the classically trained chef Louis P. De Gouy.*

¼ cup catsup	1 tablespoon lemon juice
¼ cup chili sauce such as Heinz	1 tablespoon finely chopped green onions or scallions
¼ cup mayonnaise	
2 tablespoons prepared horseradish	1 tablespoon finely chopped red onion
1 tablespoon finely chopped parsley	½ teaspoon ground black pepper
1 teaspoon grated lemon rind	10 drops or more Tabasco

Mix all the ingredients together well. Chill, covered, for at least 2 hours in the refrigerator before serving. Keeps for 1 week.

MAKES ABOUT 1¼ CUPS.

Lobsters Boiled in Light Ale

Picture yourself a New England tavern keeper in colonial times with some leftover ale in the bottom of a barrel and the sabbath coming on. Lobsters are cheap and plentiful. Why not use the ale to cook up the lobsters, you think, and egad! a new dish is born—Lobsters Boiled in Ale, a New England favorite.

However it happened, ale's malty flavors and underlying bitter notes of hops balance the sweet and succulent lobster beautifully. Serve the lobsters simply, with drawn butter and plenty of cold light ale—Blonde Ale from the Commonwealth Brewing Company of Boston or Catamount Gold Ale from Vermont.

3 bottles light ale	3 bay leaves
6 cups water	4 1½- to 2-pound live lobsters
½ teaspoon salt	½ pound butter, melted
2 medium onions, whole and unpeeled	2 lemons, cut into wedges

Put all the ingredients but the lobsters, butter, and lemons in a 3- to 4-gallon pot and bring the liquid to a rolling boil. Drop in the lobsters, and boil gently over medium heat for 20 minutes. Remove with tongs and serve at once with melted butter and lemon wedges.

SERVES 4 GENEROUSLY, WITH LEFTOVERS TO MAKE LOBSTER ROLLS. (SEE PAGE 250).

Cod and Potato Gratin

This hearty New England gratin of codfish, potatoes, and leeks is just what's needed on a cold night along with a mug of Pale Ale, such as Yuengling's Lord Chesterfield Ale.

4 tablespoons butter, melted
1½ pounds codfish fillets,
   skin and bones removed
Salt and pepper
2 tablespoons olive oil
3 cups cleaned and thinly
   sliced leeks, white part only

½ teaspoon dried thyme
¼ cup chopped parsley
2 pounds red potatoes, peeled
   and sliced into ⅛-inch
   rounds

Preheat the oven to 450° F. Brush a 9- × 12-inch baking dish with about 1 tablespoon of the melted butter. Spread the cod fillets in a single layer on the bottom of the dish. Sprinkle them with salt and pepper.

Heat 1 tablespoon of the olive oil in a 12-inch nonstick skillet. Add the leeks and thyme and season with salt and pepper lightly. Cover and cook over medium heat for 5 or 6 minutes, until the leeks are soft, but not brown, stirring frequently. Spread the leek mixture over the fish and sprinkle with the parsley.

In the same nonstick pan over medium heat, put 1 tablespoon of the butter and the remaining olive oil. Add the potato rounds, spreading them evenly over the bottom. Cook for about 10 minutes, stirring and shaking the pan frequently to cook the potatoes evenly. Spread the partially cooked potatoes over the fish, and smooth them with a large spoon or spatula. Pour the remaining melted butter over the gratin, and bake for 25–30 minutes, basting 2 or 3 times with the juices. Serve when the potatoes are well browned and everything smells buttery.

SERVES 4–6.

Welsh Rarebit

One of the great classic dishes of beer cookery, this melted cheese sauce combines pungent sharp Cheddar with ale. Traditionally served over toast and accompanied by strong ale, Welsh Rarebit is also delicious spooned over poached eggs on toast and served with fried ham as a satisfying brunch or luncheon dish.

Although usually served on white bread toast, we prefer a whole-grain wheat bread, which stands up well to the sharp cheese sauce. For cheese, use a high-quality American sharp Cheddar—New York or Vermont aged white Cheddar or Wisconsin sharp Cheddar.

With this flavorful dish, drink a traditional American ale, such as Old Marlborough Brewing's Post Road Real Ale or Commonwealth Brewing's Special Old Ale.

1 pound sharp Cheddar
   cheese, shredded
¾ cup ale
1 teaspoon Worcestershire
   sauce
½ teaspoon Tabasco
½ teaspoon English dry
   mustard powder or 2 teaspoons prepared English-
   style mustard

1 egg yolk, lightly beaten
8 slices whole-grain wheat
   bread
Salt and pepper
8 poached eggs (optional)

Place the first 5 ingredients in the top of a double boiler. Heat over simmering water, stirring constantly, until the cheese is completely melted and smooth. Stir 3 or 4 tablespoons of the melted cheese mixture into the beaten egg yolk. Pour this mixture back into the cheese sauce, and stir well until the egg is thoroughly blended. Remove from the heat and taste for salt and pepper.

Meanwhile, toast the bread, and poach the eggs if you are using them. Place 2 slices of toast on each plate with an optional egg on each piece of toast, spoon on 3 or 4 tablespoons of the cheese sauce, and serve.

Another way of serving Welsh Rarebit: Put the toast into individual baking dishes, spoon over it 3 or 4 tablespoons of the cheese sauce, then broil 1 or 2 minutes until the top is bubbly and lightly browned. Serve at once.

SERVES 4–6.

Cheese Corn Cakes

These tasty cheese and cornmeal pancakes make a very nice brunch or lunch when served with some spicy grilled or pan-fried meat or chicken and a Dark Ale like Yuengling Porter. This recipe was adapted from Marion Cunningham's delightful The Breakfast Book.

½ cup yellow cornmeal
¾ cup boiling water
½ cup all-purpose flour
½ teaspoon salt
1 tablespoon sugar
1 tablespoon baking powder
1 egg, beaten

4 tablespoons (½ stick) butter, melted
½ cup milk
½ cup grated sharp Cheddar cheese
Crisco or vegetable oil

Put the cornmeal in a mixing bowl, and pour the boiling water over it, stirring briskly until well blended. Add the remaining ingredients, except Crisco or oil, and beat the batter until thoroughly combined. If it is too thick, add a little more milk. The batter should be fairly pourable to produce thin pancakes.

Heat a griddle or heavy skillet over medium-high heat, but not as high as for other pancakes. When it is hot, film the griddle with the Crisco or vegetable oil. Use 2 tablespoons of batter for each pancake. Pour the batter on and cook until bubbles break on top of each pancake. Turn and cook for another few minutes, or until the bottoms are lightly browned and set. Serve hot with Salsa Cruda (see page 308) on the side.

MAKES 2 DOZEN 3-INCH PANCAKES.

Chestnut-Stuffed Quail with Sweet Stout Gravy

Wild chestnuts were abundant in the forests of early America, and they add a rich flavor and a slightly smoky taste to food. They are especially good with game birds such as quail or squab.

Dried chestnuts can be found in Italian delis and specialty shops as well as in Chinese markets. If you can't find dried, use fresh. You will need about 2 pounds. Fresh chestnuts must be peeled, but they do not require soaking.

Sweet Stout Gravy is excellent over turkey, other game birds, chicken, and Cornish game hens. It is also delicious on roast pork or veal. Drink a Stout or Porter here: Catamount Porter from Vermont is a good choice.

Sweet Stout Gravy

½ pound Italian dried chest-
    nuts or 2 pounds fresh
4 cups Rich Chicken Stock
    (see page 203)
1 cup Stout or Porter
2 teaspoons molasses

½ teaspoon dried thyme
1 bay leaf
Salt and pepper
1 cup *crème fraîche* or sour
    cream

Roast Quail

8 quail
½ teaspoon salt
½ teaspoon ground black
    pepper

½ teaspoon dried thyme
1 bay leaf, crumbled
2 tablespoons sweet butter,
    melted

To make the gravy: Soak dried chestnuts overnight in cold water. The next day drain the chestnuts and wash thoroughly. In a medium pot bring the stock, stout, and molasses to a boil and add the chestnuts, thyme, bay leaf, and a pinch of salt and pepper. Reduce the heat to a simmer and cook, uncovered, for 1 hour or until the chestnuts are soft. Remove the chestnuts with a slotted spoon, and set them aside to be used later with the quail. Continue to cook the liquid at a moderate boil for an additional 30 minutes or until the volume is reduced by half. Add the *crème fraîche* or sour cream, and cook slowly for 3 to 5 minutes until the gravy begins to thicken and just coats a spoon. Taste for salt and pepper. The gravy may be made in advance and refrigerated, covered, for 2 to 3 days.

To prepare the quail: Preheat the oven to 450° F. Combine the seasonings and herbs in a small bowl and rub into the cavity and on the skin of the birds. Stuff the quail cavities with some of the cooked chestnuts. Brush each bird all over with some of the melted butter. Roast for 15 minutes and baste with more melted butter. The meat should still be slightly pink. Roast 10 more minutes if you prefer quail well done. To serve, pour some of the gravy over the bottom of a platter. On it arrange the quail and the chestnuts not used in the birds. Pour some more gravy over the quail and serve.

SERVES 4.

Stuffed Duck Legs in
Ale and Bourbon Gravy

Game has always been a part of American cooking, especially in rural areas. If you've already used duck breasts in a special dish, this is a good way to use up the legs. If not, you can easily substitute four chicken legs and thighs for the duck legs. The spicy stuffing and richly flavored gravy would also be delicious with rock Cornish game hens or other small birds.

We think strong ale goes best with intensely flavored dishes like this: Try Massachusetts Bay's Winter Warmer Ale or Anchor Christmas Ale.

8 duck legs and thighs

Stuffing

1 pound spicy sausage, such as hot Italian or Louisiana chaurice, casings removed	¼ teaspoon dried thyme
	¼ teaspoon dried basil
	¼ teaspoon dried tarragon
½ cup homemade dried bread crumbs	½ teaspoon cayenne
	1 teaspoon paprika
1 egg	1 teaspoon salt
¼ teaspoon dried sage	1 teaspoon ground black pepper

Ale and Bourbon Gravy

2 tablespoons butter	¾ cup amber or dark ale
½ cup chopped onion	1 cup duck or Rich Chicken Stock (see page 203)
2 tablespoons chopped green bell pepper	1 teaspoon Worcestershire sauce
¼ cup chopped celery	Tabasco to taste
½ cup bourbon	Salt and pepper

Preheat the oven to 400° F. Bone the thighs by cutting the length of the thigh on the underside, and gently scraping the meat away from the bone. Cut the bone through at the joint and discard, leaving the thigh meat attached to the leg. Do not bone the leg. Remove any connective tissue or cartilage.

In a bowl mix together the sausage, bread crumbs, and egg. Place about 3 tablespoons of this stuffing in each cavity left by the bone. Pull the meat around the stuffing, and skewer the thigh to the leg with a toothpick or small bamboo skewer. You don't have to sew or tie the opening, as the egg should bind everything together nicely. Mix the herbs, spices, salt, and pepper in a small bowl and rub generously over each leg. Place, skin side up, on a rack over a shallow pan in the oven. Roast for 30 minutes.

To make the ale and bourbon gravy: While the duck is cooking, prepare the gravy. Melt the butter in a large heavy skillet over medium heat. Add the onion, pepper, and celery and sauté for 5 minutes, until the vegetables are soft. Add the bourbon, ale, stock, Worcestershire sauce, and Tabasco to taste, and simmer, uncovered, over low heat for about 15 minutes.

Add the cooked duck legs to the pan, cover, and braise gently for 10 minutes. If the gravy seems too thin, remove the duck legs, and cook the sauce down over high heat to desired consistency. Season with salt and pepper to taste. Skim any grease off the sauce. Serve with plain rice.

SERVES 4.

Pheasant or Chicken and Wild Rice Braised in Ale

Early settlers learned about forest delicacies such as wild rice and mushrooms from Native American cooks. Today these savory products are widely available.

Both pheasant and chicken are delicious stuffed with wild rice, aromatic herbs and sausage, and dried mushrooms, then braised in light ale. A medium light ale—Ballantine or Frank Jones Ale from New Hampshire—provides malty flavors with lightly bitter undertones to complement the nutty wild rice and earthy mushrooms. Use the same ale in the dish and on the table (and perhaps a little in the cook, for quality control).

1 ounce dried mushrooms such as *porcini*

½ pound fresh sausage, such as mild Italian, casings removed

3 tablespoons butter

½ small onion, chopped

1 rib celery, chopped

2 garlic cloves, chopped

2 shallots, chopped (optional)

2 cups cooked wild rice

Salt and pepper

1 2½- to 3-pound pheasant or a 3- to 3½-pound chicken

1 cup light ale

1 cup Rich Chicken Stock (see page 203) or pheasant stock

½ teaspoon dried thyme

½ cup *crème fraîche* or sour cream (optional)

Soak the dried mushrooms or *porcini* in 1 cup boiling water for at least 30 minutes. Strain and save the soaking water; coarsely chop the mushrooms.

To make the stuffing: Fry the sausage meat in 1 tablespoon of the butter for 3 minutes. Add half the onion, celery, garlic, and (optional) shallots, cover, and cook for 3 minutes. Add 2 tablespoons of the soaking liquid, and cook another 2 minutes until the vegetables are soft. Place in a bowl to cool. Mix in the cooked wild rice and chopped mushrooms.

Salt and pepper the bird, stuff loosely with stuffing, and truss securely with string or skewers. Place any extra stuffing in a small buttered casserole. This can be covered with foil and baked 30 minutes at 350° F. to serve with the cooked pheasant or chicken.

To cook the pheasant or chicken: Preheat the oven to 350° F.

Melt the remaining 2 tablespoons of butter in a casserole or Dutch oven. Brown the pheasant or chicken on all sides, about 5 minutes total. Remove from the pan and add the remaining vegetables, sautéing them over high heat for about 1 minute. Add the ale, remaining *porcini* liquid, and stock, along with the thyme, and bring to a boil, scraping up any browned bits on the bottom of the pan. Cover and braise in oven for 1 hour, until the pheasant or chicken is tender.

Remove the pheasant or chicken to a warm platter, and reduce the sauce over high heat until syrupy. Degrease the sauce. Remove the sauce from the heat, and stir in the optional *crème fraîche* or sour cream. Cut the pheasant or chicken into quarters, and arrange on a platter with the wild rice stuffing. Serve each guest a quarter pheasant or chicken, some stuffing, and plenty of gravy.

SERVES 4.

Veal Shanks and Winter Vegetables in Ale

New England farmers stored fall crops like carrots, turnips, and parsnips in root cellars for use over the winter. Often they would pair them with tough cuts of meat, such as shank, in savory stews.

A high-hopped, malty British-style ale should underscore the spicy and earthy flavors of this dish. Mendocino Brewing's Red Tail Ale would do the job nicely, both in the pot and on the table.

¼ pound bacon, diced

4–5 pounds veal shanks, cut into 8 or 10 1-inch slices and trimmed of excess fat

3 tablespoons olive oil

3–4 tablespoons Spice Rub for Pork or Veal (see page 79)

1 large carrot, finely chopped

1 onion, finely chopped

2 ribs celery, finely chopped

1 parsnip, finely chopped

1½ cups beef or Rich Chicken Stock (see page 203)

1 12-ounce bottle ale

1 bunch (6–8) small carrots, peeled and left whole

1 celery root, peeled and cut into 1-inch dice

2 parsnips, peeled and cut into ½-inch cubes

Salt and pepper

2 tablespoons chopped parsley

Preheat the oven to 375° F. Spread the bacon pieces over the bottom of a large shallow baking dish and bake for about 10 minutes to render some of the fat. Pour off and discard most of the fat. Brush each veal shank with olive oil, and generously sprinkle each piece with some of the spice mixture. Turn the oven up to 500° F. Spread the chopped carrot, onion, celery, and parsnip over the bacon. Arrange the veal shanks over the chopped vegetables and bake for 20 minutes, uncovered, turning once, until the shanks begin to brown. Remove veal and vegetables from the oven, and turn the heat down to 350° F.

Put the veal shanks, bacon, and vegetables in a large Dutch oven or casserole and add the stock and ale. Bring to a boil over high heat, cover, and transfer the pan to the oven. After 30 minutes, add the whole carrots, celery root, and cubed parsnip. Bake, covered, for 30 minutes, or until the meat is quite tender. (At this point you may refrigerate the dish overnight. Remove any congealed fat, then proceed with the recipe before serving.)

Transfer the shanks and vegetables to a warm platter. Degrease the cooking liquid, and reduce it over high heat until it begins to get syrupy. Adjust the sauce for salt and pepper. Pour the sauce over the shanks and vegetables and garnish with the chopped parsley.

SERVES 8–10.

Onions Braised in Porter

These savory onions make a great accompaniment to roast poultry and meats. Use a rich, dark Porter or Stout—Anchor Porter or Grant's Imperial Stout.

1½ pounds small boiling onions (12 onions to a pound), peeled and left whole
2 tablespoons butter
4 bay leaves

1 12-ounce bottle dark beer, such as Porter or Stout
¾ cup Rich Chicken Stock (see page 203)
Salt and pepper

Put all the ingredients, except salt and pepper, in a deep skillet or Dutch oven, cover, and cook over medium heat for 20 minutes or until a knife can be easily inserted into the onions. Remove the onions and reserve. Reduce the liquid over high heat until there is just enough syrupy glaze to coat the onions. Pour glaze over onions. Season with salt and pepper and serve.

SERVES 6.

Turnips and Greens

This savory combination of turnips and bitter greens goes beautifully with ale, picking up the lightly astringent flavors of the hops and balancing the sweetness of the malt. Serve with roast pork, ham, or chicken, grilled or stewed beef, with a full-bodied malty ale, such as New Amsterdam Ale or Grant's Scottish Ale.

1 bunch mustard greens (any other greens like collard or turnip greens can be added or substituted)
4 tablespoons olive oil
2 garlic cloves or more, minced
4 tablespoons chopped parsley
2 large turnips, peeled, including the greens

2 tablespoons butter
1 lemon, zest and juice
1 teaspoon sugar
2 tablespoons minced chives (or minced green part of scallions or green onions)
Salt and pepper
½ cup sour cream (optional)

Wash the greens well and chop them coarsely. In a large skillet or Dutch oven, heat the oil over high heat and quickly sauté the garlic. Add the greens and cook until wilted. Add the parsley. Set aside.

Cut the turnips into equal ½-inch pieces. In a separate pan melt the butter, and add the turnips, coating the turnips with the butter. Add just enough water to cover the turnips. Cover, and cook over medium heat, about 7–10 minutes, or until cooked to taste. Uncover and evaporate any remaining liquid over high heat. Stir in the lemon juice, zest, sugar, and chives. Season to taste with salt and pepper. Combine the greens with the turnips, and stir in the optional sour cream. Serve on a heated platter.

SERVES 6.

Kathy's Strong Ale Spice Cake

In England and colonial America ale and Porter often added flavor to puddings and spice cakes. Kathy Kelly, Denis's wife, is a talented baker who likes to use ale or beer in her cakes and cookies. This spicy fruitcake includes an Amber Ale like Anchor's Liberty Ale, but a Porter or Bock would also work well.

1 cup Amber Ale	½ teaspoon nutmeg
2 cups mixed diced dried	⅛ teaspoon cloves
fruits, such as apricots,	2½ cups all-purpose flour
peaches, apples, or raisins	1 teaspoon baking powder
1 cup light brown sugar	1 teaspoon baking soda
⅓ cup vegetable oil	½ teaspoon salt
½ teaspoon cinnamon	1 egg

Preheat the oven to 350° F. In a saucepan mix together the ale, dried fruits, brown sugar, and oil with the spices and bring to a boil. Cook at a simmer for 3 minutes, and cool.

Add the flour to the fruit mixture with the baking powder and soda, salt, and egg. Stir until smooth. Pour into an oiled 9-inch square baking pan and bake, about 45 minutes, until a skewer inserted in the middle comes out clean. Cool on rack before serving.

SERVES 6–8.

Pumpkin Cookies

Another recipe from Kathy Kelly, these aromatic cookies are a family favorite, especially on cool fall days. They are delicious with dark beer like Porter or Bock or hot spiced apple cider.

2 cups all-purpose flour
2 teaspoons baking powder
½ teaspoon cinnamon
¼ teaspoon cloves
1 cup pumpkin puree (not pie filling)

½ cup vegetable oil
½ cup white sugar
½ cup light brown sugar
1 teaspoon vanilla
2 ounces dark beer
¾ cup chopped walnuts

Preheat the oven to 400° F. In a large bowl mix together the flour, baking powder, and spices. Add the pumpkin puree, oil, white and brown sugars, vanilla, and beer. Beat until smooth. Stir in the walnuts. Drop heaping teaspoons of the dough 2 inches apart on greased cookie sheets. Bake for 10–15 minutes until golden brown. Cool on racks. Store in airtight containers.

MAKES ABOUT 3 DOZEN COOKIES.

THE LAGER REVOLUTION

Smoked Fish and Potato Salad

Marlene's Three Herring Salads

Sole Stuffed with Crab in Light Lager Sauce

Fresh Beer Sausage

Warm Potato Salad with Beer Dressing

Pennsylvania Dutch Stuffed Onions

Country Spareribs and Sausage Braised with Sauerkraut
and Amber Lager

Spice Rub for Pork or Veal

Sauerkraut and Cabbage Braised in Dark Lager

The burgeoning immigrant population of America spread west during the early nineteenth century, with settlements like Pittsburgh,
Cincinnati, Cleveland, Louisville, St. Louis, and Chicago growing up
along the rivers and lakes of the fertile new land. And brewers followed
the migration west, establishing breweries and malting houses in the
growing cities to slake the thirst of the hard-working settlers, who,
increasingly, came from the beer-drinking lands of northern Europe.

Germans formed a large part of the population of the newly emerging Western cities: In 1830 5 percent of the citizens of Cincinnati were
of German birth; by 1840 Germans made up 28 percent of the population, and the city had eight breweries, most owned by German-born
brewers.

Top, an early lager brewery; note the icehouse for cool fermentation. Above, Chicago brewery, 1847. Right, malting drums, an example of the new technology introduced by German brewers.

These German-American brewers at first made ale and Porter, using top-fermenting yeast in the English style, but in the 1840's they began to experiment with a new bottom-fermenting (*untergahr*) yeast brought over from the old country. This yeast produced a new style of beer that could be fermented and aged (in German *lagern*) at cool temperatures, and the new "lager" beer eventually replaced the old style top-fermented ales throughout most of America. Americans of all ethnic backgrounds enjoyed the new beer, which was lighter and more subtle in flavor than the aggressively flavored ales. Earlier ales and Porters had been brewed as strong as possible to preserve stability and were often cloudy and turbid, with coarse and sometimes unpleasant flavors due to unsanitary brewing and improper storage. The lager brewers were proponents of the new science of brewing being developed on the continent, and they introduced the highest standards of cleanliness, scientific analysis, and quality control in their new breweries. Soon breweries all over the Midwest were making beer in the German style, using bottom-fermenting yeast and fermenting and storing the beer in cellars and icehouses at cool temperatures.

LAGER COMES TO AMERICA

My father came to this country in 1830, and located in Pittsburgh, as a cooper, in 1831. In the latter year he commenced to brew small or common beer [top fermentation] in a little copper kettle holding about one barrel. A year later he increased his plant to a ten-barrel kettle and a regular mash tub, delivering the product to his immediate customers in a wheelbarrow, as he often told me. . . . In 1848 we heard of Bavarian [lager] beer being brewed in Philadelphia. . . . With a great deal of trouble that same winter my father secured a small lot of *untergahr* yeast . . . and commenced brewing lager beer in January or February, 1849. . . . About 1850 my father first stored [lagered] about three hundred barrels, and continued to increase until 1854, in which year he made and sold eighteen hundred barrels. Ice was unknown then in the manufacture of lager beer; therefore, caves were blasted in the hills, two miles from the brewery, and all the beer brewed in the winter was carted to the *felsenkellers* [storage cellars] for summer use, the supply usually being exhausted by September 1. Then the brewer had to resort to common beer again until cold weather set in.

Memoirs of John Staub, Pittsburgh Brewing Company, *100 Years of Brewing*

There is still some discussion as to who brewed the first lager in America, but most writers give the honors to George Wagner of Philadelphia who had a small brewery in the rear of his house and brewed eight barrels at a time. Wagner had been brewmaster at a brewery in Bavaria, and in 1840 he brought the first lager yeast to the United States and began making lager beer. This new yeast was considered so valuable that Wagner's brother-in-law was "tempted beyond his strength" and stole about a pint of it to brew his own lager. For this he was arrested and convicted, serving a term of two years in the state penitentiary. This tells us something about the value and scarcity of the new yeast (and perhaps a little about Wagner's domestic relations).

The first lager brewed in Milwaukee, which soon became the lager

THE ARRIVAL OF THE FIRST LAGER YEAST IN MILWAUKEE

Finally the yeast came. It was packed in a strong wooden box about a foot and a half square. The yeast was packed in a sort of sawdust, around which were wound several folds of strong hop-sacking. The wrapping was carefully taken off, and to the astonishment of all of us, the yeast was found to be in good condition. . . . The capacity of our kettle in those days was just eighteen barrels, and we calculated that the yeast we had was just about enough for one brew. No one slept very much while we were trying the new yeast, but it was a success. . . . After our first trial, we brewed top fermentation beer at one brew and the next brew was a bottom fermentation beer.

Memoirs of Philip Best, *100 Years of Brewing*

capital of America, dates back to 1850 when Philip Best obtained some of the new bottom-fermenting yeast. Milwaukee, in the heart of the northern prairies where most of the country's barley is grown, was host to a growing German population. The city's shipping and processing facilities quickly made it the center of the emerging lager beer industry, led by Frederick Pabst (Best's son-in-law), Joseph Schlitz, and others.

The new beer was immensely successful everywhere and often in short supply. One brewer states that his brewery was "for many years the resort of the Germans of Philadelphia, who more than once drank the brewery dry; and often we were compelled to display the placard that beer would again be dispensed after a certain date."* Breweries expanded their production rapidly to fill the growing thirst for lager, and with ice readily available from frozen rivers and lakes (and later mechanical refrigeration), brewing was carried on year round.

As the taste for lager increased throughout the 1840's and 50's, large lager breweries were established in New York, St. Louis, Chicago, and Milwaukee by German-born brewers. Ale was still made, but by mid-

*This and other references in this chapter are from *100 Years of Brewing* (H. S. Rich, 1903; reprint, Arno Press, 1974).

century the new, lighter beers were taking over. In 1857 in Philadelphia, for example, 180,000 barrels of lager were made compared to 170,000 barrels of ale. In cities with large German populations, however, lager far outsold ale: Milwaukee in 1866 consumed 68,000 barrels of lager to only 3,600 barrels of ale.

This period just after the Civil War marks a tremendous expansion of lager beer brewing and drinking in the United States and the foundation of the great national breweries like Pabst, Schlitz, and Anheuser-Busch. As beer historian Victor Clark points out, "The largest plants now had a capacity approaching 200,000 barrels per annum. Steam was used for heating and sterilizing, as well as for driving pumps and elevators, and refrigeration made it possible to brew a uniform product throughout the year . . . [in] the neighborhood of the grain and hop fields of the West."

American Lager: A New Style Emerges

When German brewers brought their new style of beer to America, they found ready acceptance for their product by American consumers—German-Americans to begin with, but in time the entire population. Conditions in the United States were propitious for the new beer: ample and abundant supplies of ice on Eastern and Midwestern rivers and lakes, a great granary in the Midwest supplying huge quantities of inexpensive and excellent barley, wheat, and corn, a thriving economy expanded by the Civil War, and a new technology that would transform American agriculture and society in the late nineteenth and early twentieth century.

Ice cut from rivers and lakes was used to cool the first lagers made in America.

From the beginning American brewers had added rice and corn to the mash, and the new lager brewers followed suit, making a brew that was generally lighter in color and flavor than most European beers. These new lagers suited the growing American taste for light and delicate beers and had the added advantage of being considerably cheaper than the all-malt beers favored on the continent.

With the lager revolution came the beginnings of the trend to lighter and still lighter beers that has resulted in today's thin (some would say almost tasteless) American beer.

OUR FAVORITE BREWERY,

THE ANHEUSER-BUSCH.

Over the years the American Pilsner style evolved: highly carbonated to suit the American taste for bubbly sodas and soft drinks, light in color and flavor, slightly sweet with only a whisper of hops. German-born brewers like Joseph Schlitz, Fred Pabst, Frederick Miller, Eberhard Anheuser, and Adolphus Busch created and refined the style and founded the companies that grew into the huge national breweries that dominate the market today.

LAGER AND *GEMÜTLICHKEIT:* GERMAN-AMERICAN BEER GARDENS

German immigrants brought not only their beer to the new land but also their beer-drinking traditions. In Germany beer drinking seems as natural as breathing, and beer is consumed regularly as a pleasant adjunct to everyday life. Low in alcohol and mild in its effect, lager beer was seen as a healthful and temperate beverage to be appreciated in pleasant and salubrious surroundings. Gin parlors and dingy saloons were not for the German drinker: rather, a pleasant garden setting with good food and music, pastimes for the whole family to enjoy, and a wholesome and healthy atmosphere—in a word, *Gemütlichkeit,* or congeniality.

In late-nineteenth-century America, every German neighborhood had its beer garden, offering an idyllic place to sip lager, picnic with friends and family, and relax from the cares of everyday life. Sunday was a favorite day for family outings, often scandalizing Anglo-Saxon Puritans, and the beer gardens in New York, St. Louis, Milwaukee, and Cincinnati would fill up quickly with German families in their Sunday best listening to music, playing games, eating platters of *wurst* and *kartopfelsalade,* and calmly sipping lager beer.

The Atlantic Garden in New York's Little Germany on the Bowery was typical, with its huge hall for all-day "picnics" of over 2,500 people, garden murals on the walls, and an oompah band playing in a box that hung from the ceiling. There were games of cards and dominoes and dice at tables all around the room, along with billiard rooms, bowling alleys, and even a rifle range where family members could amuse themselves by blazing away at wooden Turks and Zouaves.

In *On the Town in New York* (Scribners, 1973), Michael and Ariane Batterberry describe lager beer served for a nickle a stein by local frauleins in short skirts and red-topped boots, and the bar "loaded with sausages, those famous snake-looking American 'Bolognas,' with cakes and bread, brown and shiny, contorted and twisted, patted and molded as only the German brain could devise; green, fresh-looking salads dripping with oil, dimpled with red beets and scarlet turnips; salads of fish, salads of meat, salads of herring."

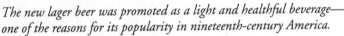

The new lager beer was promoted as a light and healthful beverage—one of the reasons for its popularity in nineteenth-century America.

Beer gardens in other cities were even more elaborate, and served, some historians feel, as models for present-day theme parks like Disneyland. Outdoor parks had ornate gazebos and picnic areas with plenty of tables for families to spread out their substantial buffets. Pabst Park in Milwaukee, one of the most famous of the country's beer gardens, had a roller coaster and Wild West shows, while Schlitz Park had a concert hall that could seat 5,000, bowling alleys, and a zoo. As Ray Oldenburg points out in *The Great Good Place* (Paragon House, 1989), "the German-American lager beer garden . . . was the basis of community. Though organized around drinking, it was . . . 'as respectable as the corner grocery store.' Unlike the Yankee saloon, which inspired so many temperance hymns and which promoted the image of Little Nell vainly searching for her father amid a throng of drunken barroom revellers, the beer garden was a unifying force in family life, not a divisive one."

Lager beer was the ideal beverage for such a setting: It was low in alcohol, light enough to be enjoyed by both men and women, and relatively inexpensive. With their pleasant atmosphere, good food and drink, and emphasis on family values, beer gardens went a long way toward making lager beer the quintessential American drink.

Early beer gardens in St. Louis (above) and on New York's Bowery (left) were favorite spots for family outings.

Smoked Fish and Potato Salad

Salads of smoked fish and potatoes in a savory vinaigrette were favorites in German-American beer gardens. The salty, smoky fish, earthy potatoes, and piquant vinaigrette provide a wonderful undertone to malty light lagers and full-bodied Bocks.

Smoked Great Lakes whitefish, often available in Jewish delis, is ideal for this dish, but smoked trout or other mild white-fleshed fish—albacore, sturgeon, cod, or halibut—are also delicious. (See Smoking Fish and Seafood, page 121, to make your own smoked fish.) This salad can also be made with pickled herring in place of the smoked fish.

Light lager or Wheat Beer is our choice of beer: Try Stroh's Signature or August Schell Weizen.

2 pounds small white potatoes	½ cup finely chopped parsley
3 tablespoons lemon juice	⅔ cup Mustard Vinaigrette
¾ pound smoked white-fleshed fish, all skin and bones removed	(see page 271)
	⅓ cup mayonnaise
	Salt and pepper
⅓ cup finely chopped red onion	1 tablespoon chopped fresh dill

Boil the potatoes in salted water until a knife point goes in easily, about 25 minutes. Drain and remove skins. While still warm, slice the potatoes into ¼-inch rounds and in a large bowl toss with the lemon juice.

Break the fish up into ¼- to ½-inch pieces, and add to the bowl with the onion and parsley. Whisk together the vinaigrette and mayonnaise to make a thin creamy dressing, and gently toss the salad with it. Don't overmix or the potatoes will break up. Taste for salt and pepper. Spoon the salad into a shallow bowl or on a platter, and garnish with the fresh dill. Serve at room temperature or refrigerate, covered, for later use.
SERVES 6–8.

Marlene's Three Herring Salads

Herring salad is a traditional German specialty and is ideal with beer. The salty, vinegary flavors of the fish balance the malty sweetness of lager, and provide just the edge of thirst to make us want another swallow. It's no wonder salted and pickled fish were favorite dishes in beer gardens and taverns—they sold more beer.

Marlene Levinson is a salad queen, supplying salads to some of the San Francisco Bay Area's best takeout food shops and upscale delis. When we asked her for a herring salad recipe, she gave us three. Since they're all delicious and easy to make, and go so well with beer, we decided to include all three. The recipes use bottled herring marinated in wine. Just drain and discard the juices and seasonings before using the fish in the salads.

Marinated herring is wonderful with full-flavored light lagers: Try Gartenbrau Special from Wisconsin or August Schell Pilsner.

Herring Salad I

1 jar (8 ounces) wine-mari-
   nated herring, chopped fine
1 hard-boiled egg, chopped
   fine

1 small tart apple, chopped fine
½ onion, or to taste, chopped
   fine
½–1 teaspoon sugar, or to taste

Mix all the ingredients together and let marinate, refrigerated, for several hours. Serve with rye bread rounds.
SERVES 4–6.

Herring Salad II

1 jar (8 ounces) wine-mari-
   nated herring, cut into ½-
   inch pieces
1 small tart green apple, cut
   into wedges and thinly
   sliced

1 small lemon, cut into wedges
   and thinly sliced
1 small onion, halved and
   thinly sliced
1 cup sour cream

Mix all the ingredients together and marinate, covered, in the refrigerator for up to 2 days. Serve with toothpicks or on rye bread rounds.
SERVES 4–6.

Herring Salad III

1 jar (8 ounces) wine-
   marinated herring,
   chopped fine
½ green bell pepper,
   chopped fine
2–3 green onions or scallions,
   thinly sliced

½ cup mayonnaise
½ cup sour cream
1 teaspoon lemon juice
1 teaspoon celery seeds, or 1
   rib celery, chopped fine

Mix together all the ingredients and let stand for 1 hour for the flavors
to develop. Serve with rye bread rounds.

SERVES 4–6.

Sole Stuffed with Crab in Light Lager Sauce

*When we think of "beer food," hearty and spicy dishes usually come to
mind. But lagers, Pale Ales, and Wheat Beers can often be part of an
elegant dish like this one, which is derived from a specialty dish served in
some of the fine fish houses in Portland and Seattle.*

*This luxurious presentation, with its subtle sauce and savory stuffing,
makes a perfect centerpiece for a formal dinner party. Serve it with a
delicate Wheat Beer such as Grant's Weiss Beer or a light lager like
Kemper Pilsner.*

6 sole fillets, no more than
   ½ inch thick, measuring
   about 3 × 6 inches each
Salt and pepper
3 tablespoons butter
½ cup finely chopped onion
1 teaspoon minced garlic
½ pound mushrooms, chopped
1 tablespoon fresh tarragon
   or 1½ teaspoons dried
¼ cup chopped green
   onions or scallions

2 tablespoons finely chopped
   red bell pepper
1 cup fresh crab meat
1½ cups bread crumbs,
   preferably fresh
1 egg, lightly beaten
1 12-ounce bottle light lager
1 cup fish stock, clam juice,
   or chicken stock
1 cup heavy cream
Lemon juice to taste

*Sole
Stuffed
with Crab
in Light
Lager
Sauce
(continued)*

Lightly salt and pepper the fillets and set aside. Heat the butter in a skillet over medium heat. Add the onion, garlic, and half the mushrooms, and cook for 5 minutes. Add half the tarragon along with the green onions and bell pepper. Cook for 2 minutes. Transfer to a bowl, and add the crab and bread crumbs. Do not overmix; the crab should stay in relatively large pieces. Add the egg and taste for salt and pepper. Moisten the stuffing with a little stock or clam juice, if it seems too dry.

Preheat the oven to 350° F.

Divide the stuffing into 6 equal amounts. Place the fish fillets skin side down, and cover with a generous layer of the stuffing. Roll the fillets up, and secure each with a wooden toothpick. Place the fillets in a nonaluminum baking dish. Sprinkle with the remaining tarragon and pour the remaining stock or clam juice and the lager over the fish. Add the rest of the mushrooms, cover with foil, and bake for 20–30 minutes, depending on the thickness. Transfer the stuffed fillets to a warm platter, and strain the cooking liquid into a saucepan. Reduce the liquid by boiling it uncovered. Add the cream and cook until the sauce is syrupy. Season with salt and pepper and lemon juice. Pour the sauce over the fish and serve immediately.

SERVES 6.

Fresh Beer Sausage

Beer and sausage are one of those natural combinations; like ham and eggs, they seem made for each other. Beer tastes so good with sausage that it is often used in sausage. Sweet malt and bitter hops add even more spice and flavor.

This sausage can be used in any recipe calling for fresh bratwurst and is especially good braised in beer with onions and served on dark bread with Honey Beer Mustard.*

The meat and spice mixture can be stuffed into casings or left in bulk to use in various recipes throughout this book. It can also be frozen in 1/2- to 1-pound portions.

We use only a little salt in this recipe, as the bacon provides most of the salt needed for preservation and flavor. Salt levels in bacon vary, however, so be sure to fry up a sample patty, and adjust the salt to your own taste.

*See Index.

Dark malty lager and an undertone of smoke from the bacon make this unique sausage a great match for a seidel of dark beer like Samuel Adams Octoberfest or Hübsch Dunkel.

1 pound pork butt with some fat (10–15%)

1 pound beef chuck with some fat (10–15%)

1 pound smoked bacon

1 cup dark lager

1 tablespoon finely chopped garlic

3 teaspoons dry mustard powder, preferably Colman's

1 teaspoon whole brown mustard seeds

½ teaspoon mace

½ teaspoon coriander

1 tablespoon fresh marjoram or 2 teaspoons dried

2 teaspoons dried sage

1 teaspoon salt

1 tablespoon coarsely ground black pepper

1 teaspoon sugar

Medium hog casings (optional)

Grind the pork, beef, and bacon through the ¼-inch plate of a meat grinder or chop them coarsely in a food processor. Mix with the remaining ingredients, and with your hands knead and squeeze until everything is thoroughly blended. Refrigerate for at least 45 minutes to allow the beer to be completely absorbed by the sausage meat. Stuff into medium hog casings and tie into 6-inch links, or leave in bulk to fry as patties or use in cooked dishes that call for sausage.

These sausages are best aged a day or two uncovered in the refrigerator before using. Will keep 3–4 days in the refrigerator, up to 3 months in the freezer.

MAKES 3–4 POUNDS.

Warm Potato Salad with Beer Dressing

Beer and potatoes make a great combination, especially when vinegar and beer dressing is added, as in this simple German-style potato salad. Be sure to dress the potatoes while they are still warm so they can absorb the dressing, which is also delicious over cold cooked vegetables such as cauliflower; garnish with a few capers. Diced fried bacon or smoked sausage would be another good addition.

Sprecher Maibock and Ambier Vienna Style Lager from Milwaukee are two malty amber lagers that would go very well with this piquant salad.

Potato Salad

2½ pounds red potatoes
½ cup finely chopped mild
   red or yellow onions

¼ cup finely chopped parsley
2 tablespoons chopped chives

Beer Dressing

6 tablespoons olive oil
½ cup finely chopped onions
¾ cup lager
3 tablespoons malt or cider
   vinegar

1 tablespoon Dijon mustard
½ teaspoon sugar
Salt and pepper

To make the salad: Cook the potatoes in boiling salted water until a knife point can be easily inserted, about 20–25 minutes. Remove, and as soon as you can handle them, slice them, unpeeled, into ¼-inch rounds. While the potatoes are still warm, gently mix them with the onions, parsley, and beer dressing. Do not overmix or the potatoes may break into pieces. Taste for salt and pepper. Garnish with chopped chives. Serve warm or at room temperature.

SERVES 6.

To make the dressing: Heat 2 tablespoons of the olive oil in a small frying pan over medium heat. Add the onions and cook until just soft, about 5 minutes. Add the lager, vinegar, and sugar and boil for 5 minutes. Put into a food processor with the mustard. With the motor running, slowly pour in the remaining 4 tablespoons olive oil. Taste for salt and pepper.

MAKES ABOUT 1 CUP, ENOUGH FOR 2½ POUNDS POTATOES.

Pennsylvania Dutch Stuffed Onions

Stuffed onions are eaten across Middle America as a side dish or light main course and are especially popular on Pennsylvania Dutch tables. Some recipes suggest that you stuff raw onions, but we find that blanching the onions first is helpful in scooping out the centers and also in the cooking.

The natural accompaniment to this savory dish is a light lager—Yuengling from Pottsville, Pennsylvania, or Stevens Point Special from Wisconsin.

6 large yellow onions, unpeeled
¾ pound fresh country-style sausage in bulk or removed from casings
½ cup grated apple
¾ cup day-old coarse bread crumbs
1 teaspoon dried sage

1 teaspoon grated lemon rind
1 egg
1 cup beef or chicken stock
⅔ cup light lager
3 tablespoons malt vinegar
Pinch each of nutmeg and cinnamon
Salt and pepper

Boil the unpeeled onions in a large pot of lightly salted water for 5 minutes. Cool under running water, remove the peel, and scoop out the centers, leaving a shell about ½-inch thick. Chop the onion centers and set the shells aside.

Preheat the oven to 350° F.

In a heavy pan fry the sausage meat over medium-high heat, crumbling it with a fork as it cooks, for 5 minutes. Add the chopped onion and cook for 5 minutes more. Transfer to a large bowl and add the apple, bread crumbs, sage, lemon rind, and egg. Stuff the mixture into the onion shells. Arrange the shells in a baking pan just large enough to hold them. Add the stock, lager, malt vinegar, and nutmeg and cinnamon. Cover with foil, and bake for 45 minutes to 1 hour, or until the onions are quite tender. Remove the pan, pour off the cooking liquid, and degrease it. In a small pot boil the liquid down until it becomes syrupy. Taste for salt and pepper.

Meanwhile, continue to bake the onions for another 15 minutes or so to brown the tops. Pour the sauce over the onions and serve.

SERVES 4–6.

Country Spareribs and Sausage Braised with Sauerkraut and Amber Lager

The schlactplat *is a dish found in German restaurants all over the Midwest. Typically it's a huge platter overflowing with sauerkraut and various cuts of pork and sausage—a reminder of the feast each autumn in the homeland when the pigs were slaughtered (*schlacten *in German) and everyone celebrated with platters of pork and kraut and foaming steins of lager.*

Full-bodied Amber Lagers in the Octoberfest style are suited to this sort of dish. The sweet malt and sour kraut balance beautifully. This dish is even more delicious prepared ahead and reheated the next day.

For the beer, choose an Octoberfest-style lager: Gartenbrau Oktoberfest from Wisconsin or Coors Winterfest.

2½ tablespoons Spice Rub for Pork or Veal (recipe follows)

3–4 pounds country-style spareribs or thick-cut pork chops, fresh or smoked

¼ cup bacon fat or olive oil

2 large onions, thinly sliced

1 large carrot, coarsely diced

5 garlic cloves, peeled

1 12-ounce bottle amber lager

2 cups beef stock

1 teaspoon dried thyme

2 teaspoons coarsely ground black pepper

2 bay leaves

1 tablespoon yellow mustard seeds

1 ham hock, sawed into 4 or 5 pieces

2 pounds sauerkraut, drained

6 links (1½ pounds) smoky sausage, such as Fresh Beer Sausage (see page 74), kielbasa, smoked bratwurst, or knockwurst

Preheat the oven to 350° F. Rub the spice mixture all over the spareribs. Heat the bacon fat or olive oil in a large Dutch oven or casserole and brown the spareribs in batches over medium heat for 5 or 6 minutes at a time, being careful not to crowd the pan. Remove the ribs to a platter as they are browned.

Pour off all but 2 tablespoons of the fat, and add the onions and carrot. Cover and cook for 10 minutes, stirring occasionally. Add the whole garlic cloves, cook for 1 more minute, and then pour in the lager and stock with the thyme, pepper, bay leaves, mustard seeds, ham hock, and sauerkraut. Bring to a boil. Return the spareribs to the pot, cover, and transfer to the oven. Braise for 1¼ hours or until the ribs and ham hock are quite tender. Add the whole sausages, and continue cooking for another 20 minutes. Remove the pot from the oven, and degrease the surface. Serve with boiled new potatoes.

SERVES 8, WITH LEFTOVERS.

Spice Rub for Pork or Veal

2 teaspoons dried thyme
2 teaspoons freshly ground
   black pepper
1 teaspoon salt
½ teaspoon dried savory

½ teaspoon dried sage
1 tablespoon sweet Hungarian
   paprika
1 teaspoon dry mustard
   powder

Mix together all the ingredients. Rub on the meat before grilling, roasting, or braising.

MAKES 3 TABLESPOONS.

Sauerkraut and Cabbage Braised in Dark Lager

By combining fresh cabbage with sauerkraut and beer you end up with a subtly flavored side dish that is wonderful with ham, roast duck, or pork. And you can always turn this into a main course simply by adding cooked sausages or leftover smoked meat like ham or smoked pork chops. This easy-to-make recipe is best made up a day ahead and rewarmed. For the beer, we suggest a Dark Lager such as August Schell Bock or Thomas Kemper Bock.

¼ pound diced bacon or
   salt pork
1 2-pound head cabbage,
   thinly sliced
2 medium onions, thinly
   sliced
1 carrot, split and thinly sliced
1–1½ pounds sauerkraut,
   drained

½ teaspoon caraway seeds
2 tablespoons Hungarian
   paprika
½ teaspoon dried thyme
1 tablespoon tomato paste
1 teaspoon coarsely ground
   black pepper
1 cup dark lager
Salt to taste

Sauerkraut and Cabbage Braised in Dark Lager (continued)

In a large nonaluminum pot or Dutch oven, fry the bacon or salt pork over medium heat until lightly browned, about 7 minutes. Add the cabbage, onions, and carrot. Cover and cook until the vegetables begin to wilt, stirring occasionally, about 10 minutes. Stir in the sauerkraut and all the remaining ingredients except the salt. Cover and simmer over low heat for 1½–2 hours, until everything is quite tender. Add more beer or liquid if needed. Taste for salt before serving. The dish can be served at once, or be refrigerated and served at a later time. SERVES 8.

OLD-TIME SALOONS AND THE FREE LUNCH

Pepper and Garlic Toasted Almonds

Popcorn with Parmesan and Garlic

Edy's Soft Pretzels

Cheese and Ale Spread

Tavern Pickled Onions

Beer and Onion Soup

Blue Cheese and Beer Croutons

Saloon Sausage

Rick's Beer-Baked Beans

Boilermaker Rabbit or Chicken Stew

Honey Beer Mustard

Porter Pot Roast

Deviled Oxtail

If the tavern was the seventeenth and eighteenth century's American drinking establishment, the saloon was the nineteenth's. From around the 1850's, the tavern—a combination of hotel, restaurant, and bar—gradually changed, especially in urban areas swelling with new immigrants, into the saloon that served drinks and a free lunch at the bar and functioned as a neighborhood workingman's club. Just as the tavern had been the focus of small-town life in early America, the saloon often functioned as a social club, union hall, political club-

The Saloon's Bleary, Beery Charm

Saloon life radiated a bleary, beery charm immortalized later in song: "Just mention 'saloon' and my cares fade away." A neighborhood saloon became the hub of a workingman's universe and he visited it daily, sometimes as frequently as morning, noon, and night. A saloon gave a man a chance to air his political opinions; it gave him masculine privacy, a feeling of belonging, easy credit (despite the curt notices on the wall to the contrary), escape from nagging household problems, and what's more, a free lunch.

Michael and Ariane Batterberry, *On the Town in New York*

house, and, in general, as a neighborhood center that, along with the parish church and the lodge hall, gave a sense of community to immigrants in a strange new land.

While most didn't survive Prohibition, some of the old-time saloons still remain. Chronicled by Toby Thompson in his monumental American pub crawl, *Saloon* (Viking, 1976), old-fashioned American saloons can be found in many American cities and towns today, and they are worth a visit.

When you walk into an old-time saloon from a busy street on a bright afternoon, it is as dim and quiet as a church, with a long bar of sleek mahogany stretching back into the darkness, a tall back bar with Corinthian columns and intricately carved entablatures towering like an altar. In the mirror (there's always a mirror), two or three old men contemplate themselves and the universe as they sip their afternoon beer. Behind the bar stands the publican; he is dignified, of a certain age, calmly awaiting whatever comes through the door, serenely in control and at peace with himself and all mankind. From time to time he wipes down the bar with a clean, white, folded cloth, carefully polishing the antique patina and inspecting its dark luster yet again.

MOPPING UP   R. L. Goldberg

When you ask for a beer, he draws a mug judiciously, pulling back the ornate enameled tap handle with a practiced hand. He pays great attention to the head, sculpting it with a twist and a flourish, and gently sets the beaded seidel of pale cool lager in front of you. He waits for a nod of approval and nods back benignly before resuming his polishing.

You sit back in the calm darkness, nursing your beer, breathing in that ineffable aroma of the old-time saloon: dark wood, spilled beer, good cigars, and ancient whiskey—the sacred incense of the drinking man.

THE FREE LUNCH (SOMETIMES IT COST A NICKEL)

Sometimes it was free and sometimes you had to come up with a nickel or a dime. It ranged from a couple of slices of stale ham and a hunk of hard cheese to a full-scale buffet with roast beef, pickled herring, pig's feet, potato salad, and salted sardines, all served with rye bread, raw onions, and pots of the hottest mustard ordinary mortals could bear. Meager or sumptuous, free or just cheap, the saloon lunch was an integral feature at virtually every bar or tavern worth its salt during the heyday of the saloon from the 1880's until that dark night of the American soul, Prohibition.

About eleven o'clock every morning a long buffet table or side bar would be piled high with eats, mostly of the salty variety (to keep the thirst level high) and heavy on the hearty. All you had to do was to sidle up to the bar, order a schooner of beer, grab a plate, and fall to.

The Ubiquitous Sardine

Just about every free lunch table, even the lowliest, had platters of salt fish, usually "sardellen," or salted sardines. George Ade describes them in *The Old Time Saloon:* "The sardellen, saturated with brine and probably sold by the hogshead, became one of the staple stand-bys of every saloon catering to a reliable beer trade. They were saltier than the Seven Seas and were served whole. No one had tampered with the heads, tails or interior arrangements. They were in great favor because a patron after he had taken a couple of them, draped across a slab of rye bread, had to rush to the bar and drink a lot of beer to get the taste out of his mouth. The sardellen were more than fish. They were silent partners."

Some of the more fashionable establishments might ask you to toss a nickel into a cigar box or bowl on the bar or tip the waiter a dime, but in most saloons the price of a beer bought you lunch. But woe betide the freeloader who slipped in through the swinging doors and headed straight for the buffet without the requisite stop at the main bar for a beer or a shot first. He would soon meet another feature of any respectable American saloon, the bouncer. This usually large and always bellicose gent's single task in life was to keep order in the saloon, according to the publican's definition of order (standards varied). But all agreed that nobody got to the free lunch counter without a glass in his hand. Otherwise it meant the "bum's rush," a quick trip back through the swinging doors, landing on one's nose on the sidewalk in the bright morning light, still hungry, certainly thirsty, sadder, and wiser than before.

Some saloons developed reputations, and a faithful clientele, from the quality and richness of their spreads. The Hoffman House in New York, for example, was famous for the plenitude of its buffet, and the better saloons offered quite a range of foods, all with the common theme of salty and spicy.

One of the most sumptuous buffets was found in that bastion of the newly affluent merchants, bankers, and stockbrokers in New York, the

Waldorf Astoria. According to *On the Town in New York,* the gentleman's bar was "an avalanche of caviar, canapes, cheeses, cold meats, anchovies, olives, radishes, and salads."

Some saloons got into the practice of handing out food with each drink the customer bought. Often a sign behind the bar read:

> *A FRIED OYSTER, A CLAM*
> *OR A HARDBOILED EGG WITH*
> *EVERY DRINK.*

One famous basement bar in Chicago even sold its beer-drinking customer huge wedges of homemade apple, huckleberry, or coconut pie for five cents each. This seems a strange combination, but we are told by George Ade in his nostalgic reminiscence *The Old Time Saloon* (Long & Smith, 1931) that "many of the boys like pastry with their suds."

The free lunch could be quite elaborate. San Francisco's Palace of Art (see menu, left) and the Hoffman House in New York (below) served sumptuous buffets.

The Palace of Art.

OUR FREE LUNCH.

Served with All Drinks, from 4 to 11 P.M.

Radishes	Crab Salad	Celery
	Clam Juice	
Pigs Head	Bolinas Bay Clams	Head Cheese
Saucisses à la Famille	Beef à la Chile Colorado	
Chili Con Carne	Honolulu Beans	
Chicken Croquette	Veal Croquette	Terrapin Stew
Fried Clams	Sardines	Boiled Ham
Saratoga Chips	Corned Beef	
Cold Tongue	Beef Stew	Pork and Beans
Chipped Beef	Smoked Salmon	
Cheese	Crackers	
Cracked Crab	Holland Herring	
Almonds	Pop Corn	Apples

FOR WINE LIST SEE LAST PAGE.

MCSORLEY'S OLD ALE HOUSE

From the sidewalk it doesn't look like much, just another New York storefront bar, on Seventh Street just east of Fourth Avenue near Cooper Union. There's a dusty, fly-specked window behind an old wire grill, a beat-up door with no sign to speak of, just "McSorley's Old Ale House" dimly painted above the door. It's easy to miss, unless you know what you're looking for.

When you push open the door, it's like stepping right into 1854, the year John McSorley opened his Old House At Home modeled on a pub back in Ireland. Mug-scarred tables are scattered all around the big front room with rickety captain's chairs clustered around a big, potbellied stove. The bar is decrepit, more like an old wooden store counter, pockmarked and warped after all the years, shored up with metal pipes and two-by-fours.

The back bar and all the walls are hung with fading newspaper clippings, old photos, horseshoes, ribbons, menus, posters, many dating back to Old John, the founder. Sawdust is scattered over the worn wood floor, old men doze at tables near the window, Irish bartenders draw mugs of golden ale that glow in the late afternoon light.

"McSorley's Cats" (1928–29), by John Sloan.

McSorley's has pretty much stayed the same over all the years it's been open, and this includes Prohibition. Somehow Old John's son Bill never got around to closing the doors, and with Irish cops, local politicians, and, it is rumored, even Treasury agents as loyal customers, nobody ever objected to the flow of good ale over the venerable bar.

McSorley's is reputed to be the oldest continually operating saloon in New York, and maybe in the whole country. Ask any of the regulars sitting around the potbellied stove on a winter afternoon, and he'll be more than happy to fill you in on the history and grandeur of the house.

Owners from John and Bill McSorley down through the years to the present day have adhered to a religion of the past in the saloon. "Old John," we are told by Joseph Mitchell in his famous essay "The Old House At Home" in *McSorley's Wonderful Saloon* (Blue Ribbon Press, 1944),

> had a remarkable passion for memorabilia. . . . Old John decorated the partition between barroom and back room with banquet menus, autographs, starfish shells, theatre programs, political posters, and worn-down shoes taken off the hoofs of various race and brewery horses. Above the entrance to the back room he hung a shillelagh and a sign: BE GOOD OR BEGONE. On one wall of the barroom he placed portraits of horses, steamboats, Tammany bosses, jockeys, actors, singers, and statesmen. Around 1902 he put up a heavy oak frame containing excellent portraits of Lincoln, Garfield, and McKinley, and to the frame he attached a brass title tag reading, THEY ASSASSINATED THESE GOOD MEN THE SKULKING DOGS. . . . The title tag on another engraving reads, "Rescue of Colonel Thomas J. Kelly and Captain Timothy Deacy by Members of the Irish Revolutionary Brotherhood from the English Government at Manchester, England, September 18, 1867." . . . Eventually Old John covered practically every square inch of wall space between wainscot and ceiling with pictures and souvenirs. They are still in good condition, although spiders have strung webs across many of them.

Old John felt that the presence of women modified the tone of a saloon and interfered with tranquil drinking and calm conversation. So, on opening, he nailed a sign up over the door: NOTICE, NO BACK ROOM IN HERE FOR LADIES. Until 1970, when the saloon was officially liberated by federal decree, women weren't served at McSorley's.

McSorley's Ale became a popular brand in New York after the Second World War.

To the best of anyone's knowledge, there were only two exceptions. Mother Fresh-Roasted, an old woman who peddled fresh-roasted peanuts in East Side saloons and whose husband died from a lizard bite in the Spanish-American War—to this venerable entity Old John sold an occasional ale on a hot day. And a brave feminist in the 1920's who came in wearing men's clothes and smoking a cigar. After sipping an ale at the bar, she took off her cap, shook her hair free, and proclaimed the freedom of women and her scorn for the clan McSorley in a loud voice to the assembled regulars before departing hastily, leaving Bill McSorley muttering for years after about the terrible perfidy of women.

Ironically, McSorley's was owned for many years by Dorothy O'Connel Kirwan, daughter of a retired policeman, a McSorley's regular, who bought the saloon from Bill just a few years before he died in 1938. She adhered to the ancient tradition and never entered the bar while it was open, visiting only on Sunday nights after closing.

McSorley's has plenty of women customers these days, and no one seems to mind. The old-timers still sit at the tables near the stove, and they chat pleasantly with all comers. The place seems a little cleaner, some say, and the tone of the conversation seems to have improved somewhat. The decor, the ale, and the famous bar lunch haven't changed though.

Ale is the drink of choice at McSorley's, and for most of its existence draft ale, specially brewed for the house, has been the only drink available. Lager was always looked on as a newfangled, Teutonic aberration. Hard liquor was served once as an experiment in 1906 or so, but it seemed to disturb the peace of mind and tranquillity of the regulars, and was discontinued.

McSorley's ale is served up in glass mugs, usually sold two at a time. The ale is cellar cool and fresh, delivered daily from the brewery, and is a satisfying and robust potation. Deep gold in color with a creamy head, it has a fruity malty flavor with a decided tang of hops. McSorley's ale is a good example of what American's drank before the lager revolution—hearty and full-bodied ale, with an individual character and flavor all its own.

The saloon lunch is a McSorley's standby, and although you have to pay a few bucks for it these days, the spread at the bar carries on the tradition of the free lunch and has varied little over the years. Raw onions are one of the constants, as the motto that once hung over the bar attests: "Good Ale, Raw Onions, No Ladies." Bill McSorley used to stick a whole raw onion into the heel of a loaf of French bread for

A quiet afternoon at McSorley's.

lunch, and munch away contentedly. It's said that wives in the old days didn't worry about wayward husbands coming home after a night on the town if they smelled of McSorley's onions. There was no worry about female companionship, and a few glasses of ale of an evening were nothing much to be concerned about.

Along with the raw onions, you're likely to find a platter of old sharp Cheddar. (So old, Mitchell suggests, that it's been on the bar since opening day in 1854.) Sliced cold cuts are usually set out: metwurst, salami, old-fashioned bologna, blood sausage, depending on what's available. Dark rye bread and hot mustard complete the buffet.

The usual procedure is to pick up a couple of mugs of ale at the bar, find a spot at one of the tables, drink one mug to satisfy the thirst, and then return to build a sandwich to eat with the other. Raw onions, dark bread, sharp cheese, and hot mustard are required for a true McSorley's sandwich; cold cuts are optional; lettuce or other additions unheard of.

The clientele at McSorley's from the beginning has always had a Bohemian bent. Students from Cooper Union, an art and engineering school, are regulars and now include a pleasant mix of both sexes. Peter Cooper, substantial citizen and founder of the school just a block west of the saloon, was a regular and good friend of Old John's. His full-length portrait still hangs in the back room, and graduating students often gather round for a final toast of McSorley's ale to the old gentleman.

Artists have always been regulars, and John Sloan painted a series of works set in the saloon, including "McSorley's Bar," with Bill tending the tap, and "McSorley's Cats," which shows Bill feeding the swarm of cats that inhabited the bar and whose descendants can still be found snoozing by the stove or lazing on the tables in the afternoon sun. Writers have always hung out at McSorley's, and it has been a favorite with authors over the years from Christopher Morley to Hunter Thompson. Paul Blackburn, the poet of the New York landscape, lived in an apartment conveniently just above the saloon, and could often be found of an afternoon sitting at a window table nursing an ale, notebook open in front of him, observing the passing scene on Seventh Street.

Pepper and Garlic Toasted Almonds

These spicy nuts are great beer snacks for almost any type of ale or lager. Make up a double batch, and keep jars of them in the freezer. Frozen, they last for months, and even at room temperature in a sealed jar they will keep for two to three weeks. Add more red pepper if you want them hotter.

¼ cup olive oil
1 tablespoon minced garlic
½ teaspoon ground black pepper
½–1 teaspoon dried red pepper flakes

3 cups (about 1 pound) whole almonds
Salt to taste

Heat the olive oil in a large heavy frying pan over medium-low heat. Put in the garlic, pepper, and red pepper flakes, and stir them around until well distributed. Add the almonds, and stir and shake the pan until the nuts begin to brown lightly and develop a toasty-nutty aroma. Taste to be sure they are roasted enough. Drain almonds on paper towels, and lightly salt the nuts to your taste. Cool and serve, or pack into airtight jars for later use.

MAKES 3 CUPS.

Popcorn with Parmesan and Garlic

This tangy popcorn is just what you need for an afternoon of baseball and beer—any kind will do.

10–12 cups plain, not buttered, popped popcorn
¼ cup olive oil
2 teaspoons minced garlic

Salt
⅓ cup freshly grated Parmesan cheese

While the popcorn is popping in the microwave, on the stove, or in a popcorn machine, heat the olive oil in a small pan over medium heat. Add the garlic and a pinch of salt, and cook for 30 seconds, stirring constantly. Pour the flavored oil directly over the hot popcorn, add the grated Parmesan, and mix gently. Taste for salt, and serve.

SERVES 2–4.

Edy's Soft Pretzels

Soft pretzels have to be the ultimate saloon food, especially when paired with a hot mustard like our Beer and Horseradish Mustard* and a traditional neighborhood beer like Brooklyn Lager. You can make the pretzels yourself with this simple recipe from Edy Young, an accomplished professional baker and candymaker from San Francisco. Like bagels, pretzels are first boiled, then baked.

1 package (1 ounce) active dry yeast	2 quarts water
½ cups warm (about 110° F.) milk	2 tablespoons baking soda
1 tablespoon sugar	1 egg, lightly beaten with 2 tablespoons water for egg wash
3½–4 cups all-purpose flour	Coarse salt
1 teaspoon salt	

In a large measuring cup mix the yeast with the milk and sugar. Let the yeast proof for 10 minutes. Place 3½ cups of the flour and the salt in a food processor bowl. Insert the metal blade. With the motor running, pour the yeast/milk mixture through the feeder tube. Pulse intermittently until the dough forms a ball and it cleans the sides of the bowl. If the dough is too sticky, add a bit more flour, pulsing intermittently. Turn the dough into a oiled bowl, cover, and put in a warm place. Let the dough rise until double in size, about 1 hour.

Punch down the dough and divide it into 20 pieces. Hand-roll each piece into a 20-inch long rope. To form a pretzel, make a large loop using about two-thirds of the length. Twist the ends around each other once, pick the joined ends up, and place firmly down on the top of the

*See Index.

loop, forming a pretzel shape. Place the pretzel on a lightly floured surface, and let rise for about 30 minutes, until almost double in size. Make pretzels with the remaining dough in the same manner.

Meanwhile, preheat the oven to 400° F. In a large deep skillet bring the water and baking soda to a simmer. Place 2 or 3 pretzels at a time in the water, and simmer for 30 seconds on each side. Flip the pretzels gently. Remove the pretzels and drain on a rack.

Place the pretzels on a cookie sheet covered with baking parchment, being sure to keep the original top sides up. Brush each pretzel with some of the egg wash, and sprinkle lightly with the coarse salt. Bake 18–20 minutes until nicely browned. Serve while still warm.

MAKES 20 PRETZELS.

Cheese and Ale Spread

This zesty spread blends four American cheeses with spices and strong ale. It's delicious on crackers or with chips at a baseball game or picnic, or when just sitting in front of the tube watching the home team beat the bejabbers out of the other guys. With it, drink a powerful, hoppy ale—Sierra Nevada Pale Ale or Anchor Liberty Ale.

2 ounces Maytag Blue or
    other blue cheese
1 ounce fresh American *chèvre*
    or other fresh goat cheese
6 ounces aged New York State
    white Cheddar or other
    sharp Cheddar, diced
1 ounce Philadelphia-type
    cream cheese

½ teaspoon celery seeds
½ teaspoon caraway seeds
2 teaspoons Hungarian
    paprika
½ teaspoon coarsely ground
    black pepper
½ cup strong ale

Process all the ingredients in a food processor until smooth. If the spread is too thick, add more beer. Pack into a crock or small bowl, and let sit several hours or overnight in the refrigerator before using. Serve at room temperature.

MAKES ABOUT 2 CUPS.

Tavern Pickled Onions

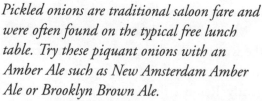

Pickled onions are traditional saloon fare and were often found on the typical free lunch table. Try these piquant onions with an Amber Ale such as New Amsterdam Amber Ale or Brooklyn Brown Ale.

Pickled onions are easy to make; the problem lies in peeling innumerable small onions. We therefore suggest pickling sliced large onions instead. The flavor is just as lively, and they remain crunchy and delicious. Make a few quart jars at a time and store the onions in the refrigerator. This is easier than making huge batches and going through all the trouble of canning.

Use the sweetest onions you can find. Some favorites are Walla Walla, Vidalia, Maui, or Texas U-38. If you can't find these, don't worry. Regular yellow onions will do just fine, since the pickling tends to mellow some of the harsh flavors of raw onions.

Not only are pickled onions good with strong cheeses, they are a great condiment to use on meat loaf sandwiches (see page 286) or as a side dish with pâtés.

2 pounds mild onions, peeled
and cut into ¼-inch slices

Spice Mixture

6 bay leaves, crushed
1 teaspoon whole black
  peppercorns
12 whole cloves
1 teaspoon whole allspice

1 teaspoon whole coriander
1 teaspoon mustard seeds
2 teaspoons celery seeds
½ teaspoon dried red pepper
  flakes

2½ cups malt vinegar, cider
  vinegar, or distilled white
  vinegar
1 cup water

1 cup sugar
2½ teaspoons salt
Pinch cinnamon

Separate the onion slices into rings and pack into 4 scalded, very clean pint canning jars or 2 quart-sized canning jars. Mix together all the spices for the spice mixture, and sprinkle about 1 tablespoon into each jar.

In a nonreactive saucepan mix the vinegar, water, sugar, salt, and cinnamon, and bring to a boil. Reduce the heat and simmer for 2 or 3 minutes. Pour the hot liquid into each jar, allowing about ¼-inch headspace. Let the jars cool, cover the mouths with plastic wrap, and screw on the lids. Store in the refrigerator up to 3 months. Although the onions can be eaten immediately, they are even better after aging in the reefer for about a month.

MAKES 2 QUARTS.

Beer and Onion Soup

In taverns from Buffalo to Boise, hearty soups are often served to patrons to nourish the inner man and counteract the effects of last night's carouse. We made this soup with Dark Lager, but an Amber Ale would do just as well. Samuel Adams Octoberfest or Boulder Brewing's Amber Ale are good choices.

¼ cup olive oil, or more if needed
3 large onions, thinly sliced (about 6–8 cups)
Salt and pepper
6 cups beef or Rich Chicken Stock (see page 203)

2 bottles Dark Lager
2 bay leaves
½ teaspoon dried thyme
Pinch allspice
Blue Cheese and Beer Croutons (recipe follows)

In a large soup pot heat the oil over medium-high heat. Put in the onions, sprinkle them lightly with salt and pepper, and cover the pot. Stirring from time to time, cook the onions until light brown, about 30 minutes. Add all the remaining ingredients, except the croutons. Bring to a boil, and reduce to a simmer. Cook for 30 minutes, or until the onions are quite soft and the broth has a nice onion flavor. Season with salt and pepper, and a little vinegar if desired. To serve, garnish with the croutons.

SERVES 6–8.

Blue Cheese and Beer Croutons

You can eat these cheesy croutons as is as a bar snack or use them as a garnish in soups and salads (check Index for recipes). Vary the cheese as you wish. We used Maytag Blue from Iowa, but you could use other blue cheeses such as Oregon blue, Stilton, or Roquefort—or even non-blue cheeses such as grated sharp Cheddar or aged Gruyère.

A full-flavored ale works best here: We suggest Winchester Brewing's Red Ale or Massachusetts Bay Harpoon Ale.

4 cups stale bread, cut into ½-inch cubes	1 cup finely crumbled blue cheese
1 12-ounce bottle ale	Olive oil

Preheat the oven to 400° F. Dip the bread cubes in the ale to barely moisten them, then roll them in the crumbled cheese. Generously brush a cookie sheet with olive oil. Spread the cubes over the pan, and drizzle a little oil over them. Bake about 10 minutes until golden brown and crispy. In a sealed container the croutons will keep for 2 weeks. MAKES 4 CUPS.

Saloon Sausage

Try this aromatic sausage grilled on a hard roll with Horseradish Mustard,* along with a hoppy Pilsner-style lager, such as Baderbrau from Pavichevich Brewing of Chicago or a fruity ale such as Redhook Ale from Seattle.

1½ pounds pork butt in pieces	2 tablespoons bourbon
½ pound pork fat in pieces	2 tablespoons chopped fresh herbs, such as chervil, tarragon, and/or basil
1 teaspoon coarsely ground black pepper	
2 teaspoons salt	¼ teaspoon nutmeg
2 teaspoons minced garlic	Medium hog casings (optional)
¼ cup chopped parsley	
¼ cup beer	

*See Index.

Grind the meat and fat through the ¼-inch (small) or ⅜-inch (medium) plate of a meat grinder or process them in a food processor until coarsely chopped. Add the remaining ingredients and knead well. Stuff the mixture into hog casings, and tie into 5-inch links, or make into patties. To cook, pan-fry the sausage for 7 or 8 minutes, turning often, or grill over medium coals until done. The sausage keeps 3 days refrigerated or 2 months frozen.

MAKES 2 POUNDS.

Rick's Beer-Baked Beans

Rick Rodgers, a New York–based caterer, cooking teacher, and cookbook author, gave us this recipe for zesty, beer-baked beans. With the beans, we suggest a light ale.

1 pound dried white cannellini beans, or other white beans such as Great Northern, or navy beans

½ pound salt pork, rind removed

¼ cup honey

¼ cup molasses

2 tablespoons catsup

2 tablespoons prepared spicy brown mustard

1 tablespoon plus 1½ teaspoons imported dry mustard powder

2 medium onions, chopped

1 12-ounce bottle lager or light ale

In a large bowl cover the beans by several inches with cold water; let stand overnight and drain. Cut half the salt pork into ¼-inch slices. Score the remaining salt pork with slashes ¼-inch deep.

Preheat the oven to 300° F. Whisk together the honey, molasses, catsup, and mustards. Line the bottom of a large casserole with the pork slices. Put in the beans and onions and toss to combine (do not disturb the pork slices). Add the honey mixture, beer, and enough water to barely cover the beans. Place the scored piece of salt pork, cut side down, on top of the beans. Cover the casserole tightly and bake, adding additional water if the beans begin to dry out, until the beans are tender and the sauce is thickened, 6 or 7 hours.

SERVES 8–10.

Boilermaker Rabbit or Chicken Stew

A traditional saloon favorite that is knocked back in bars from Hoboken to Coos Bay is the ubiquitous boilermaker—a shot of whiskey followed by (and sometimes, shudder, combined with) a glass of cold beer. While we don't exactly recommend this potent combination even to boilermakers just getting off shift, the sharp and aromatic flavors of bourbon, America's contribution to the world of spirits, and a hoppy ale do combine nicely in this flavorful stew.

This dish was originally inspired by the savory German rabbit stew, Hasenpfeffer, which was first brought to the United States by German immigrants. The German and Alsatian settlers who founded New Braunfels and Castroville in Texas gave it a lively twist and a bit of a kick with the addition of a some of the local hooch.

Our adaptation goes well with a full-bodied Pale Ale like Mendocino Brewing's Blue Heron Pale Ale or Summit Brewing's Extra Pale Ale. The recipe works equally well with rabbit or chicken.

Seasoned Flour

1 teaspoon salt
1 teaspoon ground black pepper
1 teaspoon dry mustard powder
½ teaspoon cayenne
½ cup flour

1 rabbit or frying chicken, cut into 6 pieces
1 tablespoon butter
1 tablespoon olive oil
½ cup bourbon
1 carrot, chopped
1 rib celery, chopped
3 medium onions, chopped
2 garlic cloves, chopped
1 cup Rich Chicken Stock (see page 203) or rabbit stock
1 12-ounce bottle light ale
1 sprig fresh rosemary or ½ teaspoon dried
2 leaves fresh sage or ½ teaspoon dried
1 sprig fresh thyme or ½ teaspoon dried
2 tablespoons Creole or German-style mustard
1 cup sour cream
Salt and pepper
Lemon juice
Chopped chives or green onions for garnish

Mix together the ingredients for the seasoned flour, then coat the rabbit or chicken in it. In a large heavy skillet or Dutch oven brown the meat in the butter and olive oil over medium-high heat 4 or 5 minutes a side. Pour the whiskey over the meat, light it, and flambé the rabbit or chicken, shaking the skillet continually. When the flames die down, remove the rabbit or chicken and add the carrot, celery, onions, and garlic to the skillet. Cover and cook over medium heat, stirring occasionally, for 10 minutes. Add the stock, ale, rosemary, sage, and thyme. Return the rabbit or chicken to the pot, cover, and simmer for 45 minutes until it is quite tender. Transfer to a warm platter. Degrease the sauce, and boil it down if it is too thin. When the sauce is the desired consistency, whisk in the mustard. Remove the pan from the heat and whisk in the sour cream. Season with salt and pepper and lemon juice to taste. Pour the sauce over the rabbit or chicken. Garnish with the chopped chives or green onions and serve with plain buttered noodles or rice.

SERVES 4–6.

Honey Beer Mustard

This tangy sweet-and-sour mustard will enhance the flavor of just about any sandwich, salad, or sauce. Try it with a full-flavored ale or lager: Rainier Ale or Rolling Rock Extra Pale Lager.

¼ cup dry mustard powder, preferably Colman's
½ cup beer
¼ cup malt vinegar
½ teaspoon finely ground black pepper

2 eggs
1 tablespoon honey
Salt

Mix together the dry mustard, beer, vinegar, and pepper. Let it sit at room temperature for at least 3 hours. Scrape the mustard mixture into a double boiler and heat over simmering water. Stir in the eggs and keep stirring until the mixture thickens. Stir in the honey and taste for salt. Pack into a jar, cool, and refrigerate. The mustard will improve with age in the refrigerator. Keeps for 1 year.

MAKES 1½ CUPS.

Porter Pot Roast

One of the classics of beer cookery is the Belgian dish carbonnade flamande, *a savory stew of beef, beer, and onions. The onions and beer cook down into a velvety sauce that goes wonderfully with dark beer or ale.*

The secret ingredients for great carbonnades *are a little molasses to bring out the malty taste of the beer and mustard and vinegar to balance the sweetness and underline the hop flavors.*

We've Americanized this recipe by calling it pot roast, and suggest you use boned chuck, bottom round, or rump roast, along with a Dark Ale like Pete's Wicked Ale or Anchor Porter. Serve with Garlic and Horseradish Mashed Potatoes. *

4–5 pound chuck roast, bottom round, or rump roast, boned and tied
Salt and pepper
Dried thyme and ground sage
3 tablespoons olive oil
2 pounds onions, peeled, halved, and thinly sliced
1 carrot, diced
1 rib celery, diced
6 garlic cloves, chopped
1 tablespoon molasses
4 bay leaves
2 12-ounce bottles Porter or other dark ale or beer
2 tablespoons Dijon or coarse-grained mustard
1 tablespoon malt or red wine vinegar, or to taste

Season the meat generously with salt and pepper, thyme, and sage. In a heavy Dutch oven or casserole large enough to hold the meat heat the oil over medium-high heat. Put in the roast, and sear it on all sides. Remove the roast, and add the onions, carrot, celery, garlic, and molasses. Cover and cook over medium heat for about 10–12 minutes, until the onions are soft and beginning to color. Put the meat back in with the bay leaves and beer. Cover and cook for 1½–2 hours over low heat until the meat is tender. Remove the meat and keep it warm. Degrease the liquid in the pot, and stir in the mustard and the vinegar. Boil the sauce until it just becomes syrupy. Taste for salt and pepper and vinegar. Slice the roast. Pour some of the sauce and vegetables over the meat and serve. Pass the rest of the sauce separately.
SERVES 6–8.

*See Index.

Deviled Oxtail

Oxtail is one of those dishes that are part of America's past, like tongue and pig's feet—cuts of meat that were cheap and very tasty, but are out of favor in these purified and squeamish days.

With the increase in popularity of bistro and brasserie foods, however, the homey oxtail is coming back into favor. And it's no wonder. When oxtails are cooked to succulent tenderness, they are absolutely delicious, the essence of beef flavor.

San Francisco food writer and teacher Loni Kuhn gave us this recipe. She first braises oxtails to perfection in Dark Ale, then coats them the next day with mustard, spices, and bread crumbs, broils them, and serves them with the braising sauce. Serve this dish with our Garlic and Horseradish Mashed Potatoes* and Red Cabbage Braised in Cider and Beer.* The beer? What else but Devil's Brew, a devilishly delicious porter from the California microbrewery Devil Mountain.

2 oxtails, disjointed, about 5–6 pounds
Salt and pepper
2 tablespoons olive oil
2 medium onions, chopped
8 garlic cloves, chopped
2 or 3 12-ounce bottles dark ale or beer
2 cups fine dry bread crumbs

4 tablespoons chopped parsley
1 teaspoon dried thyme
½ teaspoon dried sage
½ teaspoon cayenne
1 teaspoon dried tarragon
1 teaspoon coarsely ground black pepper
1½ cups Dijon mustard

Season the oxtails with salt and pepper. In a Dutch oven or large casserole heat the olive oil over medium-high heat, and brown the oxtails on all sides in batches. Remove the oxtails from the pan, and pour off all but 3 tablespoons of the fat. Put in the onions and garlic, cover the pot, and cook, stirring occasionally, until the onions begin to brown. Add the beer and oxtails, cover, and cook over low heat 1½–2 hours until the oxtails are quite tender. Remove the oxtails, and let them cool. The

*See Index.

Deviled Oxtail (continued) dish may be made ahead up to this point and refrigerated. Degrease the sauce and boil it down until it is reduced by half and beginning to thicken. Taste for salt and pepper.

While the sauce is reducing, preheat the broiler. In a small bowl mix together the bread crumbs, herbs, and seasonings. Brush each oxtail with mustard, then roll it in the seasoned bread crumbs. Place the oxtails on a broiling pan, and cook under the broiler until crisp, turning to brown all sides. Place the deviled oxtails on a serving platter, and spoon the sauce over them.

SERVES 6–8.

The Northwest: An Ale Lover's Dream Kingdom

Smoked Salmon and Corn Crepe Rolls

Green Bean and Red Pepper Salad with Caesar Dressing

Cold Leeks in Horseradish Vinaigrette

Potato and Fennel Gratin

Margaret's Potato Pizza

Willy's Beery Bread

Basic Brine for Fish

Smoked Fish Steaks or Fillets

Smoked Whole Small Fish

Bainbridge Island Smoked Fish Chowder

Smoked Shellfish

Fish and Oyster Croquettes

Spicy Tartar Sauce

Cornish Hens in Stout

Pork Chops with Fresh Pimiento

Chocolate Porter Cake

Black Velvet

Shandygaff

Wheat Beer with Fruit Syrup

The Pike Place Market is a maelstrom of color, sound, and delicious smells swirling down a steep hill to Seattle's docks and harbor. We make our way slowly through stalls of bright vegetables and flowers, glistening salmon, piles of orange and white crabs, slabs of fresh meat, strings of salamis festooned from hooks. We stop often to sample and talk with vendors: Indians who smoke salmon over alderwood fires, fishermen who go out into the sound every morning, old Italian women who make pasta and fresh pastries. We're looking for the legendary Athenian Saloon, a beer drinker's paradise that offers hundreds of different beers to thirsty shoppers and stall holders at the market.

When we find it we can hardly get through the door. The beat-up old bar is crowded with noontime beer drinkers, all calling for their favorites. As we pass through the bar to the upstairs dining room, we count the taps: There are 15 beer pulls, over half of them tapping kegs of locally brewed ales.

When we sit down we ask to see the beer list: It includes beers from all over the world, including such out-of-the-way brews as South Pacific from New Guinea, Niksicko Pivo from Yugoslavia, and Xingu from the Amazon, along with an array of beers and ales from England, Germany, Australia, and the United States. There are about 250 beers on the list with over 30 American microbreweries represented in bottle and on draft.

We choose two local brews: Ballard Bitter made by Redhook Brewery in Seattle's old Scandinavian neighborhood, Ballard, and Hale's Ale made by Mike Hale in Colville, Washington. The mugs of ale arrive along with platters of smoked black cod, fried local oysters, mussels broiled with bacon and anchovies, huge chunks of deep-brown fried potatoes, and spicy cocktail sauce. The combination of the amber-colored, high-hopped, and malty ales with the flavorful fish and seafood is well nigh perfect.

After lunch we walk downhill through the market, looking for a tiny new microbrewery we've heard about, Pike Place Brewery. We know we've found it when we see Charlie Finkel striding out the door of a storefront on Western Avenue at the edge of the market. Finkel is a legend among beer-lovers. The energetic, sartorially elegant beer marketer, writer, promoter, and editor of *Alephenalia,* a popular Seattle-based beer newspaper, is one of the most important figures in the American beer scene today. He is the owner of Merchant du Vin, the company responsible for the popularity of many imports, including Samuel Smith Yorkshire Ales, Ayinger Beer from Bavaria, Lindemans and Orval Abbey beers from Belgium. He's also sold and promoted many of the finest beers of small American regional breweries.

We've heard that Charlie has recently founded his own microbrewery in the Pike Place Market, and we have arrived to take a look (and have a taste). Inside the brewery, we meet Vince Cottone, author and beer columnist for the Seattle *Post-Intelligencer* and brewing consultant to many of the Northwest's best micros, and Pike Place's talented young brewers, Jason Parker and Fal Allen.

The brewery is certainly tiny, but it is efficiently designed with malt storage and grinder on the top floor and burnished copper brew kettle, mash tun, and storage tanks on the ground floor. Pike Place Brewery produces a complex and carefully balanced Pike Place Pale Ale, a deep black, intense XXXXX Stout, and a powerful, malty Old Bawdy Barley Wine. The brewers use only the flavorful two-row English barley malt preferred by many microbreweries, and English and European hops. Beers are brewed according to the Bavarian Purity Law of 1516 and include only water, malt, hops, and special yeast developed and maintained at the brewery. All the brewing is done by hand, and no filters, additives, or preservatives are used. Pike Place is typical of the Northwest's microbreweries in its respect for ingredients and its emphasis on handmade, carefully crafted beers. While sampling their brews, we plan a pub crawl with Vince Cottone to taste our way through the rich array of ales and other beers offered by Seattle's thriving beer community.

The evening began at Pacific Northwest Brewing Company, a beautifully appointed brew-pub in the recently restored Pioneer Square area near the Kingdome. Owner Richard Wrigley was involved in the highly successful Manhattan Brewing Company in New York City, and has put together a handsome new brewery and restaurant here in Seattle. All the beer is made on the premises and dispensed only on draft from shining copper brew kettles obtained from small German breweries.

The ales are excellent and in the English tradition favored by Wrigley, who is British born. A Strong Brown Ale was the special of the evening, full and malty, still cloudy with yeast, and with an excellent balance of hops and malt. A classic English pub Bitter, hoppy and aromatic, and a rich and malty Stout made with dark roasted malt were staunchly in the English ale style preferred by many Northwest brewers.

Food at Pacific Northwest Brewing is much above the usual run of brew-pub food. The fry cook uses impeccable ingredients and has a very sure hand: crispy fried calamari with ginger rémoulade was perfectly executed and a great match with the lighter ales. Batter-fried Alaskan halibut with garlicky coleslaw was a fine and greaseless rendition of English fish-and-chips, and a natural match for the pub Bitter, especially when a dash of English malt vinegar was splashed on the fish and fries.

Seafood in general was first-rate, perfectly fresh and cleanly presented. Penn Cove mussels steamed in blond ale with bay leaf, lemon, and clove were light and delicately flavored, especially when accompanied by the Pale Ale they were steamed in. Alder-smoked salmon with daikon sprouts and sesame seed vinaigrette, and salt and pepper tiger prawns rounded out the excellent seafood selection, and were nicely matched the Gold and Amber Ales.

Along with draft beers, the pub serves interesting beer mixers, such as Gold & Lime—Gold Ale with a splash of lime juice—Black & Gold—Gold Ale with sweet black currant juice—and that classic drink of the Bright Young Things of the 1920's, Black Velvet—a blend of Stout and Champagne (see page 132).

The evening continued with stops at various pubs, where we tasted local beers on draft and ales of every variety imaginable, including a red chile–laced ale and a memorable blackberry-flavored stout. We finished up the evening at the Red Door Ale House, which sports 20 pump handles, at least half of them local brews. Standouts there were two cask-conditioned ales, BridgePort's Blue Heron Ale from Portland, and Hale's Pale Ale. These naturally conditioned ales were hand-pumped from the cellar and had the creamy consistency and richly layered flavors of a true handmade ale.

Early the next morning we were out on the docks to catch the ferry to Bainbridge Island and Poulsbo, the location of Thomas Kemper Brewing Company, one of the few Northwest breweries specializing in lagers. Riding across Puget Sound in the invigorating cool morning breezes with raucous gulls dipping in and out of the wake of the ferry and cormorants scudding low across the dark water is a sure way to clear the night's vapors from the brain. By the time we reached tree-covered Bainbridge Island, we were ready to taste again.

Thomas Kemper is located way out in the forest near Poulsbo, a tiny town on the Olympic Peninsula just west of Bainbridge Island. The brewery, taproom, and beer garden are located in an old meat-packing plant, and like so many of today's microbreweries all the work is done by hand by dedicated beer fanatics. Beers at Kemper are all lagers made in the Bavarian draft style, emphasizing malt flavors and full body.

Brewed according to Germany's *Reinheitsgebot* purity law, Kemper lagers are cool fermented and lagered for months at 33° F. Made with American six-row barley malt, Yakima Valley hops, pure-culture lager yeast, and deep well water fed from melting snow from the Olympic Mountains, the beers are smooth and malty with a refreshing tang of Cascade hops.

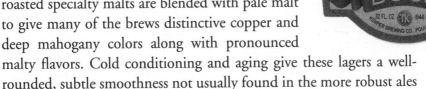

Kemper uses none of the corn or rice adjuncts so often found in modern American Lagers. Deep-roasted specialty malts are blended with pale malt to give many of the brews distinctive copper and deep mahogany colors along with pronounced malty flavors. Cold conditioning and aging give these lagers a well-rounded, subtle smoothness not usually found in the more robust ales of the region.

Lagers at Thomas Kemper include Helles, or Light, a bright golden beer with fragrant malty nose, medium body, and a smooth creamy texture. Dunkel, or Dark, is a deep mahogany color from roasted malt with hints of sweetness in the finish, in the classic dark Munich style. Kemper Pilsner is a hoppy pale lager with clean herbal aromas and a dry finish. Rolling Bay Bock is described as "Billy-goat strong," and like most German bocks it has deep color, lots of malt, high alcohol, and complex nutty flavors.

Returning from Kemper we stopped by Bainbridge Island Seafood, a store that features fresh-caught fish and locally smoked seafood. While waiting for the return ferry, we picnicked on the cool, wind-swept docks on delicious smoked mussels, chunks of alder-smoked salmon, slices of sweet Walla Walla onions, and sharp Cheddar, washed down with Kemper's Bock. The smoky seafood, tangy onions, and sharp cheese were wonderful counterpoints to the sweet and malty beers.

The next day we visited one of the oldest and most successful microbreweries in the Northwest, Seattle's Redhook. Redhook Ale Brewery's popular Ballard Bitter features on the label a mustachioed gentleman in a wing collar with the words, "Ya Sure Ya Betcha," celebrating the brewery's new location in a refurbished red brick trolley barn in the historic Ballard neighborhood, home of Seattle's large Scandinavian population.

Redhook is one of the largest microbreweries in the Northwest with state-of-the-art German brewing equipment, which is thoroughly computerized and extremely high tech. The beers, however, are very much in the English style, with plenty of body, flavor, and individual character. Redhook's ESB (Extra Special Bitter), a full-flavored ale with a characteristic nip of hops, is a favorite throughout the Northwest and California. Blackhook Porter is deeply colored with a tangy, hoppy undertone, and is available all along the West Coast. Redhook also offers specialty beers: Wheat Hook Wheaten beer, which incorporates over 50 percent English wheat malt in the brew, is light, dry, and delicate; Winterhook, a powerful and spicy Christmas Ale, is brewed seasonally, and is a solace on cold, gray winter days.

The Yakima Valley, just east of the Cascade Range, is known for extensive hop fields that supply brewers all over the world with spicy, aromatic Cascade hops and other varieties. Less known is the fact that the valley is also thriving wine country with over 20 wineries and hundreds of acres of vineyards growing top-quality Merlot, Cabernet Sauvignon, Sauvignon Blanc, and Semillon grapes. The area also boasts rich fruit orchards and lush fields of vegetables, and its roads are lined with stands selling fresh produce.

As we drive into the valley, pale-green hop vines stretch out for miles on either side of the road, and the air is filled with the spicy scent of their blossoms. Hop vines grow 20 feet straight up, trailing on wires and tall poles, with the yellow-green flowers scattering sticky and pungent pollen with each gust of wind. After walking through a hop field we were fragrant for hours, dispensing hop aromas with each step, making heads turn as we walked down the hot and dusty streets of downtown Yakima.

When we open the door to the Yakima Brewing and Malting Company, however, nobody notices. Here at the home of one of the country's first microbreweries and brew-pubs, the smell of Cascade hops is almost overpowering. And that's as it should be: The founder, Bert Grant, is one of the world's experts in hops—their history, production, and use. The feisty, outspoken brewer has worked over the years with major hop producers and breweries in the United States and Canada. Grant brews English- and Scottish-style ales using locally grown Cascade hops, prime malted barley, and carefully selected English ale yeasts.

Grant's Scottish Ale is the brewery's most famous product, and one of the best of the hand-crafted ales that define the Northwest style.

Hop pickers in the Yakima Valley at the turn of the century.

Brown to amber in color, Scottish Ale is heady with Cascade hops, but the bitterness is balanced by rich malt flavors. It is one of the most satisfying ales in America, and Bert Grant views it as his "personal ale"—the brew he proclaims "the best ale in the world."

Grant's Imperial Stout is thick and rich, with an alcohol level around 7 percent. Made in the tradition of strong Stouts brewed in England to be shipped to the Russian imperial court, this is a "serious" beer for lovers of richly flavored dark beers. A warning: It is best sipped, not quaffed, as it is one of the most potent brews available.

Grant's Celtic Ale is a lighter brew, both in color and alcohol, nicely balanced and full of flavor; Grant's India Pale Ale is an excellent version of the heavily hopped Pale Ale that used to be sent from England to Britons defending the flag of empire East of Suez. Grant's Weis Beer, the lightest in color and flavor, is a pleasantly refreshing wheat beer, just right for quenching the thirst on a hot summer day in the Yakima Valley, especially when the beer is garnished with a slice of lemon or a squeeze of lime.

South of the Yakima Valley lies the Columbia River Gorge on the border between Washington and Oregon. Here the great river cuts through steeply sided gorges and creates some of the most exciting and dramatic river views in the world. At Hood River Brewing Company on the Oregon side, you can sit on the deck of the pub and watch the windsurfers scudding before the winds that whip down the gorge, all the while sipping some of the microbrewery's Full Sail Ales. Available on draft at the brewery, Hood River's ales are also found throughout the Northwest in bottles.

The leader is Full Sail Golden Ale, crisp and medium bodied with a good bite of hops and clean fresh flavors. The Amber Ale is ample and full-bodied with spicy, butterscotch aromas and flavors. Both are all-malt beers made only from select Northwest hops, malted barley, and Mt. Hood spring water. Specialty beers are also available on a seasonal basis.

Portland is a paradise for beer lovers where even ordinary neighborhood taverns boast of 10 to 15 beers on tap, many of them brewed at microbreweries in the Northwest. Friendly beer drinkers are happy to describe their favorite brews and give travelers directions to local breweries. Downtown near the river you can see the huge Henry Weinhardt silos rising up above the red brick industrial landscape; nearby are three of Oregon's finest microbreweries: BridgePort Brewing Company, Widmer's Brewing Company, and tiny Portland Brewing Company.

BridgePort Brewing Company, owned by Dick Ponzi (also proprietor of a fine Oregon winery), is Oregon's oldest operating microbrewery. Its best-known brew is Blue Heron Pale Ale, available on draft and in bottles throughout most of the Northwest. It is a rich, golden amber ale with a pronounced bite of Northwest hops and full malty flavors. Blue Heron is very popular at BridgePort's crowded brew-pub, along with a range of other ales brewed in small batches and available on draft.

Widmer Brewing Company, also operating within the shadows of Henry Weinhardt's towers, is family owned and concentrates on German-style beers. Kurt Widmer studied brewing in Düsseldorf, home of the traditional German ale, Dusseldorfer Alt, and Widmer makes classic *Altbiers,* or ales, in the old style.

Widmer Alt is a richly flavored, copper-colored brew: dry, malty, and satisfying on the palate. The brewery also makes a light and refreshing Weizen, using a blend of malted wheat and barley. An unfiltered version, Hefeweizen, also called "liquid bread" at the brewery, is cloudy with the natural yeasts (*hefe*); it is more robust and aromatic than the clear, cold-filtered Weizen.

Widmer also makes an array of specialty beers depending on the season: Fest—dark, full bodied, and malty—for the winter holidays; Oktoberfest—deep amber, with powerful malt and hop flavors; Bock—amber, heady and high in alcohol—for the spring; and Maerzen—deep amber, strong, and traditionally made in March to be drunk over the hot summer months.

Widmer's full-flavored but subtle beers are a fine match with food, especially at the unique B. Moloch–Heathman Bakery & Pub, a col-

Henry Weinhardt, early Portland brewer.

laboration between the Heathman Hotel and Widmer Brewing. Beer is brewed and dispensed on draft on the premises, and dishes to match the beers are especially created by the talented executive chef/manager, Greg Higgins. Wonderful breads and pizzas are baked in wood-fired ovens, and Higgins smokes sausages, poultry, hams, and other meats in the chimneys of the ovens. B. Moloch is more than a brew-pub. It is one of a growing number of American beer restaurants, a new category that is proving to be one of the most exciting developments on the food scene today.

Also worth a visit are Portland Brewing Company, a tiny micro that brews full-bodied ales and stouts, and the many McMenamin brew-pubs that have sprung up in recent years. Mike McMenamin is a creative and successful entrepreneur who specializes in buying up run-down neighborhood taverns and refurbishing them, while still keeping their funky charm. He then installs a tiny brewing set-up with a ten-gallon capacity brew kettle, and a brewer/manager to run things. These small neighborhood brew-pubs have proved very popular in the Portland area. We sat in one on a Sunday morning and watched what seemed to be the whole neighborhood troop through for a pint of ale or a mug of Stout or to pick up a quart Mason jar or two of draft to take home to drink while watching football on TV. The McMenamin concept of small, neighborhood brew-pubs seems to be a real success in beer-loving Portland and might prove a model for other cities that want to preserve the traditions of good local beer.

A trip north across the mouth of the Columbia River into

A Western saloon in the days before Prohibition.

Washington brings you to one of the Northwest's finest small breweries, Hart Brewing in Kalama. Hart produces a full line of delicious ales and one of the best Stouts brewed in the country, Sphinx Stout. Hart's Pyramid Pale Ale has a rich amber color, balancing lots of malt with a generous undertone of Cascade hops. Pacific Crest Ale is a pleasantly drinkable Mild Ale, lightly malty with light hop flavors. Pyramid Wheaten Ale is made with 50 percent wheat malt and is refreshing, complex, and smooth. Hart's Sphinx Stout is a noble brew: a dry, black, extra-rich Stout, full and creamy with hints of chocolate and roasted malt. We tasted this at the brewery and on draft in pubs in Portland and Seattle, and rate it among the best stouts made in America, one of the few that can rival Guinness for depth of flavor, balance, and true Stout character.

We continued on from Kalama to Willapa Bay and Nahcotta, home of one of the Northwest's finest restaurants, The Ark, a favorite of James Beard, who hailed from this rugged and beautiful coast. Here Nanci Main and Jimella Lucas serve up the freshest seafood imaginable (the restaurant is built on a spit of land composed largely of oyster shells that juts out into the bay). Their list of local beers is extensive, and we spent a fascinating evening eating local oysters and matching their creative seafood dishes with their beers.

Smoked Salmon
and Corn Crepe Rolls

These stuffed crepe rolls are eaten cold and make great appetizers or party snacks with robust Northwest ales like Redhook Ale or BridgePort Coho Pacific Light Ale. The rolls can be prepared a few hours ahead and kept refrigerated until your guests arrive. Besides smoked salmon, you could also make these with thinly sliced smoked sturgeon or smoked black cod (sablefish).

Corn Crepes

3 eggs, beaten
3 tablespoons butter,
   melted
½ cup milk
¼ cup cornmeal
¼ cup all-purpose flour

1 cup fresh corn kernels or
   frozen corn, thawed
2 green onions, finely chopped
¼ teaspoon salt
½ teaspoon black pepper
Peanut oil

Stuffing

½ pound cream cheese
2 tablespoons milk
½ pound thinly sliced
   smoked salmon

2–3 bunches watercress, curly
   cress, or arugula, leaves and
   stems, well washed (about
   3 cups)

To make the crepes: Mix together the eggs, butter, and milk. Gradually beat in the cornmeal and flour until smooth. Stir in the corn, green onions, salt, and pepper. The batter should be thin enough to pour; add more milk if necessary. Over medium-high heat heat a thin film of oil in a 7-inch nonstick pan. Ladle in just enough batter to cover the bottom of the pan. Cook 2–3 minutes until lightly brown. Turn the crepe, and cook 1 minute more. Spread each crepe out on the work surface as it is done. Continue cooking until all the crepe batter is used. There should be about 6–8 crepes.

To make the rolls: Soften the cream cheese by beating in the milk. With a rubber spatula or broad knife, spread each crepe with a thin layer of cream cheese. Cover the cream cheese with slices of smoked salmon, and lay several sprigs of cress or arugula on top. Roll each crepe up fairly tight, and slice into 4 or 5 ¾-inch pieces. Arrange artfully on a platter and garnish with the cress or arugula.

MAKES 30–40 BITE-SIZE ROLLS.

Green Bean and Red Pepper Salad with Caesar Dressing

This colorful salad makes a fine side dish with grilled chicken or fish, and can stand on its own as a light lunch or dinner. Match the salad's tart, garlicky flavors with a crisp Wheat Beer, such as Widmer Weizen or Hart's Pyramid Wheaten Ale.

1½ pounds green beans, cut into 2-inch pieces
1 red bell pepper
1 cup cubed sourdough French bread, each cube ¾ inch

¼ cup olive oil
2 garlic cloves, minced
¼ cup freshly grated Parmesan cheese

Caesar Dressing

1 garlic clove
3 anchovy fillets
3 tablespoons red wine vinegar
1 tablespoon Dijon mustard

6 drops Worcestershire sauce
½ cup olive oil
¼ cup freshly grated Parmesan cheese

1 tomato, sliced for garnish
5 anchovy fillets for garnish

Blanch the green beans in a 4-quart pot of boiling salted water for 3 minutes. Remove and cool under cold running water. Drain and set aside. Cut the pepper into ¼-inch strips, and set aside.

To make the croutons: Preheat the oven to 400° F. Toss the bread cubes, olive oil, and garlic in a medium bowl until the bread is well coated with the oil. Spread the cubes on a baking sheet, and bake for 15 minutes or until the croutons are crisp. Remove from the oven, and sprinkle with the Parmesan. Set aside.

To make the dressing: Mince the garlic in a food processor fitted with the metal blade. Add the anchovy fillets, and process until minced. Add the red wine vinegar, mustard, and Worcestershire sauce. With the motor running, pour in the olive oil gradually to produce a creamy dressing. Blend in the cheese.

To assemble the salad: Mix together the green beans, croutons, pepper strips, and dressing in a shallow serving bowl. Garnish with the tomato and anchovies.

SERVES 4–6.

Cold Leeks in Horseradish Vinaigrette

These zesty leeks make a great accompaniment to grilled beer-marinated steaks and poultry. Serve with a hearty Pale Ale, such as Hale's Pale Ale or Full Sail Golden Ale.

8 medium leeks, trimmed, white part only
1 recipe Horseradish Vinaigrette (see page 195)

1 tablespoon capers for garnish

Split the leeks in half to about 1 inch from the root end, and wash well under running water. Put the leeks in a pan in 1 or 2 layers, and cover with water. Add a large pinch of salt. Bring to a boil, and reduce to a simmer. Cook 10–12 minutes until the leeks are just tender. Cool and drain well. Shake out any excess water from the leeks, and place them on a serving platter. Pour the dressing over them and garnish with the capers. SERVES 6–8.

Potato and Fennel Gratin

The mild licorice flavor of fennel blends well with potatoes to make a good accompaniment for full-flavored roasted or grilled meats or poultry. A hearty ale like Ballard Bitter from Redhook would pair up nicely here.

The gratin can be finished an hour or two before dinner and be rewarmed for 15 minutes in a 350 ° F. oven.

2 medium bulbs fresh fennel
1½ pounds boiling potatoes
Salt and pepper
1 cup freshly grated Parmesan
    cheese

1 cup heavy cream
1–2 cups Rich Chicken Stock
    (see page 203)

Trim the stems from the fennel bulbs along with any bruised or discolored areas. Cut the bulbs lengthwise into ¼-inch slices. Finely chop any leafy green fronds. Bring 2 quarts of lightly salted water to a boil, and blanch the fennel slices for 2 minutes. Drain well and reserve. Peel the potatoes and cut them into thin slices.

Preheat the oven to 325° F. Lightly oil a 9- × 14-inch baking pan or gratin dish. Make a layer of fennel slices and lightly sprinkle with salt and pepper, some Parmesan, and the chopped fennel leaves. Cover this with a layer of potatoes and repeat the salt and pepper, cheese, and fennel leaves. Continue layering until you fill the pan.

Combine the cream with 1 cup of the stock and bring to a boil. Pour over the potatoes and fennel. The liquid should just come up to the level of the top layer. Add more if needed. Sprinkle the top of the gratin generously with the remaining cheese. Bake for 1½ hours or until the top is brown, the liquid is absorbed, and the vegetables are tender. Serve at once. Or make 1 or 2 hours ahead and rewarm for 15 minutes before serving.

SERVES 6.

Margaret's Potato Pizza

Margaret Miller, a cooking teacher from Fort Wayne, Indiana, gave us this superb pizza recipe that uses a simple dough made in a food processor and red new potatoes and onions in the savory topping.

Since home ovens usually don't put out enough heat to produce a crisp pizza crust the way commercial ovens do, we prefer to bake pizzas at home in a heavy cast-iron 12-inch frying pan. Brush the pan well with olive oil, and let the dough come slightly up the sides. If you prefer, you can also bake the pizza on a pizza stone, perforated pizza pan, oiled cookie sheet, or on a cookie sheet sprinkled with cornmeal.

With this appetizing pizza, drink a full-bodied light lager like Kemper Helles.

Pizza Dough

1 package (1 ounce) active dry yeast
Pinch sugar
2½ cups bread flour
1 teaspoon salt

1 tablespoon chopped fresh rosemary or 2 teaspoons dried
2 tablespoons olive oil

Topping

6 tablespoons olive oil
4 cups thinly sliced red potatoes
4 garlic cloves, minced
2 cups thinly sliced red onions
3 tablespoons chopped fresh rosemary or 1 tablespoon dried

2 teaspoons dried red pepper flakes (optional)
Salt and pepper
4 cups shredded mozzarella
½ cup freshly grated Parmesan cheese

To make the dough: Sprinkle the yeast into ¾ cup warm water and the pinch of sugar. Stir and let proof for about 10 minutes. In the meantime, place the steel blade in the processor bowl, and add the flour, salt, and rosemary. Once the yeast has proofed, add the oil to the yeast mixture, stirring until well blended. With the food processor running, pour the yeast mixture in a slow steady stream through the feed tube. Process until the dough forms a ball and the sides of the bowl come clean. If the dough is too sticky, add more flour, one tablespoon at a time, pulsing after each addition. If the dough is too tight and dry, add water, one tablespoon at a time, pulsing after each addition. Once the dough is smooth and silky, process again for about 40 seconds to knead. Remove the dough from the processor and place in a oiled bowl. Cover loosely with plastic wrap or a cotton towel, and let the dough rise in a warm place until double in size, about 1 hour. Once the dough has risen, punch it down, and make the pizza.

To make the pizza: Preheat the oven to 450° F.

Heat 3 tablespoons of the olive oil over medium heat in a large heavy frying pan. Spread the potato slices over the surface of the pan, and sprinkle on the garlic, red onion, 1 tablespoon of the rosemary, optional red pepper flakes, and salt and pepper. Cook for 3 minutes, stirring frequently. Add 2–3 tablespoons water, cover, and cook 6–7 minutes more, stirring occasionally, until the potatoes are just tender. Remove the lid, and cook off any excess water. Taste for salt and pepper and set aside.

Divide the dough in half. Roll or stretch each piece of dough on a floured surface to cover the bottom of 2 oiled 12-inch cast-iron frying pans. The dough should make 2 pizzas, 12 inches in diameter. Or you can freeze half the unbaked dough for future use. Brush the dough surface with olive oil and sprinkle with shredded mozzarella, leaving a 1-inch border around the edge. Spread a layer of the sliced potatoes topping over the cheese. Brush with more oil, and sprinkle with the optional red pepper flakes and remaining rosemary. Bake the pizzas 12–15 minutes until the edges are golden. Sprinkle with the Parmesan, and bake 3–5 minutes, until the top is golden brown and the edges and bottom of the crust are nicely browned. Serve at once.

MAKES TWO 12-INCH PIZZAS.

Willy's Beery Bread

Willy Hinds, an old friend and Bruce's fellow grad student at the University of California at Santa Cruz, needed some diversion from the long hours of studying for his qualifying exams. Bread-making was perfect: It took plenty of time, but only a little bit at each step. On those endless nights of study Willy came up with this beer bread and was so proud of it that he entered it in the Santa Cruz County Fair and won a blue ribbon. He didn't fare so well on his exams, though, and had to take them over. This recipe uses the bread-making technique of starting off with a sponge. It takes a bit more time, but creates great texture and delectable bread.

2 tablespoons active dried
  yeast (Willy prefers
  Red Star)
½ cup warm tap water
3 cups whole-wheat flour
9 cups unbleached white flour
4 eggs, with 1 egg white
  reserved

3¾ cups beer (Willy
  uses Anchor Steam or
  Rainier Ale)
½ cup honey
6 tablespoons (¾ stick)
  butter, melted
5 teaspoons salt
½ cup or more sesame seeds

To make the sponge: Mix together the yeast and warm water. Set aside to proof.

Put all the whole-wheat flour and 3 cups of the white flour into a large bowl. Stir in the proofed yeast, the eggs (reserving the egg white), the beer, honey, and butter. Beat with a wooden spoon 100 strokes or with an electric mixer fitted with a paddle 3–5 minutes. The purpose is to introduce plenty of air into the sponge. Cover and let rise in a warm place for 1 hour.

Mix or sift together the remaining 6 cups white flour and the salt. Gradually work this flour into the sponge. Turn the dough out on a floured surface and knead for 15 minutes until smooth and elastic. If the dough seems too wet and sticky, add a little more flour. Place the dough in a lightly oiled bowl, cover, and let rise in a warm place for 1 hour, or until double in size. Preheat the oven to 350° F.

Punch down the dough and turn it out onto a floured surface. Shape it into 4 equal balls. Let rest 5 minutes. Knead each ball 5 or 6 times. Roll each ball into a loaf, and place in a greased 9- × 5-inch bread pan. Let the loaves rise 15–20 minutes in a warm place. Slash the top of each loaf lengthwise, and brush with the reserved egg white mixed with a little water. Sprinkle with the sesame seeds. Bake for 45–50 minutes until the loaves are light brown. Tap the bottom of each loaf. If done, it should sound hollow. If not, bake for 5 minutes more. Turn the loaves out onto racks to cool. This bread freezes well and makes great toast.

MAKES 4 LOAVES.

SMOKING FISH AND SEAFOOD

Germans and East Europeans long ago discovered the affinity between smoked food and beer. In particular, smoked fish and seafood go well with many styles of beers from light lagers to heady Stouts. (Pike Place XXXXX Stout and smoked oysters are a great match, for example.) On the coasts, good smoked fish is easily found in delis and fish markets, but it can be hard to come by in other parts of the country. And even if you have good sources for commercial smoked fish, you might want to try smoking your own: it's decidedly cheaper and can be considerably less salty than store-bought kinds. If you have a kettle-type barbecue (a Weber, for example), a water smoker, or a small home-smoker, smoking fish or seafood at home is easy to do, and the results can be very gratifying.

Smoking any food generally involves two steps: brining or salting, and the actual smoking. Since most fish and seafood are small, they can be brined quickly and smoked quite easily at home.

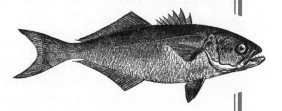

Brining

Brine is a solution of salt, water, sugar, spices, and other flavorings. Soaking fish in brine gives it the salty flavor characteristic of smoked food and replaces some of the fish's natural moisture with salt. This process is called curing, and before refrigeration, curing was essential for food preservation.

Several variables can affect curing time: the thickness of the food, the temperature during curing, and the saltiness of the brine. To eliminate two of these variables, do all the brining in the refrigerator and don't vary the salt in the formulas provided below. This leaves thickness as the guide to how long to leave fish or seafood in the brine. We provide estimates based on thickness, but taste for yourself, judge the salt levels you prefer, and adjust the curing time on the next occasion you do more smoking.

Smoking

Smoking is a process in which smoke from aromatic hard-woods is deposited on and incorporated into the food. Smoking also dries food, thus concentrating the flavor and changing its texture and appearance. If you use a kettle-type barbecue or water smoker, smoking usually takes place in a temperature range between 150° F. and 200° F. This process, called hot smoking, ensures that the food cooks slowly as it is smoked. Because of the wide temperature range, smoking times will vary considerably. For best results, take the shortest cooking times as your guide, then sample the food. If it is cooked sufficiently, remove the food from the smoker. If not, continue smoking the food until it is done. Use an instant-read thermometer to regulate smoking temperatures and to tell when the food is done.

You can also smoke fish using a stove-top smoker. If you own one of these, consult the manual for instructions on smoking fish and seafood.

The Process

Since the covered kettle-type barbecue (Weber) is the most common backyard barbecue, we'll use it as our main example. If you own a water smoker or small electric smoker such as a Little Chief, they come with excellent directions for smoking fish and seafood. Consult the manual for instructions.

Place the barbecue well away from the house, so smoke does not come in. Soak 3 or 4 cups of aromatic hardwood chips or 4 to 6 chunks of aromatic hardwood in water. Good woods for smoking fish are alder, hickory, cherry, maple, or oak. Soak the wood for at least 30 minutes or up to several hours. Remove the top rack from the barbecue and mound 10 to 15 charcoal briquettes on the bottom to one side. Light them, and allow the coals to burn down to the medium-low point; they should be covered with gray ash. This should take about 30 minutes. Spread the coals in a single layer on one side of the bottom rack. Place a pan to catch the drippings on the other side. Sprinkle 2 or 3 cups of the soaked wood chips or put 2 or 3 chunks of wood on the coals. Replace the top rack. If you are smoking small items like shellfish, place a piece of wire mesh or foil with small holes over the top rack so that the food does not fall through.

Spread the food over the top rack with the drip pan underneath. Cover the barbecue, making sure the vent in the lid is directly above the food. Open the top and bottom vents about ¼ inch. Slip an instant-read thermometer into the partially opened top vent, and monitor the temperature as the food smokes. It should be between 150° F. and 200° F. Regulate the heat by closing the vents to lower the heat and opening the vents or adding more coals to raise it. Add more chips or chunks of wood as needed. The smoke should be billowing and continuous. Check the recipes for approximate smoking times.

Basic Brine for Fish

1 gallon water	2 bay leaves
1½ cups kosher salt	12 peppercorns
1 cup sugar	Zest from 2 lemons
½ cup soy sauce	

Pour the water into a plastic tub or other nonreactive container (i.e., not aluminum or cast iron). Add the salt and sugar, stirring constantly until completely dissolved. Stir in the remaining ingredients. Chill the brine in the refrigerator. Brine will keep 2 weeks.

Smoked Fish Steaks or Fillets

Fish should be cut into steaks or fillets no more than 1–1½ inches thick. Good fish for smoking are halibut, rock cod, sea bass, striped bass, salmon, bluefish, tuna, albacore, mahimahi, swordfish, shark, cod, sablefish (also called black cod), drum, and sturgeon. The skin should be left on the fish so the pieces do not fall apart during smoking. Fillets should be smoked skin side down. Fish smoked this way is best eaten cold.

6–8 pounds fish fillets or steaks
1 recipe Basic Brine for Fish (see page 122)

½ cup vegetable oil, such as corn, olive, or peanut

In a nonreactive container cover the fish with the brine. Weigh it down with a plate. Put the container in the refrigerator for 2½–3½ hours. Wash the fish and pat dry. Brush with oil. Following the directions above, smoke the fish for 1–2 hours. Taste after 1 hour, and be sure not to overcook the fish. Test with an instant-read thermometer; it is done at 130° F. Depending on how the fish is used, there should be enough to feed 15–20. Extra fish will keep in the refrigerator for 5–7 days, and it freezes well.

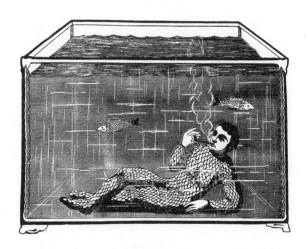

Smoked Whole Small Fish

This recipe works well with fish that weigh between ¾ to 1½ pounds each. Good small fish for smoking are trout, whitefish, bluefish, mackerel, herring, and coho salmon. For 6 to 8 fish you will need one recipe of Basic Brine.

6–8 whole fish, ¾–1½ pounds
each, gutted, with heads left
on if desired
1 recipe Basic Brine for Fish
(see page 122)

½ cup vegetable oil, such as
corn, olive, or peanut

Place the fish in a nonreactive container. Completely cover with the brine. Weigh the fish down with a plate so that they are completely submerged in the brine. Put the container in the refrigerator, and let the fish soak for 45 minutes to 1½ hours, depending on their size and the saltiness desired. If in doubt, use the shorter time, and increase the time in the brine the next time you do more smoking to add saltiness.

Remove the fish from the brine, wash, and pat them dry. Set up the kettle barbecue for smoking as described above. Brush each fish lightly with the oil, and place on the grill above a drip pan. Cover and smoke as directed for 45 minutes to 1½ hours or until the flesh is quite firm. Taste a bit to be sure if the fish is cooked to your satisfaction. The internal temperature should read 130° F. on an instant-read thermometer.

Take the fish off the grill, and brush with additional oil. The smoked fish can be eaten immediately or be refrigerated and eaten cold. Let cool first, and wrap well before refrigerating. Smoked fish will keep for 5–7 days. For a main course serving, allow 1 fish per person.

Bainbridge Island Smoked Fish Chowder

Smoked fish of one kind or another is found all over North America, and each region seems to have its favorite: smoked cod on the East Coast, smoked whitefish near the Great Lakes, smoked salmon and black cod on the Pacific Coast. Smoked fish and seafood seem made for beer, and some of the tastiest combinations we found on our travels involved smoked fish and local beer.

Smoked fish can be a bit pricey, although you can usually buy scraps and ends that don't slice nicely and aren't as pretty as the larger pieces. But they are perfectly good in soups and salads and they are a lot less expensive. Or you can make your own following our directions on pages 120–22.

We put together this hearty fish chowder using leftover bits of black cod, but almost any smoked fish will do. This richly flavored chowder is a great hit during football season, just the thing to serve to guests rooting for the home team in front of the TV on frosty autumn afternoons.

We enjoy a malty Dark Lager like Kemper Bock with this soup, but a Mild Ale such as Grant's Celtic Ale would also do well.

2 tablespoons butter
3 cups chopped onions
1 cup chopped celery
2 tablespoons flour
1 8-ounce bottle clam juice
1 teaspoon dried thyme
1 teaspoon ground black
    pepper
1 tablespoon grated
    lemon peel
½ teaspoon paprika
1 cup water
1 cup Dark Lager

3 cups diced red potatoes
1 pound mild smoked fish,
    such as black cod (sable-
    fish), cod, or trout, skin
    and bones removed, cut
    into small pieces
2 cups whole milk
2 cups half-and-half
1 cup sliced green onions
    or scallions
½ cup chopped parsley
Salt and pepper
Tabasco (optional)

In a large pot sauté the onions and celery in the butter over medium heat for 10 minutes, stirring occasionally. Stir in the flour until the vegetables are well coated. Cook 2 minutes. Add the clam juice, thyme, pepper, lemon peel, paprika, water, and lager. Bring to a boil, and reduce the heat to a simmer. Add the potatoes, and cook until tender, about 10 minutes. Add the fish, milk, half-and-half, green onions, and parsley. Cook for 5 minutes, and taste for salt and pepper. Add Tabasco if desired and serve hot.

SERVES 10–12.

Smoked Shellfish

Good types of shellfish for smoking are oysters (use larger ones), mussels, scallops (large sea scallops, not bay), or unshelled shrimp. Clams can be smoked, but they tend to get tough during the process. Once smoked, the shellfish are better cold than hot. Smoked shellfish do not freeze well.

2 pounds shucked shellfish or
   unpeeled shrimp
1 recipe Basic Brine for Fish
   (see page 122)

½ cup vegetable oil, such as
   corn, olive, or peanut

In a nonreactive container cover the shellfish with the brine. Weigh the shellfish down with a plate. Put the container in the refrigerator for 45 minutes–1 hour. Remove the shellfish, wash, and pat dry. Brush with oil.

Following the directions above, smoke the shellfish for 45 minutes–1½ hours at a temperature between 150°–200° F. The shellfish are done with they are firm and opaque. To be sure, taste a bit, or measure the internal temperature with an instant-read thermometer—it should read 120° F. Remove the shellfish from the grill and brush with oil. Cool, wrap, and refrigerate. Eat chilled as an appetizer with Creamy Horseradish Cocktail Sauce (see page 50). Enough for 6–8 as an appetizer. Smoked shellfish will keep refrigerated for 3–5 days.

Fish and Oyster Croquettes

Any firm-fleshed fish works well in these flavorful croquettes: salmon, red drum, bluefish, sea bass, striped bass, redfish, red snapper, grouper, or speckled trout are all very tasty. The recipe is a good way to use up any leftover fish, but you can poach, grill, or barbecue fish especially for the croquettes. In a pinch, you can also use canned salmon.

Serve the croquettes hot or cold with Spicy Tartar Sauce (recipe follows) or Rémoulade Sauce* and a crisp lager like Kemper Pilsner or a light ale such as Rainier.

The croquettes also make great sandwiches when sliced in half and combined with sliced tomato, tartar sauce or mustard mayonnaise, and thinly sliced red onions.

*See Index.

2 tablespoons unsalted butter

1 medium onion, finely chopped

2 ribs celery, finely chopped

1 cup thinly sliced green onions or scallions

1 teaspoon minced garlic

½ cup chopped parsley

¼ pound chopped mushrooms

1 jar (12 ounces) oysters, coarsely chopped, with liquid reserved

½ teaspoon dried thyme

¼ teaspoon dried sage

1 teaspoon dried dill or 1 tablespoon fresh

3 cups stale bread, cut into ¼-inch cubes

2 eggs

1 cup fish stock, extra oyster liquid, or bottled clam juice

2 cups flaked poached, broiled, or barbecued fish

¼ teaspoon Tabasco

Salt and pepper

1 cup olive or salad oil for frying

Melt the butter in a heavy 12-inch skillet over medium heat. Add the onion and celery, cover the pan, and cook for 5 minutes, stirring occasionally. Add the green onions, garlic, parsley, and mushrooms. Sauté, uncovered, for 5 more minutes. Add the oysters, and cook 1 minute more. In a large mixing bowl combine the vegetable and oyster mixture with the thyme, sage, dill, bread cubes, eggs, and enough fish stock or oyster liquid to make everything moist, but still firm. Stir in the flaked fish. Season with Tabasco and salt and pepper. With your hands, form the mixture into patties ½–¾ inch thick and 3 inches in diameter. In a skillet fry in oil over medium heat until brown, about 5 minutes on each side. Serve the patties immediately with Spicy Tartar Sauce.

SERVES 6–8.

Spicy Tartar Sauce

A particularly spicy version of the classic combination, this tartar sauce is delicious on all kinds of fish and seafood and is also tasty on cold chicken or salad. Tart Wheat Beers, such as August Schell Weizen and Grant's Weis Beer, go well with it.

3 tablespoons fresh lemon juice, or more to taste

2 tablespoons Creole mustard or other coarse-grained mustard

2 eggs

½ cup olive oil

1 cup peanut oil

½ teaspoon cayenne

1 teaspoon salt

½ teaspoon finely ground black pepper

½ cup finely chopped green onions or scallions

¼ cup finely chopped parsley

2 teaspoons soy sauce

1 teaspoon Worcestershire sauce

2 tablespoons finely chopped dill pickle

1 tablespoon capers, drained

2 tablespoons finely chopped fresh dill (optional)

1 teaspoon Tabasco, or more to taste

Put 2 tablespoons of the lemon juice in the bowl of a food processor fitted with the metal blade with the mustard and the eggs. With the motor running, gradually add the olive and peanut oils combined, very slowly at first, and then in a steady stream as the sauce begins to thicken. When all the oil has been emulsified, the sauce should be thick and fluffy. Remove the lid, and add the cayenne, salt, pepper, green onions, parsley, soy sauce, Worcestershire sauce, pickle, capers, optional fresh dill, and Tabasco. Replace the lid and pulse the processor for a second or two 2 or 3 times, just until everything is nicely blended. Taste the sauce and add more lemon juice, Tabasco, or salt if you think it needs it. The sauce keeps, covered, in the refrigerator for 2 to 3 days.

MAKES 3–4 CUPS.

Cornish Hens in Stout

*Make this dish with a full-flavored Stout—Hart's Sphinx Stout or Pike
Place XXXXX Stout—and, of course, drink the same beer with your
meal. The Stout, mushrooms, and cream combine to make a magnificent
sauce, and the ale's rich, caramel flavors tie everything together beautifully. Serve with Garlic and Horseradish Mashed Potatoes.**

4 1-pound Cornish game
   hens
Salt and pepper
2 tablespoons butter
1 medium onion, finely
   chopped
2 garlic cloves, minced
½ pound mushrooms,
   chopped

½ teaspoon finely chopped
   juniper berries
1 bay leaf
1 12-ounce bottle Stout, Porter,
   or other dark beer
1 cup heavy cream

Season the birds generously with salt and pepper. Melt the butter in a
Dutch oven or large casserole over medium heat and in it brown the
game hens on all sides until golden brown, about 10 minutes. Remove
the birds and all but 3 tablespoons of the fat. Add the onion and garlic
and cook until soft, about 5 minutes. Add the mushrooms, stir, and
cook for 2 minutes. Add the juniper berries, bay leaf, and beer,
and bring to a boil. Put in ¼ cup of the cream and the game hens, and
lower the heat to a simmer. Cover and cook 30 minutes until the birds
are done. Remove the hens to a warm platter and skim off any fat on
the sauce. Pour in the remaining cream and cook the sauce until it just
begins to thicken. Taste for salt and pepper. Serve some of the sauce
over the birds, the rest over the mashed potatoes.

SERVES 4.

*See Index.

Pork Chops with Fresh Pimiento

Fresh pimientos are heart shaped and have a thicker skin and a more robust flavor than red bell peppers. The pimientos appear in Northwest markets like Pike Place in late September and are sometimes still available as late as Thanksgiving. If you can't find fresh pimientos, use red bell peppers, which are at their best in late summer or early fall.

Drink a full-bodied Pale Ale with this robust and spicy dish—Pike Place Pale Ale is a natural choice.

Salt and pepper
4 loin pork chops (about 2 pounds)
1 tablespoon Dijon mustard
2 tablespoons sweet Hungarian paprika
Pinch each of dried thyme, savory, basil, and dill
2 tablespoons butter

1 medium onion, thinly sliced
2 garlic cloves, chopped
1 fresh pimiento or red bell pepper, thinly sliced
1 medium ripe tomato, sliced
1 cup Pale Ale
1 cup sour cream (optional)

Lightly salt and pepper the chops, brush with the mustard, and sprinkle generously with some of the paprika and the herbs. Brown the chops over medium-high heat in the butter in a heavy frying pan 2–3 minutes on each side. Remove and set aside. Add the onion to the pan, and fry until soft, about 5 minutes. Stir in the garlic and the remaining paprika, and cook for 1 minute. Add the pimiento or bell pepper, and sauté briefly. Arrange the chops over the vegetables, and cover the chops with the tomato slices. Sprinkle lightly with salt and pepper, and pour in the ale. Cover, and cook over low heat 45 minutes or until the meat is done. (Pork should read 155–60° F. on a meat thermometer.) Transfer the chops to a warm platter. Reduce the sauce until it is just syrupy. Remove from the heat, and stir in the optional sour cream. Taste for salt and pepper. Pour the sauce and vegetables over the chops and serve with buttered rice.

SERVES 4.

Chocolate Porter Cake

Edy Young, who gave us this recipe, is both a professional candymaker and baker. She grew up in a household where nothing went to waste. When her dad left some beer, it would be used in cooking breads, stews, and stuffing, and even to make chocolate cake!

Although almost any beer will do, this rich cake is best made with a dark beer like Porter whose roasted malt, caramel, and chocolately undertones provide lots of flavor in both the cake and frosting. Save some Porter to drink along with the cake—it's a delicious combination.

We made the cake with one of our local favorites in California, Sierra Nevada Porter, but you could use any other Porter, Stout, or dark beer you prefer.

¾ cup plus 2 tablespoons *salted* butter

2½ cups cake flour

2 teaspoons baking powder

½ teaspoon baking soda

½ teaspoon salt

3 eggs, separated, at room temperature

1⅓ cups sugar

3 ounces unsweetened Baker's chocolate, melted

1 cup Porter or other dark beer, flat

Chocolate Chip and Porter Cake Frosting

1 pound semisweet *real* chocolate chips

2 tablespoons *salted* butter

5 tablespoons Porter

5 tablespoons milk

To make the cake: Preheat the oven to 375° F. Lightly grease two 9-inch cake pans with the 2 tablespoons butter and dust with ¼ cup of flour. Shake out and discard any excess flour, and set the pans aside.

Mix together the remaining 2¼ cups flour with the baking powder, baking soda, and salt. Beat the egg whites with 2 tablespoons of the sugar until stiff peaks begin to form.

With an electric mixer, cream together the remaining sugar with the ¾ cup butter until light in texture. One at a time, beat in the egg yolks. Stir in the melted chocolate, the beer, and then gradually beat in the flour mixture. With a rubber spatula, fold in the egg whites. Scrape half the batter into each of the cake pans, and bake in the middle of the oven 30–35 minutes, until a toothpick inserted in the center comes out clean. Remove the pans from the oven and let the cakes cool while you prepare the frosting.

To make the frosting: Soften the chocolate chips and butter in a double boiler. (The chips should be soft, but still hold their shape.) Remove from the heat. Using an electric beater, beat the chocolate and butter until smooth, about 1 minute. Beat in the Porter and milk, one tablespoon at a time, until the mixture is soft and shiny.

Remove the cakes from the pans. Frost the layers.

MAKES A 2-LAYER 9-INCH CAKE.

BEER DRINKS

Black Velvet

In a large wineglass or goblet mix ⅓ part Stout, such as Hart's Sphinx Stout or Pike Place XXXXX, with ⅔ parts sparkling wine.

Shandygaff

In a beer mug or large glass mix together equal parts sparkling lemonade (or lemon soda) and Pale Ale, such as Hart's Pale Ale.

Wheat Beer with Fruit Syrup

In a large goblet or mug mix together 2–3 ounces fruit syrup, such as raspberry, strawberry, lime, or lemon, with 8–12 ounces Wheat Beer, such as Widmer Weizenbeer or Hart's Pyramid Wheaten Ale.

CALIFORNIA: BILLY THE BREWER, STEAM BEER, AND NEW ALBION ALE

Bay Wolf BBQ Potato Chips

Crunchy Sausage Bites

Lemon and Lager Marinade for Fish or Chicken

Ale Marinade for Steak or Lamb

Porter or Stout and Molasses Marinade

Bourbon Stout Marinade for Chicken

Chinese Hoisin Marinade for Pork, Chicken, or Lamb

Tandoori Marinade

Smoky Rauchbier Marinade

Asparagus and Shiitake Mushrooms in Sesame Dressing

Rice, Corn, and Watercress Salad

Smoked Chicken and Orzo Salad

Szechuan Chicken Salad

Duck and Roasted Walnut Salad

Chinese Fish Salad with Chui Chow Vinaigrette

California Calamari Salad

Cold Roast Beef and Scallions in Ginger Dressing

Stuffed Pork Loin in Imperial Stout

Beef Brisket with Lemon and Spices

Lamb Chops with Whole Garlic Cloves and Summer Herbs

Solianka—Russian Beef Stew

Hangtown Fry

Carrots and Leeks in Steam Beer

Garlic and Horseradish Mashed Potatoes

Roasted Garlic and Shallot Soup

**Dry Fried Green Beans and Chinese Noodles with
Smoky Black Bean Sauce**

Beer and brewing in California date from the Gold Rush, when hopeful miners flooded the state, dreaming of finding the Mother Lode and working up quite a thirst in the process. San Francisco was quickly transformed from a small town into a roaring city filled with forty-niners who wanted, if not all the comforts of home, at least their suds.

Saloons sprang up on every corner of the burgeoning metropolis, and establishments like the Bella Union, The Empire Saloon, Denny O'Brien's, and The Bank Exchange offered patrons everything from the cancan and fandangos to dogfights and bull-baiting, Shakespeare by Junius Brutus Booth, and terpsichorean extravaganzas by Lola Montez. And with their cultural entertainments, the boys wanted beer.

Although there is mention in Bill Yenne's *Beers of North America* (W. H. Smith, 1986) of a legendary Billy the Brewer McGlore making beer in the 1830's in San Francisco, the first commercial brewery in California dates from 1849. It was started by A. Schuppert, a German forty-niner who found making beer in San Francisco more profitable than grubbing for gold in the Sierras. Within a few years, breweries abounded in California, with substantial ones thriving in San Francisco, San Jose, Stockton, Sacramento, and up in the Mother Lode Country among the thirsty miners. One brewery in Placer county even had its cellars dug out by eager argonauts who pooled their gold nuggets to get the brewery going.

And when the miners struck it rich and came back to the bright lights of San Francisco for a spree and good eats, they had plenty to choose from. There were Monkey Warner's Cobweb Palace on Meiggs Wharf, the Old Tadich Grill and the Oakdale Clam House, where you could find the freshest grilled fish, Hangtown Fry,* and seafood chowders and soups. For those who wanted more elaborate fare, elegant hotels and fancy restaurants served grilled steaks, succulent stews and braised dishes, freshly made salads, and flavorful sautés. For the more adventurous there was always a trip to San Francisco's bustling Chinatown, North Beach for Italian food, or to Luna's on Telegraph Hill for spicy Mexican dishes.

*See Index.

Above, San Francisco's finest, hands outstretched but uncharacteristically empty, at the Bank Exchange Saloon. Right, Abe "Monkey" Warner's Cobweb Palace on Meigg's Wharf in old San Francisco.

Early San Francisco brewers pose with their families. Notice the cotton "head of steam" on the steins and barrels.

With this rich array of food, Californians drank an amber-colored, powerfully flavored beer with plenty of head, or steam, as they called it.

The 1850's saw the establishment of lager as *the* American brew, and most of the brewers in California were of German extraction. They naturally wanted to brew lager for their customers, but they faced a serious problem: no ice. Before refrigeration, lager required a long slow fermentation over the winter or, in summer, ice to maintain the cool temperatures necessary for proper aging. In the East, the winter's ice was cut on lakes and rivers, and stored in huge icehouses for summer brewing. California's sources of ice were by boat from the Sierras or Alaska, or from New England around the Horn—all prohibitively expensive.

So early California brewers did the next best thing: They fermented the beer at warm temperatures, sometimes using the old ale yeasts, sometimes the newer lager. The resulting "common beer" was a cross between the lager and ale styles—not as subtle or smooth as lager, not as aggressively flavored as ale. The higher temperatures and faster fermentation also produced more CO_2 pressure in the keg, and this natural carbonation, and the hiss when the keg was tapped, gave the beer its nickname—Steam Beer.

Ale and porter were also brewed in California, and by the 1880's, with the advent of mechanical refrigeration, lager as well. As the century progressed, lager became the dominant brew, just as in the rest of America, but a few of the old-style steam breweries hung on in the Bay Area in Northern California.

ANCHOR STEAM BEER

The last survivor was Anchor Brewing Company. In the early 1960's, it was a small run-down brewery located near the railroad tracks south of Market Street in San Francisco. Anchor Steam Beer was served in a few bars and saloons in North Beach, the old Italian section of the city, which at that time was filling up with the writers and artists who would later be called the Beat Generation. To this poor but discriminating population, Anchor had some advantages: It was cheap, it was sold on draft, and it had character. In hangouts like Vesuvio's and the Old Spaghetti Factory you could get a mug of amber, hoppy Steam Beer for about a quarter. A plate of spaghetti, a hunk of sourdough French bread, and a schooner or two of Anchor Steam could provide plenty of nourishment and good cheer for surprisingly little money.

One of those who discovered Anchor Steam Beer in those days was an ex-philosophy student from Stanford, Fritz Maytag. When Anchor was facing bankruptcy in 1965, Maytag, twenty-six at the time and a member of the family

that made Maytag washers and Maytag Blue Cheese, bought the decrepit 600-barrel brewery for a few thousand dollars, more to save a bit of California's heritage than to found a business. Within a few years he had transformed the brewery and its product.

Emphasizing quality and coupling traditional brewing practices with modern techniques and sanitation, Maytag created a beer that showed beer lovers that an American brewery could make beer equal to or better than the imported ones. Anchor Steam became the standard, a benchmark of quality for lovers of fine beer. Brewed at "ale" temperatures using lager yeast, amber-colored and with a rich, creamy head, full bodied and malty, aggressively hopped and beautifully balanced, Anchor was the beer that inspired imitation among the growing number of serious home brewers in the Bay Area. Anchor Steam Beer became the model for the many microbreweries that followed Maytag's example in the years that followed.

Today, Anchor Steam is recognized as one of the finest beers made in America, and production is in the 50,000 barrel per year range. Located in a showpiece brewhouse gleaming with copper and tile, the brewery now makes, in addition to its main product, Anchor Steam Beer, the following: an intense, deeply colored Porter; Liberty Ale, hoppy and full flavored; Christmas Ale, different every year and available only during the holidays; Old Foghorn Barley Wine, heady,

slightly sweet, and very powerful; and a light and refreshingly tart Anchor Wheat Beer.

Inspired by Anchor Steam Beer, and impressed with the growing number of European and British beers available in the U.S. market, home brewers in California and other areas began to make beers that were a far cry from the old Prohibition brewed-in-the-bathtub types. As more and more products became available—malt extracts from England and Germany, specialty malts from pale to black patent, fresh hops from the Yakima Valley, Germany, and Czechoslovakia, pure strains of lager and ale yeasts—home brewers began to experiment in a serious way, making beers that rivalled the products of German and English breweries.

Home-brew clubs like the San Andreas Malts, The Maltose Falcons, The Draft Board, Cinque Zanni (Five Fools) Brewers with its legendary poet-brewmaster, Nestor Marzipan, and others created world-class beers in home kitchens and cellars. Books were written, competitions held, and an informed and enthusiastic beer culture grew up all over the United States that cared for fine beer and knew how to make it. (For more information about home brewing, see Appendix III, Brewing Beer at Home.)

THE FIRST
MICROBREWERIES:
CALIFORNIA ALE

I n 1977 Jack MacAuliffe, an avid home brewer who developed a taste for English and Scottish ales while serving in the Navy, opened the first microbrewery in America, New Albion Brewery.

Jack, a colorful character whose command of profanity was equaled only by his ability to weld, scrounge, and improvise brewery equipment, founded his tiny brewery in an old barn near the town of Sonoma north of San Francisco. Just about everything at New Albion was haphazard and improvised, but the ale that Jack and his partner Suzie Stern made was

A nineteenth-century California lager brewery. Mechanical refrigeration led to the spread of lager brewing throughout the West. Many breweries also sold ice as a sideline.

impressive by any standard. It was sometimes cloudy, occasionally funky, it didn't last very long if you left it out of the fridge, and in some batches the hops would take the enamel off your teeth, but New Albion ale had *character* above all else. When you drank New Albion, you knew you were tasting something real: This was no mass-produced, technologically perfect brew. Here was a handmade, downhome kickass ale, American and real and full of flavor.

New Albion didn't last more than a few years: A combination of money problems and difficulties with distribution, sales, and marketing finally sank it. But it was the first, and it showed the way to a whole host of home brewers who went on to create California microbreweries and brew-pubs.

In the years that followed, microbreweries sprang up all over California. One of the first was Mendocino Brewing Company in the aptly named town of Hopland, about a hundred miles north of the Bay Area. In 1982, brewers Don Barkley and Michael Lovett of the then recently closed New Albion and three other partners took advantage of a law newly passed in California permitting breweries to sell their own products to the public.

They opened the state's first brew-pub in a hundred-year-old brick saloon on Highway 101, bringing with them much of the equipment from New Albion and the tradition of full-bodied hoppy ales fostered by MacAuliffe. Within a few years, the brew-pub had quite a following, drawing ale aficionados from all over Northern California, and the partners began to bottle their vastly popular Red Tail Ale.

Today Mendocino Brewing Company/The Hopland Brewery is packed with visitors on the weekends, who are offered pub food and ales in the outdoor hop garden restaurant, and blues and jazz in its spacious, wood-paneled bar. In addition to the amber Red Tail Ale, the brewery makes a full line of ales, all of which are named after the raptors that circle over the vineyard-covered hills surrounding the town: Blue Heron Pale Ale, Eye of the Hawk Special Ale (8 percent alcohol), Peregrine Ale, and Black Hawk Stout. Depending on the season, the ales can be found at the brewery in Hopland and throughout Northern and Southern California.

The name Hopland, by the way, reflects a once-thriving hop-growing industry in Northern California. Earlier in the century hops were cultivated all through Sonoma and Mendocino counties, but a combination of a hop blight and bad economics made hop growers move north to Washington's Yakima Valley. When you drive through the region, however, you can still see the distinctive hop kilns and oast-houses that once processed this aromatic harvest.

Another microbrewery/brew-pub located in the old hop-growing country is Anderson Valley Brewing Company in the tiny Mendocino County town of Boonville. Located on the site of the old Buckhorn Saloon, a popular tavern of the 1860's, Anderson Valley Brewing makes full-bodied, hoppy ales: Poleeko Gold, a light, gold ale with sweet malt flavors balanced by tangy hops; Boont Amber, a reddish-amber ale in the English style; Deep Enders Dark, a rich, dark Porter; and High Rollers Wheat, a light and refreshing Wheat Beer. The names of the beers derive from "Boontling," a local lingo created by Boonville hop pickers, farmers, and saloon-goers, and still used by local wags when giving directions to "flatland furriners."

Full-bodied ales and the cool coastal climate of Mendocino County seem suited for each other North Coast Brewing in the seacoast town of Fort Bragg produces one of the most flavorful of the California-style ales, Ruedrich's Red Seal Ale. The distinctive copper-colored ale is rich in malt and hops with excellent balance and a smoother finish than most. It is available bottled throughout Northern California. The brewery also makes excellent India Pale Ale, Old 45 Stout, Christmas Brown Ale, and Scrimshaw Pilsner-style Beer.

One of the great success stories among California microbreweries is Sierra Nevada Brewing Company of Chico, a lively college and farming town in the foothills of the Sierra Nevada mountains north of Sacramento. Partners Paul Camusi and Ken Grossman founded their brewery in 1978, soon after New Albion was established. Generously supported by Fritz Maytag of Anchor, who sold them equipment and materials at low prices and donated much time and advice, the partners soon established a reputation for making top-quality ales.

Their Sierra Nevada Pale Ale has become the paradigm of the California Ale style: amber-gold in color with intense caramel malt flavors balanced by powerful Cascade hop aromas and a beautiful dun-colored head that just won't quit. And it is the ale that has the greatest reputation among San Francisco Bay Area food fanatics: It's on draft at the Chez Panisse Café, Oliveto, and many of the area's finest restaurants. Sierra Nevada Pale Ale is a fine match for California-style food: light and spicy salads (see Index for Duck and Roasted Walnut Salad), and flavorful grilled fish, poultry, and meats (see Marinating and Grilling, page 155).

The brewery has grown over the years and now produces upwards of 25,000 barrels a year, making it one of the largest and most successful of California's microbreweries. (Tom Dalldorf, the ebullient editor/publisher of *The California Celebrator Beer News,* calls Sierra Nevada a "macro-micro.") In addition to its popular Pale Ale, Sierra Nevada also bottles Celebration India Pale Ale, a malty and unusual Pale Bock, a

chocolatey Porter, a deeply colored Stout, and a slightly sweet and very strong (8 percent) Bigfoot Barley Wine.

Other microbreweries producing full-bodied ales in California include Lind Brewing of San Leandro, whose Drake's Ale is a favorite in Bay Area taverns and restaurants, San Andreas Brewing, whose brewmaster Bill Millar makes a number of distinctively flavored ales including fruit ales made with cranberries and apricots, and Devil Mountain Brewery of Benicia, with its popular Devil's Brew Porter and Railroad Ale Strong Ale. Winchester Red Ale from San Jose is also much appreciated by local ale fanciers.

One California contract brewery whose products are widely available is Pete's Brewing Company of Palo Alto. Pete's Wicked Ale is a Dark Ale with roasted malt flavors and a good undertone of hops; Pete's Gold Coast Lager is full bodied and tangy, while Pete's Pacific Dry is a light lager in the crisp Mexican style so popular on the West Coast.

ALTBIERS AND LAGERS IN THE GERMAN TRADITION

While most California microbreweries produce ales in the English and California styles, an increasing number of micros and brewpubs are making German-style *Altbiers* and lagers.

Germany, and specifically the city of Düsseldorf, famous for Düsseldorfer Alt, an old-style German ale, was the inspiration for Stanislaus Brewing Company's St. Stan's Alt. When owner/brewer Garith Helm, a physicist working at the Lawrence Livermore Lab, married German-born Romy Graf, he tapped into a tradition that predated the lager revolution.

Altbier, made in Düsseldorf and a few other places in Germany, is a leftover from the older ale tradition, but incorporates some lager-making techniques. Brewers use a special top-fermenting ale yeast, but make the beer using the low temperatures and aging usually associated with lager. The result is a distinctive, richly flavored beer that has characteristics of each style: It is fruity and robust like ale, yet smooth and subtle like lager.

Helm returned from visits to his wife's family in Germany a convert to the *Altbier* style and began his career as a home brewer. Within a few years, however, like many in California in the 1980's, he went professional and founded his Stanislaus Brewing Company in Modesto in California's Central Valley.

St. Stan's Amber Alt, Dark Alt, and Festbier are named after a mythical brewer St. Stan who is occasionally seen in full robes and tonsure at the brewery; the beers are among the most popular of California's microbrewed products. The brewery has a substantial yearly production of 12,000 barrels, and is widely distributed throughout the West. St. Stan's is also available on draft in a new 15,000-square-foot beer restaurant Helm opened recently in downtown Modesto.

Lager is definitely the main attraction at Sudwerk Privatebrauerei Hübsch Brewery in the university town of Davis near Sacramento. Both a German beer garden and a lager brewery, Sudwerk/Hübsch offers one of the finest lagers made in the U.S. today with its Hübsch-Brau Lager, a malty golden lager in the Munich Helles style.

German-born brewmaster Karl Eden, an immensely erudite yet unflaggingly jolly brewer, is a product of Munich's Paulaner Brewery and the Dinckelacker Brewery of Stuttgart. He and assistant brewer Dave Morrow produce and bottle the popular Helles, along with a heady Dopplebock, crisp Wheat Beer, and seasonal Oktoberfest. The beers are currently available at the brewery and in select Northern California locations.

Another microbrewery specializing in lagers is Santa Cruz Brewing, located in the popular beach resort city on Monterey Bay south of San Francisco. It was founded in 1984 by Bernie and Gerry Turgeon, father and son, who sold their interest in a thriving South Coast winery, Turgeon-Lohr, to create handcrafted American lagers. With prize-winning home brewer Scotty Morgan, they designed a handsome modern brewery along with the Front Street Pub, a brew-pub and beer restaurant modeled on an English public house.

The 1,500-barrel-a-year brewery produces Lighthouse Lager, a European-style golden lager; Lighthouse Amber, malty and with a clear undertone of bitter Northern Brewer hops; and Pacific Porter, made from caramel malt, black roasted barley, and an aromatic mix of American and European hops.

The restaurant in the adjacent Front Street Pub offers a variety of spicy grills and deep-fried foods that go well with beer, including homemade onion rings (check Index for our Onion Rings), tortilla chips and fresh salsa (see our Salsa Cruda*), spiedies (marinated pork chunks, skewered and grilled), oyster shots (Pacific oysters in spicy sauce), shark bites (thresher shark in beer batter) (see our Beer Batters for Fish*), and pub shrimp poached in porter (see our Shrimp Boiled in Beer and Spices*).

Southern California's hot climate and laid-back style seems suited

*See Index.

for crisp, light lagers. One of the region's largest microbreweries is the Alpine Village Brewing Company of Torrance, which produces a malty Bavarian-style lager, Alpine Village Hofbrau Lager, a high-hopped Hofbrau Pilsner, and a light lager, Hofbrau Light.

The Alpine Village is an Old World shopping complex with shops, restaurants, and markets offering a wide variety of German and other European products. The brewery supplies the Alpine Village Bavarian Beer Garden and the Alpine Inn Restaurant, where diners can enjoy German specialties, such as schnitzels, sauerbrauten, and tangy German-style salads (check Index for our Sauerkraut and Apple Salad and Warm Potato Salad in Beer Dressing) with their steins of lager.

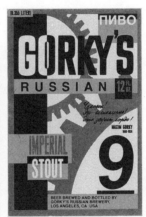

GORKY'S: SLAVIC SUDS
AND PUNK ROCKERS

Gorky's Cafe and Russian Brewery in Los Angeles' downtown wholesale flower district is a special kind of place. The brew-pub and restaurant caters to a mixed clientele of beer fanatics, émigré Russians, local warehouse workers, students from nearby colleges, punked-out musicians, hungry actors, and lovers of hearty food and beer. The decor is definitely L.A. post-modern funk, with rickety tables and beat-up booths, Soviet agitprop posters from the 1920's, punk-rock posters, and tattered announcements for concerts and conceptual art happenings all over the walls. A busy cafeteria line offers omelets and an array of Russian specialties day and night, and a long bar with full-bodied draft ales and lagers serves a bustling clientele.

The tiny brewery at Gorky's produces Baltic Light Ale, a pleasant blonde ale with good malt/hop balance, Golden Pilsner, a crisp, full-bodied lager, Red Star Ale, a hoppy amber ale, and Russian Imperial Stout, dark, thick, and very flavorful.

Gorky's Russian Imperial Stout is one of the best Stouts we found on our travels: deep black, malty, with a toasty undertone from roasted barley. At the pub we ran into a Russian friend who took us home to his artist's loft in the produce district for a meal. We brought along a couple of liters of Red Star Ale and Gorky's Imperial Stout, and the result was a memorable beer banquet that featured Solianka,* a delicious Russian soup/stew made with beef and prunes, and Stuffed Pork Loin in Imperial Stout,* a dish fit for a czar, or at least a commissar.

WOLFGANG PUCK'S EUREKA: CALIFORNIA BEER CUISINE

California cuisine, an exciting, eclectic blend of Asian, South-western, and Mediterranean flavors on a California base of grills and salads, is popular in restaurants from Spokane to Singapore these days. The emphasis on light and spicy dishes easily prepared and served casually in no particular order is a formula that is also suited to beer with its many styles and compatibility for intensely flavored foods.

Wolfgang Puck, one of the creators of the new California style, recently opened Eureka in West Los Angeles, a restaurant and micro-brewery devoted to what Puck calls "beer cuisine." Featuring Eureka Lager, a pale gold, lightly malty beer in the Continental Pilsner style, the wildly popular and very trendy restaurant offers a wide array of signature Puck dishes, all created with beer in mind.

*See Index.

Diners in the brightly lit room with its gleaming copper bar and bustling open kitchen are offered dishes like Muscovy duck chile with black beans (check Index for our O'Shea's Black Beans), red curry chicken quesadillas (see our Quesadillas), Grandpa Puck's cheese ravioli with hazelnut butter, and Garlic Horseradish Mashed Potatoes* along with Puck's innovative piz-

zas, and a startling mix of sausages, including Cajun shrimp sausage, Chinese almond-duck sausage, and fiery Yucatan sausages flavored with smoky chipotle chiles.

Composed salads, especially with Oriental and Latin ingredients, are particularly compatible with the California lifestyle and seem naturally suited to light lagers. Our Asparagus and Shiitake Mushrooms in Sesame Dressing,* California Calamari Salad,* Szechuan Chicken Salad,* and Smoked Chicken and Orzo Salad* all provide the bright flavors and spicy tastes that complement malty, lightly hopped beers. Cold cooked meats are often incorporated in Oriental salads such as our Thai Beef Salad* and our Cold Roast Beef (or Pork) and Scallions in Ginger Dressing.*

Grilling is quintessentially Californian, and some of the best dishes in the California style are barbecued on backyard patios, on picnics, or in upscale restaurants. Fish and seafood are particularly delicious when briefly grilled (see our Skewered Scallops with Red Pepper Coulis*), especially when previously marinated to pick up flavorful undertones of beer, herbs, and spices (see Marinating and Grilling, page 155).

Marinades add complexity to grilled food and can transform a simple piece of barbecued meat, poultry, or fish into an interesting ethnic dish; our Chinese Hoisin Marinade for Pork, Chicken, or Lamb* and Tandoori Marinade* are good examples. Marinating foods in powerfully flavored beers or ales also provides flavor interest and a liaison between the food and the beer drunk with it, as in our Porter or Stout and Molasses Marinade,* Ale Marinade for Steak,* and Smoky Rauchbier Marinade.*

Garlic, and plenty of it, is one of the key ingredients in many California dishes, and the odiferous bulb seems to have a special affinity with beer. Beer tends to be the drink of choice at the jam-packed

---

* See Index.

Gilroy Garlic Festival, where happy allophiles gorge on garlic in every form imaginable, from garlic fritters and roasted garlic to garlic ice cream and chocolate-covered garlic cloves. A full-bodied ale such as Sierra Nevada Pale Ale is a fine match for the garlicky intensity of our Roast Garlic and Shallot Soup* and Lamb Chops with Whole Garlic Cloves and Summer Herbs.*

Gordon Biersch Brewing Company of Palo Alto and San Jose is one of the most successful of California's brewery/restaurants that matches beer with California cuisine. The restaurant was opened in 1988 by partners Dan Gordon and Dean Biersch in Palo Alto and was an immediate success. Concentrating on German-style lagers and serving a varied menu of California- and Oriental-influenced grills, sautés, and salads, the restaurant and bar are packed every night with noisy crowds of Stanford students, lawyers, and young professionals from the affluent suburbs south of San Francisco. The beers, which vary from light Pilsner styles through heavier Maerzens and Doppelbocks, complement the spicy salads and grilled meats and seafoods served from the busy open kitchen. Popular appetizers offered to throngs at the bar include fresh grilled prawns with spicy Coral Island sauce, chicken wings with chipotle chile sauce and honey mustard dip (see our Adobo Chicken Wings* and Honey Beer Mustard*), raclette and caramelized onion quesadilla and chunky salsa (see our Quesadillas* and Salsa Cruda*), and Maui Onion Rings (see our Onion Rings*).

Entrées are very much in the eclectic, California cuisine style, with dishes like red tiger prawn curry with coconut milk, lime, and cilantro, lamb chops with garlic (see our Lamb Chops with Whole Garlic Cloves and Summer Herbs*), and chicken breast on a bed of black beans with salsa fresca (see O'Shea's Black Beans*). The Palo Alto location has proven so successful that Gordon Biersch has recently opened a new restaurant/brewery in San Jose, an expanding community southeast of San Francisco, and another this spring on the San Francisco Embarcadero.

Asian cooking has had a tremendous influence in California. In the early days many professional cooks of both Oriental and American food were Chinese, and the Chinese culinary influence is seen almost

*See Index.

everywhere today, notably in fashionable East/West restaurants, such as Wolfgang Puck's Chinois in Los Angeles and China Moon and Monsoon in San Francisco. Chinese restaurants in virtually every regional style—from Szechuan to Hakka, from tiny family-run neighborhood restaurants to huge Hong Kong–style seafood palaces—are found in almost every city on the Pacific Coast.

Chinese cooking is eminently suited to beer. The range of ingredients and flavors, the use of sweet/sour combinations, the spicy dishes favored by many regional cooks all tie in beautifully with beer's great range of styles and flavors. Our Szechuan Chicken Salad,* Chinese Fish Salad with Chui Chow Vinaigrette,* and Dry Fried Green Beans and Chinese Noodles with Smoky Black Bean Sauce* all reflect the rich tradition of West Coast Chinese cooking.

Other Asian cultures have enriched West Coast cooking immeasurably in recent years. The Japanese influence, with its emphasis on absolutely fresh food, beautifully prepared and presented, is especially important. Japan is a beer-drinking country, and much Japanese food, from *sushi* to tempura (see our Tempura recipe*), is suited to the light lagers so popular in Japan.

Vietnamese, Thai, Cambodian, Burmese, and Indian cooking are also popular, and the spicy character and vivid flavors of these cuisines are nicely complemented by beer. California cooking draws heavily on these cuisines, and our California Calamari Salad,* Thai Beef Salad,* Cold Roast Beef (or Pork) and Scallions in Ginger Dressing,* Asparagus and Shiitake Mushrooms in Sesame Dressing,* Curried Fish Chowder,* and Tandoori Marinade* all have their roots in this exciting addition to American cooking.

CALIFORNIA: BREW-PUB COUNTRY

BUFFALO BILL'S BREW PUB
HAYWARD, CALIFORNIA
BEER

There's no way we can keep track of all the brew-pubs in the state: Some have opened and closed with the speed of radishes sprouting and going to seed within a couple of days. We'll list below some of our favorites and try to give you an idea of the lively brew-pub scene in California.

*See Index.

One of the first brew-pubs in the country was Buffalo Bill's in Hayward, a hotbed of home brewing and beer fanatics south of Oakland in the Bay Area. Bill Owens, a successful professional photographer and enthusiastic home brewer, started his vest-pocket brew-pub in an old saloon just a few weeks after Mendocino Brewing opened up in 1982.

Bill has been a vocal spokesman for small brewers both locally and on the national scene and has been a consultant to many interested in

starting brew-pubs on their own. He brews a wide array of ales and lagers in his tiny brewery and has made some of the most interesting beers around. In addition to his regular Buffalo Brew Lager, he offers Amber Lager, Tasmanian Devil Lager, Wheat Beer, and Stout along with specialty beers—Pumpkin Ale, deep orange in color and flavored with pumpkin and spices, and a smoky Rauchbeer in the German tradition. As with most brew-pubs, beers are available on draft only on the premises and vary according to a seasonal brewing schedule. Food tends to be simple pub grub with flavorful sausages and sandwiches that complement the full-bodied ales and lagers.

Pacific Coast Brewing is located in a neighborhood of restored Victorians in downtown Oakland. The beautifully appointed pub and restaurant not only serves its own forthright ales but offers a range of draft and bottled beers from local breweries along with Draft Guinness and Fuller's E.S.B. from England.

Brewer Don Gortemiller specializes in English- and California-style ales: Blue Whale Ale, the house favorite, is a copper-colored, high-hopped Amber Ale with powerful, malty flavors and hints of oak from chips added during fermentation; Killer Whale Stout is a strong, black Stout with undertones of coffee and chocolate, roasted malt flavors, and plenty of hops in the finish. Specialty beers are available seasonally and some feature spices and other flavorings: Neptune's Nectar uses ginger in the brew with sweet maltiness and light touches of hops; Amber Alt is lightly sweet with caramel malt flavors and undertones of European hops.

Food in the restaurant includes a range of tangy appetizers such as marinated herring (see our Marlene's Three Herring Salads*), warm

*See Index.

potato salad (see our Warm Potato Salad with Beer Dressing*), and a traditional plowman's platter of cheese, fruit, and sausage.

California-style salads are popular and include a spinach and smoked chicken salad with honey-lime dressing as well as papaya stuffed with Dungeness crab in fresh ginger vinaigrette. Sandwiches are a favorite beer food (see our Sandwiches*), and Pacific Coast's restaurant offers an extensive choice of sausage, pâtés, roasted and smoked meats, and cheeses on its sandwich menu. Popular at all times are Cornish pasties—a traditional English pastry stuffed with beef, potatoes, and vegetables.

Triple Rock, located in Berkeley near the University of California, specializes in hearty ales much appreciated by the dart-playing college crowd. Favorites are Pinnacle Pale Ale and Red Rock Ale, robust and hoppy ales in the California style, to accompany the sandwiches, soups, and chili served at the crowded bar. Brewer Reid Martin also makes a richly colored Black Rock Porter and full-bodied Lodestone Stout.

Marin Brewing at Larkspur Landing near San Francisco Bay just north of the Golden Gate uses American two-row barley from the Pacific Northwest, fresh hops from the Yakima and Willamette valleys, and clear Marin County water in its beers. It brews mostly English and California-style ales, German-style Wheat and *Alt* Beers, and unusual and delicious Fruit Ales from blueberries and raspberries.

The most popular ale in the lively pub is Albion Amber, an Amber Ale with lots of malt and a high hop level, named in homage to New Albion Ale, the first of the California-style ales. Other favorites are: Mt. Tam Pale Ale, bright gold in color and perfectly balanced; Marin Weiss and Hefe Weiss, filtered and unfiltered Wheat Beers served with a slice of lemon in the glass; San Quentin's Breakout Stout, black in color with a creamy texture and long-lasting head; St. Brendan's Red Ale, a full-bodied, powerful red ale in the Irish tradition; Blueberry Ale and Raspberry Trail Ale made from fresh fruits added at the end of the boil; and Happy Holidaze Ale, traditional spiced Christmas Ale.

Marin Brewing's menu has a special section entitled Beer Buddies, dishes made with beer in mind. It features clams steamed in Amber Ale (see our Clams or Mussels Steamed in Beer and Spices*), ceviche (see

*See Index.

Alice's Ceviche*), chips and fresh homemade salsa (see our Bay Wolf BBQ Potato Chips* and Salsa Cruda*), and onion rings in beer batter (see our Onion Rings*). The pub's salads include oriental chicken salad (see our Szechuan Chicken Salad*), sandwiches, sausages, pizza, and spicy main courses, including a flavorful cilantro chicken—chicken breast marinated in cilantro and lemon juice and grilled (see Marinating and Grilling, page 155).

Other noted brew-pubs in the San Francisco area include Kelmer's Brewhouse in Santa Rosa, Brewpub on the Green in Fremont, and the Tied House in Mountain View. Rubicon Brewing in Sacramento, Butterfield Brewery in Fresno, and Okie Girl Brew Pub in Lebec are found in California's Central Valley. The thriving southern California scene features Heritage Brewing of Dana Point, Karl Strauss' Old Columbia Brewery and Grill, and the La Jolla Brewing Company.

The microbrewery and brew-pub revolution really began in California, and brewers in the state are at the forefront of this constantly changing and exciting new industry. While most California brews are still only available locally, more and more are making their way into national markets. And for true beer fanatics, a pilgrimage to California's new breweries and pubs is like a wine fancier visiting Bordeaux or an Elvis fan at Graceland—not exactly heaven, but close.

*See Index.

Courtesy of *Colliers*

THE BUNG-STARTER

Bay Wolf BBQ Potato Chips

These crisp, savory chips are wonderful appetizers for an outdoor barbe-cue with full-bodied California-style ales, such as Sierra Nevada Pale Ale or Anchor Liberty Ale.

Chefs Nathan Peterson and Joseph Nouhan of the Bay Wolf Restaurant in Oakland contributed this recipe.

3 large Russet or other boiling potatoes, peeled (about 2½ pounds)

Peanut oil for deep frying

Spice Mixture

2 teaspoons salt
2 teaspoons onion powder
2 teaspoons paprika

½ teaspoon finely ground black pepper
½ teaspoon cayenne

Cut the potatoes into ⅛-inch-thick slices. Soak the slices in cold water. Before frying, pat them dry between paper towels. Heat 3 inches of oil in a skillet or deep fryer to 360°–375° F. Fry the potatoes in batches until golden brown and crisp. Drain on paper towels.

While the potatoes are frying, mix the spices together in a small bowl. Put the chips in a large bowl or on a serving platter, and toss thoroughly with the spice mixture. Serve while still hot, with plenty of beer and napkins.

MAKES ABOUT 10 DOZEN CHIPS. SERVES 4–6 AS AN APPETIZER OR BAR SNACK.

Crunchy Sausage Bites

Crunchy, nutty bits of sausage with sweet chutney make a great snack or appetizer with a glass of Bock Beer. Try Santa Cruz Beacon Bock or Samuel Adams Double Bock.

5 spicy sausages, such as bratwurst, Kielbasa, Fresh Beer Sausage (see page 74), bockwurst, or duck sausage
½ cup sweet mango chutney

½ cup chopped roasted peanuts
½ cup finely chopped cilantro (optional)

Fry the sausages in a skillet over medium heat, turning frequently until lightly browned, about 10 minutes. Remove from the pan, and cut each sausage into 5 or 6 bite-sized chunks. If using the cilantro, mix it with the peanuts in a small bowl. Skewer each piece of sausage on a toothpick. Dip in the chutney to coat, and then roll the sausage bite in the peanut mixture. Serve immediately.

MAKES 25–30 PIECES, ENOUGH TO SERVE 6–8 AS A SNACK OR APPETIZER.

MARINATING AND GRILLING

Barbecue parties on warm summer evenings with platters of grilled fish or seafood, steaks, burgers, or chicken are natural settings for beer. The food and the beer taste even better when the fish or meat is marinated in a spicy marinade with the assertive flavors of herbs, lemon juice, garlic, and beer. Combine this with the smoky tastes from the coals and some hardwood chips, and you can see why beer is definitely the beverage of choice for most barbecues.

Marinades serve two important functions: They tenderize food and they enhance flavors. Most marinades contain some high-acid ingredient such as lemon juice, vinegar, or wine, which tenderizes the food and also gives it a special tang. And many marinades incorporate spicy and powerfully flavored ingredients, such as hot peppers, mustard, garlic, Worcestershire sauce, bourbon, or beer. Full-flavored beers complement spicy foods, and thus these marinades create foods especially suited to full-bodied ales and malty lagers. And as we've seen, food cooked or marinated in beer usually goes beautifully with the beer used in the preparation.

Lemon and Lager Marinade for Fish or Chicken

2 teaspoons minced garlic
1 12-ounce bottle lager
½ cup olive oil
⅓ cup fresh lemon juice
1 teaspoon salt
1 teaspoon ground black pepper

1 tablespoon mixed chopped fresh herbs (for fish: tarragon, chervil, basil, or oregano; for chicken: rosemary, thyme, tarragon, or sage), or 2 teaspoons mixed dried herbs

Mix all the ingredients together in a nonreactive bowl or pan. For chicken pieces, marinate at least 6 hours or overnight in the refrigerator. For fish, marinate for 2 hours at room temperature. Use the marinade to baste the fish as it grills.

MAKES 2½ CUPS, ENOUGH FOR 2 CHICKENS OR 3 POUNDS OF FISH.

Ale Marinade for Steak or Lamb

This marinade is also excellent with pork.

1 cup oil	2 teaspoons brown sugar
3 garlic cloves, crushed	3 tablespoons Worcestershire
1 cup ale	sauce
½ cup lemon juice	2 teaspoons salt
1 teaspoon dry mustard powder	2 teaspoons coarsely ground
½ cup soy sauce	black pepper

Use a steak at least 1½ inches thick. Poke the steak all over with a fork. Mix together all the marinade ingredients. In a nonreactive pan or bowl marinate the steak overnight in the refrigerator. If the marinade doesn't cover the steak, turn it once or twice. Before grilling, bring the steak to room temperature.

MAKES 3 CUPS, ENOUGH FOR 4–5 LARGE PORTERHOUSE OR RIB STEAKS OR 1 BUTTERFLIED LEG OF LAMB.

Porter or Stout and Molasses Marinade

This sweet marinade with slightly bitter overtones is best used to marinate ham steaks, smoked pork chops, venison, wild boar, duck, or fresh pork. Serve with a full-bodied Dark Ale, Porter, or Stout.

3 tablespoons Dijon mustard	1 tablespoon Worcestershire
¼ cup molasses	sauce
1 cup Porter, Stout, or Dark	2 bay leaves, crumbled
Ale	1 teaspoon Tabasco
⅓ cup malt or red wine vinegar	½ cup finely chopped onion

In a small saucepan mix together the mustard and molasses. Gradually stir in the remaining ingredients. Bring to a boil, and simmer for 2 minutes. Cool before using. Marinate venison, wild boar, duck breast, or fresh pork overnight in the refrigerator. For ham or smoked pork chops, marinate 2 hours at room temperature or up to 6 hours in the refrigerator.

MAKES 2 CUPS.

Bourbon Stout Marinade for Chicken

This marinade is also good for beef, lamb, pork, or duck.

½ cup Stout or Porter
¼ cup bourbon
¼ cup soy sauce
2 tablespoons Dijon or coarse-grained mustard
3 tablespoons brown sugar

½ teaspoon salt
2 teaspoons coarse black pepper
½ teaspoon Worcestershire sauce
¼ cup minced green onions or scallions

Mix together all the ingredients. Cut boned chicken, duck, or other meat into 1½-inch cubes or marinate in whole pieces if you don't intend to make skewers. Marinate 2–3 hours in the refrigerator for small pieces of chicken or duck, overnight for whole poultry pieces, beef, lamb, or pork. Skewer chunks with red and green bell peppers before grilling. Grill and baste these or whole pieces with remaining marinade.

MAKES 1½ CUPS, ENOUGH FOR 1 CHICKEN OR 2–3 STEAKS.

Chinese Hoisin Marinade for Pork, Chicken, or Lamb

¼ cup hoisin sauce
2 tablespoons sweet sherry
⅓ cup Dark Lager, such as Bock, Maibock, or Maerzen beer
2 tablespoons minced green onions or scallions
2 teaspoons minced garlic

2 teaspoons finely chopped fresh ginger
1 tablespoon soy sauce
1 tablespoon Chinese black bean paste (optional), or 2 more tablespoons soy sauce
1 tablespoon sesame oil
1 teaspoon sugar

Mix together all the ingredients. This marinade is particularly good with pork tenderloins, spareribs, chicken thighs, or lamb rib chops. Marinate the meat overnight in the refrigerator, turning occasionally if it is not covered by liquid.

MAKES 1 CUP, ENOUGH FOR 8 CHICKEN THIGHS, A SIDE OF SPARERIBS, 3 PORK TENDERLOINS, OR 8 RIB CHOPS.

Tandoori Marinade

This spicy Indian marinade is used for foods such as chicken, fish, or lamb that are cooked in tandoori ovens, the traditional terra-cotta ovens of Northern India. Excellent results can also be obtained by marinating and grilling chicken or meat in a covered kettle-style barbecue. This is an excellent marinade for chicken wings, good as bar snacks or finger food.

2 cups plain yogurt
¼ teaspoon cinnamon
2 tablespoons Hungarian paprika
1½ teaspoons cayenne
1 tablespoon grated fresh ginger
1 tablespoon minced garlic
½ cup fresh lemon juice

2 teaspoons cumin
1 teaspoon cardamom
1 teaspoon coriander
½ teaspoon clove
1 teaspoon ground fenugreek
¼ teaspoon nutmeg
1 teaspoon finely ground pepper

Mix together all the ingredients. Marinate pieces of fish, skinless chicken pieces, chicken wings, 2-inch cubes of lamb, or small rib or loin lamb chops overnight in the refrigerator.

MAKES 2½ CUPS, ENOUGH FOR 16 WINGS, 2 CHICKENS, OR 4–5 POUNDS LAMB.

Smoky Rauchbier Marinade

Rauchbier is a specialty beer made with smoke-flavored malt in Germany and by a few American producers (for example, Buffalo Bill's Rauchbeer, The Vermont Pub's Smoked Porter, and Alaska Brewing's Smoked Porter). Powerfully flavored and unusual, it is definitely an acquired taste and makes a smoky marinade particularly good with shrimp, scallops, or fish. If you can't find one of the German or American Rauchbiers, you can use a bottle of Amber Lager and a few drops of liquid smoke.

1 bottle Rauchbier or American smoked beer, or 1 bottle Amber Lager plus 1 or 2 drops liquid smoke

¼ cup salad oil
2 teaspoons salt

Mix together all the ingredients. Marinate shrimp, scallops, or fish for 2–3 hours in the refrigerator. Brush with additional oil before grilling.

MAKES 2 CUPS, ENOUGH FOR 2–3 POUNDS FISH OR SEAFOOD.

Asparagus and Shiitake Mushrooms in Sesame Dressing

This garlicky sesame dressing is wonderful with asparagus and mushrooms, but also combines well with shredded cabbage, cold noodles, or seafood. The dressing needs a full-bodied, malty lager such as Hübsch Märzenbier to stand up to the intense flavors of the garlic, sesame, and ginger.

Sesame Dressing

1 garlic clove, finely chopped
2 teaspoons chopped fresh
   ginger
2 tablespoons malt vinegar

2 tablespoons sesame oil
4 tablespoons soy sauce
2 teaspoons sugar
2 tablespoons peanut oil

1 pound asparagus spears, cut
   on the diagonal into thirds
8 fresh or dried *shiitake* mushrooms

¼ cup sesame seeds

Whisk together all the dressing ingredients. Blanch the asparagus pieces in rapidly boiling salted water for 4 minutes. If the mushrooms are fresh, wash them and pat dry, then cut into ¼-inch strips. If dried, soak them in boiling water for 10 or more minutes, drain, and dry. Remove stems, and then cut the caps into ¼-inch strips. Toss the asparagus and mushrooms with the dressing in a shallow bowl. Toast the sesame seeds lightly in a nonstick frying pan over medium heat, being careful not to scorch them. Garnish the salad with the toasted sesame seeds.

SERVES 6.

Rice, Corn, and Watercress Salad

When reaching into the refrigerator for a beer, you might find stacked-up boxes of rice from Chinese take-out meals. If so, use it to make this recipe. The tiny, rice-shaped pasta called orzo can also be used and is flavorful. Try the salad with a light ale—Anderson Valley's Poleeko Gold, for example.

⅓ pound pine nuts
2 cups cooked rice or orzo
½ cup Mustard Vinaigrette
   (see page 271)
1 bunch watercress, leaves only

3 green onions or scallions,
   thinly sliced
2 ears cooked fresh corn, kernels removed or the equivalent frozen, thawed

Toast pine nuts in a dry frying pan over medium heat, shaking pan continuously until lightly browned. Transfer to a bowl to cool. Mix together all the ingredients, tossing well with the vinaigrette.

SERVES 6.

Smoked Chicken and Orzo Salad

Orzo, a small rice-shaped pasta, is combined with smoked chicken, nuts, feta, and olives in this tasty salad. It makes a dramatic centerpiece for an al fresco lunch with a glass or two of light lager like Eureka.

1 pound smoked chicken, diced
2 cups cooked orzo or other
   small pasta (orzo triples in
   volume when cooked)
⅓ cup shelled pistachio nuts
   or pine nuts, roasted (see
   preceding recipe)
½ cup Mustard Vinaigrette
   (see page 271)

6 green onions or scallions,
   thinly sliced
¼ pound feta cheese, crumbled
10 Kalamata olives, pitted and
   coarsely chopped
1 bunch watercress, leaves
   only, chopped

Mix together all the ingredients, except the watercress. Arrange in a shallow bowl or on a platter and sprinkle on the chopped watercress.

SERVES 4–6.

Szechuan Chicken Salad

This Chinese chicken salad was popular at Poulet in Berkeley when Bruce was chef there. Its gingery flavor and spicy assertiveness make it a natural with high-hopped ales like Devil Mountain's Gayle's Pale Ale.

4 chicken breasts, boned and skinned

2 cucumbers, peeled, seeded, and thinly sliced

Dressing

2 tablespoons minced fresh ginger

2 teaspoons minced garlic

1 tablespoon sugar

2 tablespoons soy sauce

1 tablespoon Chinese black vinegar or malt vinegar

2 tablespoons Chinese red chile oil

3 tablespoons dark sesame oil

6 tablespoons sesame butter or peanut butter

½ teaspoon Szechuan peppercorns

1 bunch cilantro, coarsely chopped (1 cup)

2 tablespoons sesame seeds, toasted

Poach the chicken breasts in lightly salted water for 15 minutes. Remove breasts, let cool, and slice thin. Save the stock for later use.

To make the dressing: Process the ginger, garlic, sugar, soy sauce, and vinegar in a food processor for 30 seconds. Add the chile oil, sesame oil, sesame butter, and Szechuan peppercorns, and process 1 minute.

Lightly toss the cucumbers in ⅓ cup of the dressing and spread on a large platter. Lay the chicken slices over them, and dress with the remaining dressing. Garnish with the cilantro and toasted sesame seeds.

SERVES 4–6.

Duck and Roasted Walnut Salad

*This composed salad of duck, cucumber, and walnuts makes a stunning
first course or lunch and is especially delicious with a dark malty beer
like St. Stan's Dark Alt.*

2 duck breasts (use legs and
thighs in Stuffed Duck Legs
in Ale and Bourbon Gravy*)

Salt and pepper
½ cup walnuts

Dressing

1 tablespoon raspberry vinegar
2 tablespoons walnut oil
1 tablespoon peanut oil

1 teaspoon soy sauce
2 teaspoons sugar

1 cucumber, halved, seeded,
and thinly sliced

2 tablespoons chopped green
onions or scallions

Preheat the oven to 350° F. Salt and pepper the duck breasts and roast
on a rack for 45 minutes. Let cool and slice thin.

Spread the walnuts on a cookie sheet and roast at 350° F. for 10–15
minutes until brown and giving off a rich nutty aroma. Stir once or
twice during cooking.

Whisk together all the dressing ingredients and toss (reserve 2 tablespoons) with the cucumber slices. Arrange on a platter, and fan the
duck slices on top. Spoon reserved dressing over them and garnish with
the roasted walnuts and chopped green onions or scallions.

SERVES 4.

*See Index.

Chinese Fish Salad with Chui Chow Vinaigrette

The flavors of this salad—a sort of Chinese ceviche—are sweet, sour, and spicy, just right for a malty Dark Lager like Hübsch Dark. The salad can be served in small portions as a first course or as part of a buffet or multicourse Chinese dinner. For the fish, use mild-flavored, firm-fleshed fish or seafood, such as bass, rock cod, halibut, red snapper, or scallops. For an elegant presentation, serve the salad over crisp, deep-fried Chinese cellophane noodles or on a bed of finely shredded iceberg lettuce.

The Chinese ingredients are available in Chinese groceries or by mail order (see Appendix IV, Mail Order Sources).

1 pound fresh fish fillets or scallops

Juice of 8–10 limes (about 1¼ cups)

Chui Chow Vinaigrette

¼ cup Chinese chiles packed with salted black beans

¼ cup pickled red ginger

2 teaspoons Chinese black bean paste

2 tablespoons soy sauce

2 tablespoons rice wine vinegar

2 tablespoons dry sherry

1 teaspoon sugar

1 tablespoon sesame oil

3 tablespoons peanut oil

2 cucumbers peeled, seeded, and cut into thin 2-inch strips

3 cups shredded iceberg lettuce, or 1 package Chinese cellophane noodles

Peanut oil for deep frying

½ cup dry roasted peanuts

¼ cup chopped cilantro

Cut the fish on the diagonal into thin pieces roughly 2 inches wide. Cut each piece into strips ¼ inch by 2 inches. Do the same for large scallops; if small, leave whole. Mix the fish with 1 cup of the lime juice and let marinate for 2 hours in the refrigerator.

To make the vinaigrette: Mix together the remaining ¼ cup lime juice with all the vinaigrette ingredients, except the oils. Whisk in the sesame oil, then the peanut oil. Set aside.

When the fish is ready, it will appear opaque or "cooked." Pour off the lime juice and discard. Mix together the fish, cucumber, and dressing. Spread the shredded lettuce on a platter or in a shallow bowl.

*Chinese
Fish Salad
with Chui
Chow
Vinaigrette
(continued)*

Spoon the fish mixture over the lettuce, sprinkle with the peanuts, and garnish with chopped cilantro.

Or for a more elegant presentation: Heat 2–3 inches peanut oil to 350° F. in a wok or high-sided frying pan. Add the cellophane noodles. In only a few seconds they will expand to many times their original size. Remove immediately, and drain on paper towels. Spread out on a platter and arrange the fish salad on top. Sprinkle with the peanuts and garnish with the cilantro.

SERVES 4–6 AS AN APPETIZER, 8–10 AS PART OF A BUFFET OR MULTI-COURSE CHINESE MEAL.

California Calamari Salad

Calamari, or squid, are easily overcooked, so pay attention to the cooking process. As soon as the flesh goes from translucent to opaque, about 20 seconds in boiling water, squid is fully cooked, yet still tender. To clean calamari, see Fried Calamari, page 244.

Serve this piquant salad with a crisp light lager: Pete's Pacific Dry or Lighthouse Lager from Santa Cruz Brewing.

2 pounds small squid
1 tablespoon salt
1 medium red or yellow bell pepper, quartered, seeded, and cut crosswise into ⅛-inch strips
1 medium green bell pepper, quartered, seeded, and cut crosswise into ⅛-inch strips
2 green onions or scallions, finely chopped

½ cup chopped parsley
1 small red onion, finely chopped
2 teaspoons minced garlic
Juice of 2 lemons
2 tablespoons chopped fresh oregano or 2 teaspoons dried
1 cup olive oil
Pepper

Cut each squid body lengthwise into 4 strips, and leave the tentacles whole. Bring 3–4 quarts water to a boil in a 6-quart pot. Add the salt. Add the squid, stir, and cook very briefly, 20 seconds or so, until it turns from translucent to opaque. Drain the squid in a colander and cool under cold running water. When cool, pat dry with paper towels.

In an attractive serving bowl mix together the squid, vegetables, lemon juice, oregano, and oil. Taste for salt and pepper and lemon. Serve at once.

SERVES 6.

Cold Roast Beef and Scallions in Ginger Dressing

This Chinese-influenced salad makes a good luncheon dish, especially when paired with a full-flavored ale like North Coast Brewing's India Pale Ale. The ginger, onions, and sesame flavors tie in beautifully with the pronounced hop flavors and fruity maltiness of the India Pale Ale style.

2 cups water, ale, or beer
Salt
2 ribs celery, thinly sliced on the diagonal
3 bunches green onions or scallions, cut into 3-inch lengths

4 cups shredded rare roast beef or leftover rare steak
2 tablespoons sesame seeds

Ginger Dressing

1 garlic clove, minced
3 teaspoons minced fresh ginger
1 tablespoon sugar
1 tablespoon malt vinegar

2 tablespoons beer
1 tablespoon soy sauce
1 tablespoon sesame oil
1 tablespoon peanut oil

Bring the water, ale, or beer and a pinch of salt to a boil. Add the celery and blanch for 2 minutes. Add the scallions, and blanch for 15 seconds. Drain the vegetables, plunge them into cold water, and drain. Dry thoroughly by patting them with a kitchen towel. In a shallow serving bowl or on a platter mix together the beef, celery, and scallions. Toss with the sesame seeds.

To make the ginger dressing: Mix together in a small bowl the garlic, ginger, sugar, vinegar, beer, and soy sauce. Gradually whisk in the sesame oil and peanut oil.

Pour the dressing over the salad, mix well, and serve.

SERVES 6.

Stuffed Pork Loin in Imperial Stout

This elegant dish makes a dramatic main course for a small, special dinner party. The rich flavors of pork, prunes, and Stout come together magnificently, and this dish could serve as a centerpiece for a Russian banquet.

Because the dish does take some time and effort to make, why not keep the rest of the meal simple, but up to the standards of the main course. Start off with caviar or smoked salmon, pickled mushrooms, and marinated artichokes, accompanied by black bread and sweet butter. With this, drink a crisp Pilsner, such as Santa Cruz Pacific Pils. Serve the pork loin with buttered carrots or carrot purée and rice flavored with butter and dill. Gorky's Imperial Stout, Grant's Imperial Stout, Anchor Porter, or another flavorful Dark Ale would be an excellent match.

5- to 6-pound center-cut
   boneless pork loin, untied

Marinade

¼ cup fresh lemon juice

2 tablespoons honey

2 teaspoons dried mustard
   powder

½ teaspoon dried marjoram

½ teaspoon dried thyme

1 teaspoon coarsely ground
   black pepper

1 teaspoon kosher salt

Stuffing

3 cups pitted prunes

1 tablespoon sugar

1 cup Imperial Russian Stout
   or other dark beer

1 green apple, peeled, cored,
   and diced

2 cups coarse fresh bread
   crumbs

1 egg

Basting Sauce

½ cup dry sherry

⅔ cup chicken stock

Remaining marinade

Sauce

Deglazed pan juices
Liquid from cooking prunes
¼ cup vodka, kirsch, or
  anisette

½ cup heavy cream
1 tablespoon Dijon mustard

To make the marinade: Combine all the marinade ingredients and rub all over the pork loin. Place in a shallow pan, cover, and refrigerate for at least 2 hours or overnight.

To stuff the loin: Boil the prunes with the sugar in the Stout for 10 minutes or until tender. Drain the prunes and save the liquid for the sauce. Coarsely chop 1 cup of the prunes, reserving the rest for the sauce, and combine them with the apple, bread crumbs, and egg. Remove the pork from the marinade and save any remaining marinade for the basting sauce. Butterfly the loin, and spread the stuffing over the full length of the meat. Close the loin around the stuffing, tie the roast in several places with kitchen string, and place in a roasting pan.

Preheat the oven to 350° F. Make the basting sauce by combining the sherry and chicken stock with any leftover marinade.

Roast the loin for 1¾–2 hours, basting every 15 minutes or so. Pork is done when it reaches an internal temperature of 155–160° F. Remove the roast from the pan, and keep it warm on a platter covered with foil while you prepare the sauce.

To make the sauce: Pour off all the liquid from the roasting pan into a saucepan, and skim off the fat. Deglaze the roasting pan with the Stout reserved from the prunes, scraping up any brown bits that cling to the bottom of the pan. Strain through a sieve into the saucepan. Add any leftover basting sauce and the vodka or other liqueur to the pan. Bring to a boil. Add the cream mixed with the mustard, and continue to boil until the sauce is thickened slightly. Add the reserved 2 cups prunes, and warm them through for about 1 minute. Taste for salt and pepper.

To serve, slice the roast into ½-inch slices and arrange them on a warm platter. Spoon some of the sauce and prunes over the meat, and serve the rest in a sauceboat. This dish makes superb leftovers: To rewarm, place the pork slices in a heavy pan. Cover with the sauce. Cover the pan and gently heat for about 10 minutes.

SERVES 8–10.

Beef Brisket with Lemon and Spices

A tart Wheat Beer like Hübsch Wheat Beer or August Schell Weizen with a slice of lemon in the glass is a natural pairing for this spicy, lemon-infused dish inspired by Moroccan tagines. Like many braised dishes, it is even better reheated: Just slice the brisket and gently warm it with the sauce and vegetable. Serve this tangy dish with couscous, grits, or rice.

4–6 pounds well-trimmed beef brisket

2 teaspoons salt

2 tablespoons New Mexico or California chile powder or a commercial blend such as Gebhardt's

1 teaspoon powdered ginger

½ teaspoon cinnamon

2 teaspoons turmeric

1 teaspoon ground coriander

½ teaspoon cumin

½ teaspoon cayenne

1 teaspoon ground black pepper

4 tablespoons olive oil

2 large onions, halved and thinly sliced

4 carrots, quartered and cut into 2-inch pieces

½ teaspoon saffron threads

1 cup Rich Chicken Stock (see page 203)

1 cup Wheat Beer or lager

1 bunch cilantro, stems finely chopped, leaves coarsely chopped and kept separate

6 fresh mint leaves or 2 teaspoons dried mint

1 lemon, quartered lengthwise

⅓ cup fresh lemon juice

Trim the fat from the brisket, leaving about ¼ inch. Mix the salt and the dry spices, except the saffron, in a small bowl. Rub about half the spice mixture over all sides of the meat. Let the brisket marinate at room temperature for 2 hours or covered in the refrigerator overnight.

Heat the olive oil over high heat in a Dutch oven or high-sided skillet large enough to hold the brisket. Brown the brisket 5 minutes on each side. Remove. Put the onions and half the carrots in the pot and reduce the heat to medium. Cover and cook until the onions are soft, stirring occasionally and scraping up any brown bits that cling to the bottom of the pot. This should take about 5–10 minutes. Sprinkle the remaining spice mixture and the saffron over the onions and carrots, and cook, uncovered, 2 minutes. Add the stock, beer, cilantro stems, mint, and brisket. Bring to a boil, reduce to a simmer, cover, and braise for 2 hours. Add the lemon quarters, lemon juice, and remaining carrots, and continue to cook, covered, for another 20 minutes. Taste a slice of meat to see if it is tender. If not, remove the vegetables so they don't overcook, and continue to cook the meat until tender. (At this point the dish can be cooled and refrigerated.)

Transfer the meat to a cutting board, and to the vegetables and sauce in the pot add all but 2 tablespoons of the chopped cilantro leaves. Cook at a moderate boil for 5 minutes. Taste for salt and pepper. Meanwhile slice the meat, arrange on a serving platter, and cover with carrots, lemon pieces, and some of the sauce. Garnish with remaining cilantro. Pass any extra gravy for guests to pour over couscous, grits, or rice.

SERVES 6–8.

Lamb Chops with Whole Garlic Cloves and Summer Herbs

Aromatic summer herbs and whole cloves of garlic provide plenty of flavor to balance the rich hoppiness and fruity character of English-style ale in this easy-to-make lamb dish. Try it with Red Hook's Extra Special Bitter (ESB) or Drake's Ale from Lind Brewing in San Leandro.

In a medium hot skillet brown the chops in 2 tablespoons of the olive oil. Remove from pan. Add the remaining oil and sauté the red pepper.

8 rib or loin lamb chops (about 2½ pounds)	1 teaspoon *each* of fresh chopped oregano, tarragon, savory, or ½ teaspoon *each* of same herbs dried
¼ cup olive oil	1 cup ale
1 large red bell pepper, seeded and cut into strips	Salt and pepper
1 head garlic, separated into cloves and peeled	Chopped chives for garnish

Add the garlic and herbs, and deglaze the pan with the ale. Put the chops back in, cover the pan, and cook for 10 minutes. Season with salt and pepper and serve with the chives sprinkled on top.

SERVES 4–6.

Solianka—Russian Beef Stew

This hearty Russian soup/stew makes a satisfying one-pot meal on a cold evening. The combination of meat, sausage, prunes, and cucumbers might sound a bit unusual, but all the ingredients go amazingly well together. The prune/meat combination is common in many Eastern European dishes (see Stuffed Pork Loin in Imperial Stout, page 166), and lends a richness and complexity to many recipes. Use a mildly smoky sausage for this dish, such as our Beer Sausage, kielbasa, or smoked bratwurst. Drink Dark Ale—Gorky's Russian Imperial Stout or Pete's Wicked Ale—and accompany the dish with black bread, sweet butter, whole scallions, and sliced radishes.

4 cups beef or Rich Chicken Stock (see page 203)

1 12-ounce bottle Dark Ale

1½ pounds beef or veal stew meat or a combination of both, cut into 1-inch chunks

2 bay leaves

4 tablespoons butter

1 medium onion, thinly sliced

3 tomatoes, peeled, seeded, and chopped

2 tablespoons tomato paste

¾ pound Fresh Beer Sausage (see page 74), kielbasa, or smoked bratwurst, sliced in ½-inch rounds

4 cucumbers, peeled, seeded, sliced, and lightly salted

10 pitted prunes, soaked in hot water

12 Kalamata olives, pitted and sliced

2 teaspoons capers

Salt and pepper

Lemon slices, fresh dill or parsley, sour cream or yogurt for garnish

Bring the stock and ale to a boil in a large soup pot, and put in the meat and bay leaves. Reduce the heat to a simmer, and cook, uncovered, for 1½ hours. Meanwhile, heat the butter in a heavy frying pan over medium heat, and cook the onion for 5 minutes until soft. Add the tomatoes, tomato paste, and the sausage. Simmer for 10 minutes. Degrease the pan, and add the contents to the soup, along with the cucumbers, prunes, olives, and capers. Cook for 2–3 minutes, and taste for salt and pepper. Serve in individual bowls and garnish with the lemon slices, sour cream or yogurt, and dill.

SERVES 6.

Hangtown Fry

You can still see the hanging tree in Hangtown in the Gold Country in the foothills of the Sierras, even though the town is now called Placerville and the Miner's Court has been out of business for some years now. But "Hangtown Fry" continues to be a popular favorite in the Gold Country and in seafood restaurants in San Francisco and throughout the West.

A good match for this rich and flavorful omelet is a bottle of hoppy Sierra Nevada Pale Ale and a crusty loaf of sourdough French bread.

2 tablespoons butter
½ cup finely chopped onion
¼ cup finely chopped green
    bell pepper
6 shucked small oysters

¼ pound bacon, diced,
    cooked until crisp, and
    drained
4–6 eggs, beaten
Salt and pepper

Heat the butter in a nonstick pan. Add the onion and cook over medium-high heat for 5 minutes. Add the bell pepper and sauté for 2 minutes. Add the oysters and cook until just plump, about 3 minutes. Add the bacon and pour in the eggs. Cook until the eggs begin to set. Flip the omelet over by inverting it onto a plate or the pan lid and sliding it back into the pan. Cook the second side for 1–2 minutes. Serve at once.

SERVES 2–3.

Carrots and Leeks in Steam Beer

Anchor Steam Beer, amber colored, malty, and with a decided bite of hops, has become an American classic. We love to drink it and are always looking for ways to cook with it. Braising carrots and leeks in this full-flavored beer produces a great vegetable side dish that is especially good with roast meats and chicken. With it drink, what else, Anchor Steam! If you can't find Anchor Steam Beer in your market, another full-bodied amber beer or ale will do almost as well.

1½ pounds leeks, cleaned,
    trimmed (white parts only),
    and sliced
2 tablespoons olive oil
2 carrots, thinly sliced
4 bay leaves

½ teaspoon coarsely ground
    black pepper
½ bottle Anchor Steam Beer
    or other amber beer
¼ cup chicken stock
Salt and pepper

Cook the leeks in the olive oil over medium-high heat for about 5 minutes, or until they just begin to wilt. Stir in the remaining ingredients, and simmer over medium heat until the carrots are tender, about 15 minutes. Taste for salt and pepper. Serve at once.

SERVES 4-6.

Garlic and Horseradish Mashed Potatoes

The idea for these savory, creamy mashed potatoes came from Eureka, the Los Angeles brewery and beer restaurant owned by chef Wolfgang Puck. There the potatoes are served with grilled sausages and a sauce of caramelized onions and beer.

These potatoes also make a great side dish with our Pork Chops in Beer with Mustard and Onions,* Lamb Chops with Whole Garlic Cloves and Summer Herbs,* or roast chicken, beef, or pork.

Serve the potatoes with a light lager—Eureka or a flavorful California-style ale like Mendocino Brewing's Peregrine Pale Ale.

2 pounds Russet or other baking potatoes, peeled and quartered
1 head garlic, left whole but with cloves peeled

2 tablespoons butter
½–⅔ cup sour cream
2 tablespoons prepared bottled horseradish, or more to taste
Salt and pepper

Boil the potatoes and garlic in lightly salted water until the potatoes are quite tender, about 25 minutes. Drain, and put the potatoes and garlic in a large bowl. Add butter and mash with a potato masher, or alternatively, push the cooked potatoes and garlic through a potato ricer. Then add the butter. Spoon in ½ cup of the sour cream and the horseradish, and whip with a fork or an electric mixer (don't use a food processor, which will turn the potatoes to glue). Add more sour cream as needed, a little at a time, until the desired consistency is reached. Taste for salt and pepper, and add more horseradish if you like. If the potatoes are too cool when you are ready to serve, warm them for 10 minutes or so in a preheated 350° F. oven.

SERVES 4-6.

*See Index.

Roasted Garlic and Shallot Soup

This fragrant soup is a favorite at L'Avenue Restaurant in San Francisco. The delectable nutty flavor of roasted garlic keeps patrons clamoring for more. Full-bodied ales stand up to lots of garlic; try North Coast Brewing's Red Seal Ale.

5 heads garlic, 3 heads left whole, 2 heads separated into cloves and peeled
¾ pound shallots, half peeled and coarsely chopped, half left unpeeled
4 tablespoons olive oil
1½ teaspoons salt
1 teaspoon pepper
4 tablespoons butter
2 large onions, coarsely chopped
¾ pound Russet potatoes, peeled and quartered
3 cups Rich Chicken Stock (see page 203)
1 cup full-flavored ale
1 cup heavy cream, half-and-half, or milk
1 tablespoon chopped fresh thyme or 1 teaspoon dried
Salt and pepper

Preheat the oven to 350° F. In a shallow baking pan toss the unpeeled whole garlic heads and unpeeled shallots in the olive oil and 1 teaspoon each of salt and pepper. Spread them out in a single layer. Cover with foil, and bake 35 minutes. Check the shallots. If they are soft, remove and reserve them. If not, leave them in with the garlic and bake until all the shallots and garlic are quite soft, about another 20 minutes. Let the shallots and garlic cool.

Meanwhile, begin the soup by heating the butter in a heavy 3- to 4-quart saucepan or Dutch oven. Add the onions, and cook, stirring occasionally, over medium heat for 10–15 minutes until soft but not browned. Add the peeled separated garlic cloves and chopped shallots, cover, and cook over low heat for 10 minutes. Stir occasionally. Add the potatoes, the remaining ½ teaspoon salt, the stock, ale, cream, half-and-half, or milk, and the thyme. Cover and cook 25–30 minutes until the potatoes are quite soft.

Peel the roasted shallots. Cut the whole roasted garlic heads in half, and squeeze the cooked garlic out of the bulbs. Process the roasted shallots and garlic in a food processor, and add to the soup. Cook 10 minutes.

In a blender or food processor process the soup until smooth. Season with additional salt and pepper to taste. If the soup is too thick, dilute it with additional stock, cream, or ale. Reheat gently before serving.
SERVES 6–8.

Dry Fried Green Beans and Chinese Noodles with Smoky Black Bean Sauce

Use fresh Blue Lake, Kentucky Wonder, Romano, or Chinese long beans in this tangy side dish. Serve with Pale Ale or light lager.

Oil for deep frying
½ pound green beans, ends removed and cut into 1½-inch pieces
¾ pound fresh Chinese egg noodles or fresh thin Italian pasta like tagliarini
1 recipe Smoky Black Bean Sauce (recipe follows)
¼ cup chopped cilantro
¼ cup chopped green onions or scallions

Heat 3–4 inches of oil to about 400° F. in a wok or deep saucepan. Add 1 bean to test the temperature. The oil should sputter and sizzle when you drop it in. Add the remaining beans and fry for 2 minutes. Drain on paper towels. The beans should be wrinkled and bright green. Cook the noodles for 1 or 2 minutes in boiling salted water or until just tender. Drain. Place in a large bowl and add the green beans and hot bean sauce. Toss until everything is well coated. Garnish with the cilantro and green onions and serve at once.

SERVES 4.

Smoky Black Bean Sauce

¼ pound spicy smoked sausage, cut into chunks, or ¼ pound fresh sausage in bulk or removed from casings
2 garlic cloves
2 tablespoons Chinese fermented black beans, rinsed
4 thin slices fresh ginger
2 tablespoons peanut oil
2 tablespoons fresh lime juice
½ cup beer
½ cup chicken stock
1 teaspoon cornstarch dissolved in 2 tablespoons water

In a food processor fitted with the metal blade, process the sausage, garlic, black beans, and ginger. In a skillet fry the mixture in peanut oil for 2 minutes over medium-high heat, stirring continuously. Add the lime juice, beer, and stock and bring to a boil. Cook over medium heat 3 minutes. Add the cornstarch and water and bring to a boil, stirring well. Use immediately or reheat. Add more liquid if the sauce is too thick. Keeps in the refrigerator for 5 days or freeze.

MAKES 1½ CUPS.

THE MIDWEST: AMERICA'S BREADBASKET AND LAGER COUNTRY

Edy's Beer Rocks

Savory Bites

Liptauer Cheese

Beet and Apple Salad with Horseradish Vinaigrette

Wisconsin Cheese and Beer Soup

Balkan Chicken and Eggplant Soup

Herbed Croutons

Cauliflower and Buttermilk Soup

Margaret's Onion Cheese Bread

Greek Tavern Chicken

Chicken and Dumplings

Rich Chicken Stock

Rakott Káposzta —Hungarian Chicken with Sauerkraut and Peppers

Lecsó —Hungarian Ham and Pepper Sauté

Pork Chops in Beer with Mustard and Onions

Pork Shoulder Braised in Bock

Pork Tenderloin Brined in Beer

Great Goulash

Red Cabbage Braised in Cider and Beer

Brussels Sprouts with Bacon and Beer

Wild Rice and Corn Crepes

Spinach Torte

Curried Cauliflower

Homemade Sauerkraut

Pineapple Sauerkraut

Sauerkraut and Apple Salad

Beer and Horseradish Mustard

Gingerbread Stout Cake

Flying into Chicago from the West on a spring morning, we look down on a vast landscape of green fields neatly divided by straight black roads, dotted here and there with white farmhouses and dun-colored silos, small towns with elaborate courthouses at the center, slate-colored lakes ringed by bright sand. This is America's breadbasket, an immensely fertile land largely settled by immigrants from Northern Europe—Germany, Poland, Hungary, Russia, Norway, Sweden—who transformed the Great Plains from a grazing land for buffalo and antelope into one of the world's great granaries.

They planted wheat, corn, barley, oats, and rye in the deep black soil, and offered America and the world the seemingly inexhaustible supply of food that flows through the great trading and processing centers of Chicago, St. Louis, Kansas City, Milwaukee, St. Paul, Cincinnati. The grain itself is turned into flour, bread, and breakfast cereal. The grain transformed in the feedlots of Kansas City and Omaha becomes beef and pork. And the grain blended with water, hops, and yeast in the breweries of St. Louis and Milwaukee makes lager beer, the most popular alcoholic drink in America.

The Midwest is the center of the country's brewing industry, and the huge national breweries such as Anheuser-Busch, Miller, Heileman, and Pabst are located here. The region also contains many of the country's remaining mid-sized to large regional breweries: Leinenkugel, Berghoff-Huber, and Stevens Point in Wisconsin; Dubuque Star (Zele) in Iowa; Cold Springs and August Schell in Minnesota; Evansville Brewing (Drewery's, Fall City) and Falstaff (Ballantine) in Indiana; Hudepohl-Schoenling (Christian Moerlein) in Cincinnati; Stroh (Augsburger, Old Milwaukee, Schlitz) in Detroit.

Immense quantities of beer are made here in the Midwest: Production at the nationals is in the millions of barrels per year; at the smaller, but still substantial, regional breweries, in the hundreds of thousands. Hundreds of tons of grain are malted and processed daily, and the outskirts of brewing centers are dominated by row after row of silos. The air in cities like Milwaukee is permeated with the smell of malt, and freight trains roll through the neighborhoods of St. Louis and Cincinnati, cars heaped high with tan barley and bright yellow corn.

Increasingly these days microbreweries and brew-pubs are springing up, some brewing only a few hundred barrels per year for local beer lovers, others making substantial amounts of beer and distributing it in keg and bottle throughout the region. Just as in the West and Northwest, here handcrafted, artisan beers are much sought after and talked about by a growing numbers of beer connoisseurs.

But there is one big difference: Out West, most small brewers make robust, hearty ales with lagers decidedly in the minority; here in the Midwest, not surprisingly given the German influence, lager is king. Ales are made occasionally, but the preponderance of beers made by brewers, large and small alike, is lager.

Another difference is that most of the small brewers are graduates of the large breweries. Having put in time in production or quality control at one of the nationals or large regionals, brewmasters at Midwest

AUGUST SCHELL: A MIDWESTERN ORIGINAL

August Schell Brewing of New Ulm, Minnesota, is one of a few regional breweries still thriving in the Midwest. Founded in 1860, the 50,000-barrel brewery survived Prohibition and the fierce competition of the national brands, and now produces a line of excellent lagers that are nationally distributed.

The flagship beer is Schell Pilsner, an all-malt lager with pronounced hop accents and rich malty flavors. Schell Weizen is a

Bavarian-style wheat beer using 60 percent wheat malt. It is light and tart, a refreshing brew for summer drinking, and an excellent accompaniment to fish and seafood. Schell Bock and Octoberfest are seasonal beers, amber and malty, with full flavors and body.

micros and brew-pubs are extremely sophisticated and knowledgeable about the techniques of scientific brewing.

Thus you find very few flawed beers at Midwestern micros. Hardly ever do you come across beers with too much hops or the raw malt flavors that one occasionally finds at Western breweries, and not one beer tasted on our trip was out of condition, oxidized, or vinegary. These microbreweries and small regionals sometimes share a problem with American beer in general, though—technological purity, but lack of assertive flavors. The best are wonderfully malty, smooth, and subtle, with light undertones of aromatic hops. The worst are thin and attenuated, pleasant enough, but innocuous.

CHICAGO: SEIDELS OF BOCK AT THE BERGHOFF

Chicago, hub of the region, is truly a beer town, with taverns on every corner, and draft lager the universal drink. The local populace is knowledgeable about beer and fierce in its defense of favorite brands.

One of the oldest and best places to get acquainted with the flavor of Chicago, its food, beer, and people is the Berghoff, located on West Adams near the Art Institute and just off the lake. This venerable tavern and restaurant founded in 1898 has its own specially brewed lager on tap and serves huge amounts of high-quality German food to enthusiastic diners.

The menu features the usual German specialties—hot potato salad and red cabbage, schnitzels and sauerbraten, with a few items not often found on American tables, such as fresh pork braised in beer with sauerkraut (see our Country Spareribs Braised in Sauerkraut*) and aromatic, nutmeg-laced creamed spinach (see our Spinach Torte*). The food, dispensed at polished wooden tables in the cavernous, wood-paneled dining room, is amazingly good considering the volume and speed of service.

And the beer, Berghoff Light, Dark, and Bock on draft, is full and malty, with a decided tang of European hops to cut the richness of the food. Over a few seidels of Berghoff Bock in the tavern after dinner, we found out from an avuncular, red-faced bartender that the beer is made

*See Index.

Even though lager was the most popular brew in the Midwest by the turn of the century, ale and Porter were still made by a few breweries.

especially for the restaurant at the Berghoff-Huber Brewing Company in Monroe, Wisconsin, about 60 miles northeast of Chicago.

This decided our itinerary. We were here to find out about Midwestern lager, and we had mugs of one of the best in our hands. Our bartender pal gave us the name of the Berghoff-Huber's brewmaster, Dave Radzanowski, and directions to Monroe, along with some sage advice about Chicago street etiquette and life in general.

After threading through the dreary suburbs of Chicago with acre after acre of brick buildings yielding to endless miles of white-painted houses, we broke free into the lush countryside. Rolling green hills dotted with cows, farmhouses set in the middle of unending acres of corn, narrow roads winding through lanes of just-blooming spring roses, dirt roads and detours brought us to Monroe, a good-sized town and county seat located on the southern edge of Wisconsin.

Yodelers, Limburger, and More Berghoff Bock

Settled largely by Swiss and German immigrants, the county in the late nineteenth century boasted of having 30,000 people, 60,000 cattle, and 120,000 hogs. The town itself surrounds a courthouse and square and has three main products: farmhouse cheese, summer sausage, and Berghoff-Huber beer.

Berghoff-Huber is typical of many American regional breweries. Founded in the 1840's (nobody seems to know exactly when), it produced about 10,000 barrels of lager beer a year for the local populace and the Chicago market until Prohibition. At that point it made near beer and—it is rumored, but no one will say for sure—perhaps some more substantial brews for the thirsty countryside. Bought in the 1940's by Joseph Huber, the brewery produced one of the more popular beers in the Wisconsin and Chicago region, averaging about 100,000 barrels of draft and bottled beer annually.

It then came under pressure from the large nationals that submerged many local and regional breweries in the postwar period. Aggressive advertising and economies of scale gave the huge centralized breweries a price and market advantage over regional breweries, but Huber survived by concentrating on quality and the Chicago market. For some years it produced Augsburger, one of the first and most successful of the nationally marketed super-premium beers, until the brand was sold to a large national (a typical pattern for small breweries).

Today the brewery makes Berghoff for the Chicago restaurant and also markets bottled Berghoff Regular, Dark, and Bock as its super-

McAuley's lager beer saloon, Chicago, late nineteenth century.

premium brew throughout the Northern Midwest. In addition, it produces Huber Braumeister as its regular beer, Dempsey's Irish Ale, and a popular low-priced brew, Rhinelander. Production is in the range of 400,000 barrels per year, and this includes a number of contract beers and other brands.

Brewmaster Radzanowski, a stocky, forthright brewer with long experience at major national breweries, feels that Berghoff-Huber produces lager beers like those that were popular in the United States in the 1930's and 40's: full bodied, moderately malty, with light hints of hops in flavor and aroma. He believes that the high protein content and high levels of diastatic enzymes in American barley make adjuncts such as corn or rice advisable, but feels that beer should have enough malt for good flavor and head retention.

For skillful professional brewers like Radzanowski, malt and hop flavor are tied directly to price. (Much like in the past—remember the distinction between strong ale and small beer.) Super premium brews such as Berghoff have plenty of hops and malt, are nicely balanced, and full of flavor. Regular beers like Huber Braumeister will necessarily have more adjuncts and less hops and malt, with a pleasing but lighter character overall. Cheaper beers (called popular in the trade) will have even less malt and hops and more adjuncts to keep down costs,providing the public with a light, clean, and drinkable product. Essentially, "ya gets what ya pays for."

When we asked Radzanowski about local food, he suggested we all repair to Baumgartner's on the square, a popular tavern owned by John Huber, a descendant of the eponymous founder of the brewery. Local cheeses and summer sausage are a specialty at Baumgartner's, and the bar is amply provided with Berghoff-Huber on tap. (As Dave pointed out, they don't have to even put the kegs onto a truck, they just roll them to the square and heave them up behind the bar.)

The original Mr. Baumgartner was Swiss, and the decor of the tavern is Helvetic in the extreme. Brightly colored posters of alpine scenery cover the walls, along with racks of antlers and heads of stags, jaunty felt hats with chamois brushes, hunting horns, and the coats of arms of all the Swiss cantons are prominently displayed.

The bar was packed with friendly people who greeted us loudly as we strolled in. When it was announced that we were Californians here to taste the local beer, the atmosphere got even more jovial. Space was made and an array of beers was drawn by the owner, full of lore about Huber beer and hometown history.

Saloon on the eve of Prohibition.

We ordered sandwiches, all on thick slices of dark rye: locally made Liederkrantz, sliced red onion, and beer mustard; ripe local Limburger with onion, hot mustard, and horseradish; summer sausage with onion, horseradish mustard, and dill pickles. With these we tasted Berghoff Regular, a light lager with medium malt flavors and a light hop undertone; Berghoff Bock, a medium dark lager, full bodied with lots of malt and more hops than usual for an American bock; and Dempsey Ale, an amber Irish-style ale with plenty of caramel malt character and an aggressive hop finish on the palate.

We left before the afternoon really got going, although someone was already yodeling in a highly professional manner at a corner table, and one elderly gentleman at the bar was describing how he arm-wrestled an entire platoon of off-duty Marines (one after the other, of course) in a saloon in Twenty-nine Palms one lively evening in California in 1947. Tearing ourselves away from Baumgartner's and its obvious attractions, we headed out for Madison, capital of Wisconsin, and home of one of the most renowned Midwestern microbreweries, Capital Brewery.*

*After this was written, we learned that Berghoff-Huber had been bought by Stroh's, a large national brewery, which owns the Augsburger brand. Bottled Berghoff beer is still being produced at the Monroe brewery, while Berghoff draft is made at a new Berghoff brew-pub in Chicago (formerly Siebens), which provides beer for the pub and the Berghoff restaurant.

Gartenbrau: Wisconsin's Small-Town Brewery

Capital Brewery in Middleton, Wisconsin, a suburb of Madison, sees itself as part of a tradition of small-town breweries and has as its motto "Wisconsin's Small Town Brewery." At the brewery visitors can view an exhibit of photos and artifacts of earlier Wisconsin breweries. The list reads like a litany of past brewers and could be reproduced in almost any American community in the Midwest: Potosi Brewery producing Potosi Pure Malt Beer, closed in 1972; Walter Bros. Brewing Company of Menosha, Wisconsin, closed in 1956; George Walter Brewing Company of Appleton, producers of Adler Brau, closed in 1972; John Walter & Company of Eau Claire, closed in 1988; Leidiger Brewing Company of Merrill, Wisconsin, closed in 1948.

Kirby Nelson, the energetic brewmaster of Capital Brewing, feels that Gartenbrau, the main brand of the 10,000-barrel brewery, carries on the tradition of handcrafted, all-malt lagers that had almost died out in Wisconsin in recent years. The small but technologically advanced brewery produces a full range of lagers: Gartenbrau Lager, pale gold, smooth, and lightly hopped; Gartenbrau Dark, full bodied in the malty Munich style, a 1988 Gold Medal winner at the Great American Beer Festival; Special Pilsner, hoppy, "puts the bite back in beer"; Bock, medium-dark, hoppy, brewed January through April; Maibock, dark gold with a decided hoppy flavor, higher in alcohol than others, brewed April through May; Weizen, a light Wheat Beer brewed for summer drinking; Oktoberfest, a strong, slightly bitter, full-bodied seasonal beer with a distinctive amber color from Munich malt; Wild Rice, a special beer made only for the holidays (November through December), using wild rice.

Gartenbrau is a line of truly distinctive lagers, handcrafted, carefully brewed, and beautifully balanced. Available throughout most of Wisconsin and in the Chicago market, Gartenbrau is among the three or four finest lagers made in America today and well worth seeking out.

Urged on by Kirby Nelson, we sought and found a Madison pub located in a cellar below the Italian Veterans of Foreign Wars Hall that

was the hangout for local beer fanatics, of which there are a surprising number. Serving an impressive line of local draft beers, the unnamed tavern was a veritable hotbed of brewing information, especially since we had stumbled onto the weekly meeting of the Madison home brewers society, a hearty group, to say the least. We tasted some of the renowned local brews: Stevens Point, Leinenkugel, and Ambier from Wisconsin, August Schell, and Cold Springs from Minnesota. And we got a long list of microbreweries, brew-pubs, and taverns in Milwaukee to visit, feeling a bit like Spanish conquistadors being constantly pushed on to the great El Dorado just one town farther away.

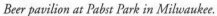
Beer pavilion at Pabst Park in Milwaukee.

MILWAUKEE: BEER CAPITAL OF AMERICA

You can smell Milwaukee almost before you can see it, and that's a compliment. The sweet reek of malt drifts out over the plains, and you start thinking of having a beer even before you see any buildings on the skyline. When you wend your way above the old brick buildings near the river on raised freeways and look down on silos and smokestacks, you smell the damp sweetness of malt, the bitter edge of hops in the wind sweeping in from the lake. And you know this is the capital of beer in America. A lager lover has come home.

One of the most interesting microbreweries in the United States, Sprecher Brewing, and one of its most interesting brewers, Randy Sprecher, can be found in an old brick tannery between the railroad tracks and the river on Oregon Street in the industrial section of Milwaukee. A wanderer and avid beer-taster in Germany in the 1960's, an oceanographer in California, a student developing yeast cultures at the University of California at Davis, a brewer at Pabst, someone who has, as he said, "done it all," Randy Sprecher is making world-class German-style beers in his 8,000-barrel brewery.

His best-seller, available in both draft and bottle, is Sprecher Special Amber, a smooth, mellow lager with a toasted malt flavor, hoppy bouquet, and lightly bitter finish. Sprecher Helles is light in body, hops, and alcohol, with fresh, clean flavors and pleasant character. Milwaukee Weiss is a very smooth Wheat Beer with tart flavors and a fruity bouquet, while Dunkel Weizen is a dark Wheat Beer, unique and interesting, with little bitterness and a roasted malt flavor. Winter Brew is a seasonal beer, very dark, with the flavor of caramel and black malts to the fore, in the style of a full-bodied Munich Dunkel. Oktoberfest and Maibock are seasonal beers, full bodied, dark, malty, and strong. Black Bavarian Style is a very deep colored, robust malt liquor with complex malt flavors, a creamy head, and distinctive aromas of coffee, caramel, and chocolate. Sprecher is careful to note that all his beers are brewed according to the Bavarian Purity Law and are nonpasteurized. They should be refrigerated to preserve freshness, and all bottles are stamped or coded with the date of bottling.

Lakefront Brewery, a tiny micro producing only 150 barrels a year, makes any array of individually styled beers on a small scale. Brewer Russell Klisch produces East Side Dark, Klisch Beer, Klisch Cherry Beer, and River West Stein Beer. Water Street Brewery, a bright and trendy brew-pub on Water Street near the river, offers a wide range of ales, stouts, lagers, and wheat beers to accompany an extensive pub grub menu.

Dave Radzanowski at Berghoff-Huber told us that if we really wanted to understand American beer we should visit one of the great malting companies in Milwaukee. He gave us the name of John Acker, director of production of Froedtert Malt, one of the largest malt producers in the country, and supplier to some of the most important regional and national breweries.

Acker's directions to the malting facility were simple: Take a certain freeway exit on the edge of Milwaukee and head for the silos, visible for miles across the plain. The first thing that strikes you about U.S. malting is simply the scale: Everything is huge, Brobdignagian; the ton seems to be the smallest unit of measurement, silos and malt houses rise up ten to fifteen stories, long plumes of fragrant steam pour out of huge ventilating ducts atop the malting towers.

We began by viewing trainloads of barley arriving from fields in North and South Dakota, Montana, Wyoming, Idaho, both the six-row barley that provides most U.S. malt, and two-row varieties, used more by European brewers and many American micros. (For more information, see Appendix I, How Beer Is Made).

Acker, a genial and extremely knowledgeable maltster with an extensive background at Canadian and American malting companies, explained the malting process to us. The aim of the maltster is to stimulate the growth of the barleycorn or seed, thereby encouraging the formation of enzymes and malt sugars, and then to stop the process by drying and roasting the malt.

The first step in malting is steeping, where the grain is conveyed to the top of the malting towers and soaks to absorb moisture in huge steeping tanks in warm water. The seeds swell over a period of one to two days, and enzymatic activity and growth is stimulated. The bottoms of the tanks then open up and drop the moist barley to the germinating floors below. Here the grain is spread out a few feet deep in football field–sized bins and is periodically stirred by gigantic machines that comb and turn the seeds. Warm, humid air constantly blows over and through the barley, encouraging growth of sprouts (called chits in the trade). The barley seed is tricked into beginning the formation of enzymes and sugars that will nourish the growing plant. When the sprout is about half the length of the seed, the germinated barley is dropped one more story to the kilns or drying floors.

Here the barley is heated to dry the malted grain and create the aroma, flavor, and final color of the malt. Specialty or coloring malts are roasted at higher temperatures for longer times to provide caramelized flavors and deeper color. After curing, the malt is shipped to breweries, distilleries, and bakeries all over the United States, Canada, and Europe.

We ended our stay in Milwaukee at one of the many ethnic neighborhood tavern/restaurants recommended by the home brewers back in Madison. From the outside, the place is not much: TAVERN GOOD

BEER HOME-COOKED FOOD flashes the sign; the windows are covered with grillwork and Pabst Blue Ribbon displays; there's sawdust on the cement floor, a long bar filled with beer drinkers, and a clutch of tables in the back near the kitchen. On a small stage in one corner a concertina band is whooping it up, all the players over sixty at least, ruddy and smiling, steins of gold lager at their elbows.

We started out with huge bowls of pungent, flavorful Wisconsin Beer and Cheese Soup,* followed by platters of Pork Chops in Beer with Mustard and Onions,* and Sauerkraut and Cabbage Braised in Dark Lager.* We washed down the hearty food with mugs of Sprecher beer on draft: toasty Special Amber with the soup, and full-bodied and heady Maibock with the pork chops and vegetables.

BREW-PUBS, BADERBRAU, AND SERBIAN FOLK DANCES

Back in Chicago, on our way home, we visited some of the city's many brew-pubs, micros, and beer taverns. Chicago has always been a beer center and these days has an active brew-pub scene with a growing clientele of knowledgeable and enthusiastic beer lovers.

Goose Island Brewing Company's brewmaster, Vic Ecimovich, is one name that we kept hearing during our trip through Midwest breweries. A graduate of Chicago's famous Siebel Institute of Brewing Technology, Ecimovich is well respected by fellow brewers and produces some of the best beers we found in any of the brew-pubs we visited. Offering a wide range of beers from Golden Goose Pilsner and Lincoln Park Lager to Honker's Ale, Old Clybourn Porter, and Chicago Vice Weizen, the pub also has a good selection of spicy foods on a menu that features daily specials and regional dishes. Beer batter walleye pike (see our Beer Batter*) and Spicy Tartar Sauce* was a nice match with the Pilsner, and an excellent, malty Maibock went well with a house-made kielbasa. A nice touch at Goose Island: We visited it on a rainy Saturday, and it was filled with families with

*See Index.

young children watching the rain and eating flavored popcorn and spicy nuts while parents sampled a couple of the house brews.

The Weinkeller Brewery is located in Berwyn, a western suburb of Chicago. Here brewer Udo Hartung makes a number of brews in various styles: Berwyn Brew Pilsner, a gold lager with hop emphasis and pleasant malt character on the palate; Aberdeen Amber Ale, a rich copper-colored ale; Düsseldorfer Doppelbock, deep amber with complex, slightly sweet, roasted malt flavors; Dublin Stout, a very dark almost opaque ale, with a bittersweet finish from dark roasted barley; Bavarian Weiss *mit hefe* (with yeast), tangy and malty; and Berliner Weisse, a Berlin-style Wheat Beer served *mit schuss* (with raspberry syrup).

Weinkeller Brewery also provides a grill and pub grub menu with sausages and smoked meats made by brewer Hartung in his own smokehouse. There is an extensive beer list in the restaurant and pub that offers over three hundred beers from all over the world and includes virtually every American microbrewery that bottles its beer.

Another beer we sampled in Chicago taverns was Chicago Legacy, a popular, all-malt lager made by the Chicago Brewing Company, and widely available in local bars and brew-pubs.

On our last day in the Midwest, we made a pilgrimage to a small suburban brewery that produces Baderbrau, one of the finest beers in the United States, a brew that world beer expert Michael Jackson pronounced "the best Pilsner in America." Ken Pavichevich is wildly enthusiastic about his beer, and his opinion is shared by just about anyone that tastes it. He makes only one beer, the full-bodied, deep-gold Pilsner called Baderbrau at Pavichevich Brewing Company in Elmhurst near O'Hare Airport.

Pavichevich, an ex-policeman and oil executive, became a true believer in handmade beer while on a tour to Europe a few years back and returned vowing to create an American version of the great Czechoslovakian lager, Pilsner Urquell.

Tasting the beer with Pavichevich in the brewery's tasting room, it's hard to argue with Michael Jackson. First of all, there's the head: Pavichevich carefully draws the beer from its tap, building a creamy, pale golden head slowly and reverently. When we bring up the old bartender's tale about being able to float a shilling on the head of a pint of Guinness, Pavichevich asks to borrow a quarter. He carefully lays it on

Midwestern beer gardens.

the head. It floats and stays there as he takes a long and careful sip, descending with the foam intact all the way down to the bottom of the glass. Belgian lace, the tracery of foam that clings to the glass as you drink a fine beer, decorates the tall Pilsner glass from top to bottom. That's impressive.

The aromas and flavors of Baderbrau are no less impressive. The deep-gold lager has beautiful hop aromas with dusty sweet malt undertones, a very full body with intense but pleasant hop bitterness that is balanced by lots of malt and hints of caramel and butterscotch. The finish is long, with hops and malt beautifully mixed, first one dominating, then the other.

Baderbrau's brewmaster, Doug Babcock, created Stroh's superpremium prize-winning Pilsner, Signature, before retiring from the brewery in 1985. After many trips to Europe, he and Pavichevich developed the formula for Baderbrau with the 1516 Bavarian Purity Law, the *Reinheitsgebot,* as a model. Using only the four permitted ingredients—yeast, hops, malt, and water—they set out to create a world-class beer in the Czech Pilsner style. They ended up using one bushel of pure malt per barrel (most U.S. breweries allow only a half bushel of all grains, including corn and rice) and three pounds of the best European hops (Saaz, Spalt, Hallertau, Tettnanger) as opposed to the usual American formula of only 1 pound of domestic hops per barrel. Cool-fermented in the modern brewhouse gleaming with copper and stainless steel, the beer is indeed one of the finest in America and worthy to stand up to the best Pilsner-style lagers in the world. Beer aficionados from both coasts often call Ken at the brewery to meet them at O'Hare with a case or two to take home when they have to make a connection at the Chicago hub.

When we asked Pavichevich (of Serbian and Montenegrin parentage) where to taste his beer with food, he reeled off a list of Eastern European nightclubs and restaurants all over Chicago, its suburbs, and the Region in northern Indiana. We took careful notes to decide where we would spend our last night in town.

As it turned out, we had to bribe the taxi driver to take us to the Eastern European restaurant Ken recommended. It's way out in a neighborhood that even a hardened Chicago taxi driver is nervous about, but we convinced him not only to take us but to pick us up afterward as well.

The neighborhood is indeed a bit daunting, with boarded-up windows and acres of empty lots, but the restaurant itself is brightly lit, its neon sign gleaming like a beacon of good cheer in the empty streets. And it is packed, even on a week night, with wall-to-wall folk having one hell of a time. A gypsy band plays a *czardas* on a stage near the bar, the waitresses are sleek and cheerful, and the bartender/host has a black handlebar mustache that would make Jerry Colonna jealous.

When we tell them Ken Pavichevich sent us, we are welcomed like long-lost cousins just down from the hills of Montenegro. Platters of Liptauer Cheese* and Onion Cheese Bread* suddenly appear, along with huge steins of Baderbrau. The band gets louder, the waitresses get sleeker, our mustaches start to curl, and plate after plate arrives from the kitchen: Balkan Chicken and Eggplant Soup,* *Rakott Káposzta,* a spicy chicken and pepper sauté, *Lecsó,* Hungarian ham and peppers, and Pork Chops with Fresh Pimientos.*

When the faithful taxi driver finally arrives, he has to fight his way through the crowd to the dance floor where we are learning Serbian folk dances. Good-byes echo through the dark streets as we walk to the cab, radiating garlic and Baderbrau in the cool, still air.

*See Index.

Edy's Beer Rocks

Beer Rocks, another recipe from baker Edy Young, are the ultimate snacks with beer. Try them at a comparative beer-tasting where you and your guests sample a crisp, full-bodied lager from the Midwest, an amber California Ale, a Porter made by Yuengling or Anchor Steam, and a rich dark Stout from Washington State like Pike Place XXXXX.

We prefer the dough on the dense side. This can be controlled by how much time you allow for the final rising: Longer time yields lighter dough, a shorter time a denser one. You should experiment to find out the temperature and amount of time that produces the consistency and texture you like. Edy uses her cold electric oven in which she places a large shallow pan of boiling water. This provides just enough heat for the dough to rise and also ensures that the surface doesn't dry out.

Filling

1½ pounds fresh sage or smoked sausage or a combination of both, removed from the casings or coarsely chopped

1 cup thinly sliced onion

4 cups shredded cabbage

Dough

⅓ cup sugar

½ teaspoon salt

1 package (1 ounce) active dry yeast (not the fast-acting variety)

1½ cups warm cooking water (at about 100° F.) from the potatoes

⅔ cup butter, softened

2 eggs

1 cup warm mashed potatoes (at about 100° F.)

7–7½ cups all-purpose flour

To make the filling: Fry the sausage over medium heat 3–5 minutes to render some of the fat. Pour off the fat, and add the onion and cabbage. Cover and cook for 5 minutes, or until the cabbage has wilted. Set aside to cool while you prepare the dough.

To make the dough: Dissolve the sugar, salt, and yeast in the warm potato water. Proof in a warm spot (80–100° F.) until the mixture becomes bubbly, about 5–10 minutes. Pour into a large mixing bowl. Blend in the butter, eggs, mashed potatoes, and 7 cups of the flour.

Knead on a floured surface until the dough becomes elastic and easy to work, about 5–10 minutes. Add the remaining flour if needed. Place the dough in a large oiled bowl and cover loosely with plastic wrap. Let rise in a warm spot for 45 minutes to 1 hour until the dough doubles in size.

After it has risen, punch down the dough and form into 30 equal balls. Pat the balls into ½-inch-thick rounds, about 2 inches in diameter. Place about ¼ cup of the filling in the middle of each round. Form the dough around the filling to make round rolls. Place on a baking sheet. Put in a warm spot and let the rolls rise for 20–40 minutes. If the surface of the dough has dried out, brush lightly with water.

Preheat the oven to 375° F. Bake the rolls for 20–25 minutes or until the beer rocks have a nice golden color and a mouth-watering aroma. The rolls freeze well.

MAKES 36 ROLLS, 3–4 INCHES IN DIAMETER.

Savory Bites

This rich, short-crust biscuit is light and flaky, a good dough to combine with spicy sausage. The piquant tidbits are great snacks for a beer-tasting of American Pale Ales: Compare Ballantine India Pale Ale, Sierra Nevada Pale Ale, Mendocino Brewery's Blue Heron Pale Ale, and Grant's India Pale Ale, or make up your own tasting.

You can cut the dough into squares and top with sausage or form it into long rolls and slice into pinwheels. Use a spicy sausage with this recipe. Serve hot as an appetizer or party snack.

Dough

2 cups all-purpose flour
½ cup (1 stick) plus 2 tablespoons butter
3 egg yolks

¼ cup half-and-half
½ teaspoon salt
Pinch nutmeg

1 whole egg, lightly beaten, for
  egg wash
1 cup freshly grated Parmesan
  cheese

1 pound spicy sausage, such
  as kielbasa, andouille, or
  linguiça

To make the dough: In a bowl add to the flour the butter, egg yolks, half-and-half, salt, and nutmeg. Mix well to make a dough. Briefly knead the dough and let it rest for at least 15 minutes.

To make little squares: Preheat the oven to 400° F. Roll the dough out on a floured surface to a thickness of ¼ inch. Brush with the egg wash, and place ¼-inch-thick slices of sausage in rows over the surface. Cut out squares a little bit larger than each sausage round. Sprinkle with the Parmesan cheese. Bake on a baking sheet for 20 minutes.

To make pinwheels: Roll the dough out ⅛-inch thick. Sprinkle generously with the Parmesan cheese and the finely chopped sausage. Roll the dough up lengthwise, then slice it into pinwheels about ⅜-inch thick. Place on a baking sheet and brush with eggwash. Bake for 20 minutes.

MAKES 48 SQUARES OR PINWHEELS.

Liptauer Cheese

This tangy Hungarian cheese spread is not only good on dark rye or pumpernickel, but is also very enjoyable on crackers, celery, or fresh young radishes. It's a great appetizer, especially when accompanied by a full-flavored, hoppy pilsner-style lager, such as Capital Brewing's Gartenbrau or Pavichevich Brewing's Baderbrau.

Try to use real Hungarian sweet paprika in this dish; it gives the cheese more flavor than the domestic product.

1 small garlic clove (about ½ teaspoon minced)
1 green onion or scallion, coarsely chopped
2 teaspoons capers
1 teaspoon Dijon mustard
1 teaspoon caraway seeds
1 tablespoon Hungarian paprika

8 ounces cream cheese, *or* 4 ounces cream cheese and 4 ounces fresh goat cheese
1 tablespoon freshly grated Parmesan (optional)
2–3 tablespoons Pilsner-style lager

With the motor of the food processor or blender running, drop the garlic, green onion, and capers into the feed tube. Process about 15 seconds. Remove the lid, and add the remaining ingredients. Pulse the machine several times, until everything is well blended and smooth. Add more beer, a tablespoon at a time, if the mixture is too thick. Pack into a small bowl. Cover and chill several hours or overnight.

MAKES 1½ CUPS.

Beet and Apple Salad with Horseradish Vinaigrette

Earthy beets, tart apples, and a spicy vinaigrette make this dish irresistible with beer. We think a malty Amber Lager goes best, but a Pale Ale would also be very nice.

6 medium beets, unpeeled, but with tops removed

2 tart green apples, such as Granny Smith

3 green onions or scallions, thinly sliced

Horseradish Vinaigrette

1 tablespoon Dijon or Creole mustard

1 tablespoon prepared horseradish

3 tablespoons red wine or raspberry vinegar

½ cup olive oil

Salt and pepper

Cook the unpeeled beets in plenty of boiling salted water until a knife point can be easily inserted. The timing depends on the size of the beets, but 15–20 minutes should be about right. Let cool and peel the beets. Cut into shreds or julienne strips. Peel and shred the apples. In a large salad bowl mix together the beets, apples, and green onions or scallions.

To make the horseradish vinaigrette: In a food processor mix the mustard, horseradish, and vinegar. With the processor running, gradually pour in the oil. Taste for salt and pepper.

Toss the salad with the dressing, and let sit for 1 hour or so in the refrigerator before serving. This flavorful vinaigrette is also good on leeks.

SERVES 4–6.

Wisconsin Cheese and Beer Soup

In one fell swoop, or more precisely, in one swell soup, you can find all the ingredients that make Wisconsin a paradise for hearty eaters and drinkers—beer, cheese, and sausage. Use a lightly smoky sausage for this recipe like our Beer Sausage, smoked bratwurst, or kielbasa and the best aged Wisconsin sharp Cheddar you can find. We'd suggest a good, full-bodied Midwestern lager like Berghoff-Huber, Stevens Point Special, or Leinenkugel, but just about any similarly styled beer will do, both in the soup and on the table.

This substantial soup is great any time, but perfect to round off a long and convivial evening of poker, raucous conversation, and, of course, beer.

4 tablespoons (½ stick) butter

1 pound Fresh Beer Sausage (see page 74) or other lightly smoky sausage, chopped

2 cups chopped onions

2 cups diced carrots

1 cup thinly sliced celery

⅓ cup flour

1 12-ounce bottle lager

3 cups Rich Chicken Stock (see page 203)

2 cups diced red potatoes

2 cups milk

3 cups grated sharp Cheddar cheese

1 teaspoon dried thyme

2 teaspoons Worcestershire sauce

2 teaspoons sweet Hungarian paprika

2 tablespoons tomato paste

Salt and pepper

Tabasco to taste

¼ cup thinly sliced green onions or scallions

In a heavy 4-quart pot or Dutch oven melt the butter over medium heat. Put in the sausage and cook for 5 minutes, stirring occasionally. Add the onions, carrots, and celery, and cook 5 minutes. Stir in the flour, coating the vegetables well with the *roux*. Whisk in the lager and stock, and bring to a boil. Lower the heat, and simmer until the soup thickens slightly, 3 to 5 minutes. Add the potatoes and cook 10–15 minutes until tender. Stir in the milk, grated cheese, thyme, Worcestershire, paprika, and tomato paste. Continue stirring until the cheese is melted and the soup is smooth. Taste for salt and pepper and Tabasco, if desired. Serve in large soup bowls and garnish with the green onions.

SERVES 6–8.

Balkan Chicken and Eggplant Soup

Eggplant and lemon provide a lively touch in this zesty soup, typical of Chicago's Balkan restaurants. The soup makes a refreshing first course or a pleasant lunch when paired with hot pita bread and a light Wheat Beer like Sprecher Milwaukee Weiss.

4 tablespoons olive oil
1 medium eggplant, diced
   (about 4 cups)
1 red bell pepper or fresh
   pimiento, chopped
2 tablespoons chopped garlic
¼ cup chopped onion
2 tablespoons sweet
   Hungarian paprika
2 teaspoons chopped fresh
   oregano or ½ teaspoon
   dried
2 teaspoons chopped fresh
   rosemary or ½ teaspoon
   dried

1 teaspoon cayenne
4 cups Rich Chicken Stock
   (see page 203)
2 cups diced cooked chicken
1 cup half-and-half
1 egg yolk
1 tablespoon cornstarch
Lemon juice
Salt and pepper
Herbed Croutons (recipe follows) (optional)

Heat the olive oil in a 4-quart pot or Dutch oven. Cook the eggplant in the oil for about 10 minutes, stirring frequently, until soft, adding more oil if needed. Add the bell pepper, and cook for 1 minute. Add the garlic, onion, and paprika, and cook for 1–2 minutes, until the vegetables are well coated with the paprika. Add the oregano, rosemary, cayenne, and stock. Bring to a boil, then reduce the heat to a simmer. Cook for 10 minutes. Add the chicken. Whisk together the half-and-half, egg yolk, and cornstarch. Ladle a little soup into this mixture, stir well, and gradually add the mixture to the soup. Do not let the soup boil after this point. Add lemon juice and salt and pepper to taste. Ladle into soup bowls and garnish with the herbed croutons if desired.
SERVES 6.

Herbed Croutons

4 slices day-old French bread or other coarse-textured bread, cut into ½-inch cubes

½ cup olive oil

¼ cup chopped fresh herbs, such as oregano, marjoram, rosemary, and thyme

½ teaspoon minced garlic

Pinch salt

Preheat the oven to 350° F. Combine the olive oil, herbs, garlic, and salt in a bowl. Toss the bread cubes with the herbed oil until they are well coated and most of the oil is absorbed. Spread the cubes on a cookie sheet and bake until lightly browned and crisp. Herbed croutons are also delicious in salads.

MAKES ABOUT 2–3 CUPS.

Cauliflower and Buttermilk Soup

This tart and flavorful soup makes a great light lunch or first course with a malty Amber Lager such as August Schell Bock or Wild Boar Special Amber.

1 large head cauliflower, trimmed, with florets separated

1 cup rice

8 cups (2 quarts) Rich Chicken Stock (see page 203)

1 cup lager

2 tablespoons butter

1 onion, coarsely chopped

1 rib celery, coarsely chopped

1 leek (white part only), cleaned and coarsely chopped

2 cups buttermilk

1 cup half-and-half

Salt and pepper

In a large saucepan cook the cauliflower and rice in the stock and lager until they are very soft, about 20 minutes. Meanwhile, in another pan cook the remaining vegetables in the butter over medium heat until soft, about 10 minutes. Add the vegetables to the cauliflower mixture, and cook 10 minutes. Purée everything in a food processor or through a food mill. Return the purée to the pan and reheat. Blend in the buttermilk and half-and-half. Taste for salt and pepper.

SERVES 6.

Margaret's Onion Cheese Bread

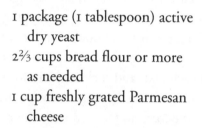

This savory bread is wonderful with cream cheese for a snack or brunch, and can be used to make sandwiches (see page 282). It also goes well with aged cheese and full-flavored ales like Dempsey's Irish Ale.

Margaret Miller is a Fort Wayne, Indiana, cooking teacher who specializes in creating recipes for great breads and other baked goods.

1 package (1 tablespoon) active dry yeast

2⅔ cups bread flour or more as needed

1 cup freshly grated Parmesan cheese

1 teaspoon salt

1 tablespoon chopped fresh herbs, such as thyme, oregano, basil, or whatever else you have on hand

2 tablespoons olive oil

Onion Filling

4 tablespoons olive oil

1 pound (2 large) onions: Sweet Texas, Vidalia, Walla Walla, or other sweet onions, sliced into crescents

Cornmeal

2 tablespoons poppy seeds

Sprinkle the yeast over 1 cup warm water and add a pinch of sugar. Stir and let the yeast proof for about 10 minutes. Meanwhile, place the metal blade in the processor bowl, add the flour, grated cheese, and salt, and pulse the machine off and on. Add the chopped fresh herbs to the bowl.

When the yeast is proofed, add the olive oil to it, stirring until well blended. With the food processor running, pour the yeast mixture through the feed tube in a slow, steady stream and process until the dough forms a ball and the sides of the bowl come clean. If the dough seems too tacky and sticky, add more flour, one tablespoon at a time, pulsing after each addition. If the dough seems too tight and dry, add water, one tablespoon at a time, pulsing after each addition. Once the right consistency has been achieved (the dough should look smooth and silky), process again to knead for about 40 seconds.

Remove the dough from the processor and place in an oiled bowl. Turn the dough to coat all the sides with oil. Cover loosely with plastic wrap or a towel. Allow the dough to rise in a warm place until double in size, about 1 hour.

While the dough is rising, preheat the oven to 375° F.

To make the onion filling: In a large frying pan add enough olive oil to cover the bottom of the pan. Heat the oil over medium-high heat, and add the onions. Sauté until softened, but still a bit crunchy, about 3–4 minutes. Remove the onions from the pan, and cool.

On a floured surface roll the dough into a 17- × 8-inch rectangle. Cover the surface with the cooled onions, reserving ½ cup for topping, leaving a 1-inch border of dough. Carefully roll the dough up like an 8-inch-long jelly-roll. Pinch the long seam together, and place seam side down. Pinch down the seams at each end, and tuck under to form a loaf. Place the bread on a cookie sheet that has been dusted with the cornmeal. Make 3 slits in the top of the loaf, and spread with the remaining onions and the poppy seeds. Bake for 30–35 minutes, until the crust is golden brown. Remove, and cool on a wire rack before slicing.

MAKES 1 LOAF.

Greek Tavern Chicken

This aromatic chicken stew is popular in Greek taverns in Chicago. Serve it over the rice-like Greek pasta, orzo, or with rice pilaf, along with a lightly hopped lager like Berghoff or Frankenmuth Old German Pilsner.

½ teaspoon salt
½ teaspoon black pepper
¼ teaspoon allspice
1 teaspoon paprika
3- to 4-pound chicken, cut
    into 8 serving pieces
3 tablespoons olive oil
2 cups sliced onions
3 cups sliced leeks
1 medium carrot, diced
2 tablespoons chopped garlic
1 cup light lager
1 cup Rich Chicken Stock (see
    page 203)

2 cups roughly chopped toma-
    toes, peeled and seeded, *or* 2
    cups canned Italian-style
    tomatoes, chopped
¼ cup tomato puree
½ teaspoon dried oregano,
    preferably Greek
Pinch each of cinnamon and
    cloves
2 bay leaves
Lemon juice to taste
Salt and pepper

Combine the salt, pepper, allspice, and paprika and rub it all over the chicken pieces. In a heavy Dutch oven or deep skillet brown them over medium-high heat in the olive oil. Regulate the heat and turn the chicken often to insure even browning and to prevent burning. This should take about 10–15 minutes. Remove the chicken and pour off all but 3 tablespoons of the fat. Add the onions, leeks, and carrot. Cover and cook for 10 minutes until the aromatic vegetables are soft and beginning to show some color. Add the garlic and lager. Boil over high heat for a minute or two, scraping up any brown bits that cling to the bottom of the pan. Add the stock, tomatoes, tomato puree, oregano, cinnamon, cloves, and bay leaves. Bring to a boil. Put the chicken back in the pot, and reduce the heat to a simmer. Cook, covered, until the chicken is tender, about 35 minutes.

Remove the chicken to a hot platter and keep warm. Reduce the liquid in the pan over high heat until it thickens slightly, about 5 minutes. Add lemon juice and salt and pepper to taste. Cover the chicken on the platter with the sauce.

SERVES 4–6.

Chicken and Dumplings

The sauce for this recipe for chicken and dumplings, an American farm-house favorite, is not thickened; it's really somewhere between a soup and a stew. The key is a wonderfully rich chicken stock. We provide a recipe, but you could use any good homemade chicken stock here. Be sure to make plenty, as it freezes well.

We used legs and thighs for the chicken itself, since the dark meat is so flavorful and moist, but use any part of the chicken you like. Remove the skin to cut down on fat and calories. We used buttermilk and a little melted butter for the dumplings, but you could use regular milk and leave out the butter, if you wish.

A light-bodied American Pilsner, mildly hopped and lightly malty, such as Dubuque Star Private Reserve or Heileman Special Export, would be a good match for this Midwestern specialty.

2 quarts Rich Chicken Stock
   (recipe follows)
6 large chicken legs and
   thighs, about 4 pounds, or
   6 chicken breasts or 1
   chicken, skin removed and
   cut up
1 onion, diced

1 carrot, diced
1 tablespoon olive oil
2 ribs celery, diced
1 teaspoon chopped fresh
   thyme or ½ teaspoon dried
Salt and pepper

Dumplings

1 cup flour
2 teaspoons baking powder
½ teaspoon salt

2 tablespoons butter, melted
1 egg, lightly beaten
Buttermilk or regular milk

To cook the chicken: In a large pot or Dutch oven bring the stock to a boil. Add the chicken, reduce to a simmer, and cover. Meanwhile, in a heavy covered skillet fry the onion, carrot, and celery in the olive oil over medium heat for about 10 minutes until soft. After the chicken has cooked for 30 minutes, stir the vegetables into the pot. Season with the thyme and salt and pepper.

To make the dumplings: Sift the flour, baking powder, and salt into a mixing bowl. Add the melted butter. Break the egg into a ½ cup measuring cup, and fill to the top with milk. Slowly add the liquid to the dry ingredients, stirring as you pour. Add more milk if necessary, but keep the batter as stiff as possible.

After the chicken and vegetables have cooked 15 minutes, drop the dumpling mixture by spoonfuls onto the surface of the stew. Cover, and continue cooking 10 minutes. Do not lift the lid until the 10 minutes are up. Then check the dumplings. They are done when fluffy, and a toothpick inserted comes out clean. Serve at once.

SERVES 6.

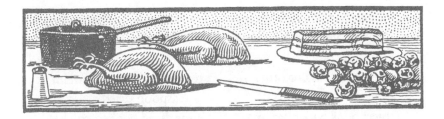

Rich Chicken Stock

4 pounds chicken backs, necks, wing tips, or bones in any combination

4 quarts water

1 whole onion, unpeeled and split

2 ribs celery, cut into chunks

1 carrot, unpeeled and cut into chunks

Stems from 1 bunch parsley

1 teaspoon dried thyme or 2 sprigs fresh thyme

6 peppercorns

Salt and pepper

Bring the chicken and water to a boil in a stockpot. Reduce to a simmer, and skim off any scum that rises to the surface. Add the remaining ingredients and simmer for about 1½ hours. Strain and discard all the solids. Taste for salt and pepper. Refrigerate the stock overnight, and remove any congealed fat from the surface. Refrigerated, the stock keeps 3–4 days, and it freezes well.

MAKES ABOUT 3 QUARTS RICH STOCK.

Rakott Káposzta — Hungarian Chicken with Sauerkraut and Peppers

We're always looking for inventive ways to present chicken. Rakott káposzta is a delicious Hungarian peasant dish traditionally made with diced fresh pork, peppers, rice, and herbs. We've substituted cooked chicken, with very good results; turkey or rabbit would be equally successful, too.

A full-bodied, malty Dark Lager would be a suitable match: August Schell Bock or Sprecher Black Bavarian from Milwaukee.

½ pound kielbasa or other smoked sausage, sliced

2 tablespoons bacon fat or olive oil

Salt and pepper

2 onions, thinly sliced

1 tablespoon chopped garlic

1 yellow or green bell pepper, cut into thin strips

3 tablespoons sweet Hungarian paprika

1 teaspoon caraway seeds

2 teaspoons fresh marjoram or 1 teaspoon dried

2 cups diced cooked chicken, turkey, or rabbit

1 cup beef stock

1 12-ounce bottle Dark Lager

1 pound sauerkraut, rinsed briefly and drained

2–3 cups slightly undercooked converted rice

2 cups sour cream

In a large skillet fry the smoked sausage in the bacon fat or olive oil over medium-high heat 3 minutes. Remove with a slotted spoon, and reserve. Pour off all but 3 tablespoons of the fat, and in it cook the onions for about 10 minutes, stirring occasionally, until they begin to brown. Add the garlic and sliced pepper, and cook 2 minutes. Sprinkle the vegetables with the paprika, caraway, and marjoram. Cook for 1 minute until everything is well coated with spices and herbs. Add the reserved sausage and cooked chicken with the stock and lager. Bring to a boil, scraping up any browned bits from the bottom of the pan.

Preheat the oven to 350° F.

Spread half the sauerkraut on the bottom of a large Dutch oven. Cover with half the chicken mixture. Cover the chicken mixture with all the cooked rice, followed by the remaining chicken mixture and then the remaining sauerkraut. At this point the casserole can be refrigerated overnight. Cover the casserole and bake for 45 minutes. Before serving, spread a layer of sour cream over the top of the casserole, and sprinkle on a little paprika. Increase the oven to 450° F. and bake for 15 minutes.

SERVES 4–6.

Lescó—Hungarian Ham and Pepper Sauté

Sautéed peppers, tomatoes, smoked meat, and paprika are often a starting point for Hungarian dishes, but the combination is delectable just on its own. Served over rice or with fried eggs, Lecsó is an excellent dish for a hearty breakfast or brunch.

The rich and intense flavor of this preparation comes from the long slow cooking of the onions and the sweet peppers along with the smoky, salty ham. We suggest a high-hopped Pilsner here: Gartenbrau Special Pilsner is a good choice.

2 tablespoons olive oil or bacon fat
1 pound smoked ham, diced
4 cups thinly sliced onions
1 tablespoon minced garlic
3 tablespoons sweet Hungarian paprika
1 pound fresh pimiento, or yellow, green, or red bell peppers, or any combination, thinly sliced

½ pound ripe Italian-style tomatoes, peeled, seeded, and chopped
2 teaspoons minced fresh marjoram or 1 teaspoon dried
Lemon juice to taste
Salt and pepper

In a large heavy skillet heat the oil, and fry the ham for 5 minutes over medium heat. Transfer to a platter, and add the onions to the pan. Cover, and cook over medium heat for 20 minutes, stirring occasionally. Add the garlic and paprika, and cook 2 minutes. Stir in the peppers and tomatoes with the marjoram and reserved ham. Cover and cook over low heat for 20 minutes, until the peppers are quite tender. Taste, and add lemon juice and salt and pepper as desired.

SERVES 4–6.

Pork Chops in Beer with Mustard and Onions

With these savory, mustardy chops we recommend a Dark Lager like Berghoff Huber Dark.

4 thick-cut rib pork chops (about 2–3 pounds total)
1 teaspoon salt
½ teaspoon black pepper
1 teaspoon dried dill
1 teaspoon dry mustard powder
1 tablespoon olive oil
1 large onion, thinly sliced

½ cup dark beer
1 tablespoon malt, cider, or wine vinegar
1 tablespoon coarse-grained or Dijon mustard
½ cup sour cream
Chopped fresh dill or chives (optional)

Season the chops generously with the salt, pepper, dill, and dry mustard. Heat the oil in a heavy 12-inch skillet over high heat, and brown the chops for 2–3 minutes on each side. Remove the chops and all but 2 tablespoons of the fat from the pan. Put in the onion, cover, and cook for 10 minutes, stirring occasionally, until soft. Arrange the chops on top of the onion, pour in the beer and vinegar, cover, and cook at a simmer for about 30 minutes or until the meat is quite tender. Transfer the chops to a platter and keep warm.

Add the remaining mustard to the pan, and reduce the sauce to a syrupy consistency. Off the heat, stir in the sour cream, and pour the sauce over the chops. Garnish with optional dill or chives.

SERVES 4.

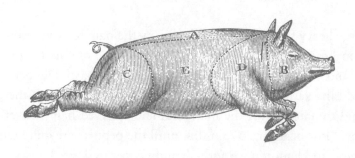

Pork Shoulder Braised in Bock

This simple but delicious way to cook smoked or fresh pork is typical of ethnic neighborhoods in American cities and comes to us from Maria Cecchini, an Italian cooking teacher and author.

Good cuts of meat to use are smoked picnic, fresh Boston butt, or fresh pork shoulder. Serve it with our Horseradish Mustard or prepared horseradish and a full-bodied Bock like Berghoff Bock or Gartenbrau Bock. You should save the stock to make bean, lentil, or vegetable soup.

1 smoked picnic, fresh pork shoulder, or Boston butt, 6–8 pounds
2 12-ounce bottles lager
6 cups water
3 bay leaves
3 whole cloves
2 whole allspice
10 whole black peppercorns
2 teaspoons salt
2 whole onions, unpeeled
2 ribs celery
12 small new potatoes
1 head cabbage, quartered
Beer and Horseradish Mustard (see page 219)

Put the meat in a large pot, and add the beer and water to cover. Add more liquid in the ratio of 2 parts water to 1 part beer, if needed. Put in the bay leaves, spices, onions, and celery, and bring to a boil. Reduce to a simmer, and cook, partially covered, until the meat is tender. Smoked picnic should take 1½–2 hours; fresh pork shoulder or Boston butt 2–3 hours. When it is done, remove the meat and keep it warm. Remove and discard the onions and celery. Cook the potatoes and cabbage in the stock in the pot until the potatoes are tender, about 20 minutes. Remove the fat from the outside of the meat, slice the pork, and serve on a platter with the vegetables arranged around the edge. Serve with the mustard.

SERVES 8-12, DEPENDING ON THE CUT OF MEAT USED.

Pork Tenderloin Brined in Beer

Pork tenderloin is lean, very tender, and takes well to a light brining. Once brined, it can be pan fried, or cooked on a grill. The loin is not in the brine long enough to become very salty, but it takes on a succulent flavor from the beer, sage, and citrus oils.

Try this dish with Garlic and Horseradish Mashed Potatoes,* Pineapple Sauerkraut,* or other braised sauerkraut dishes. Sliced cold, the cooked tenderloins make wonderful sandwiches, especially with our Tavern Pickled Onions* and Honey Beer Mustard.* Serve with Sprecher Amber or Berghoff Bock.

1 quart water	1 teaspoon dried sage
1 quart dark beer	Peel of 1 tangerine
1 cup salt	Peel of 1 lemon
½ cup brown sugar	4 whole pork tenderloins
1 tablespoon whole black pep-	(about 3–4 pounds in all)
percorns	
⅓ cup crushed fennel seeds	

Place all the ingredients, except the pork, in a large pot, bring to a boil, and then reduce to a simmer. Stir until the salt and sugar are dissolved, then simmer an additional 5 minutes. Transfer the brine to a nonreactive container, cool, and refrigerate.

When the brine is quite cool (less than 50° F.), add the pork tenderloins, and place a heavy plate on top of them to keep them submerged. Marinate the pork in the refrigerator for 3 days. Then remove the pork, wash, and pat dry. It will keep 2 days in the refrigerator before cooking.

Grill the tenderloins to an internal temperature of 160° F. or pan-fry them whole, turning frequently, until done, 10 to 12 minutes. Cut each tenderloin into thick slices on the diagonal. Each tenderloin should serve 2 people.

SERVES 6–8.

*See Index.

Great Goulash

Like most stews, this goulash is best prepared a day ahead, and it makes great leftovers. Cook up a big batch, and freeze it in dinner-size portions for later use when unexpected guests drop in. It's marvelous served over noodles, spaetzle, or parsley potatoes with a glass or two of Dark Lager like Leinenkugel Bock or Samuel Adams Double Bock. Don't forget a hunk of brown bread.

1½ pounds smoked sausage, such as kielbasa or paprika sausage, sliced into ½-inch rounds

1 pound beef stew meat, cut in 2-inch cubes

1½ pounds pork shoulder butt, cut in 2-inch cubes

Salt and pepper

3 onions, thinly sliced

4 garlic cloves, chopped

2 red bell peppers or fresh pimientos, thinly sliced

1 carrot, diced

6 tablespoons sweet Hungarian paprika

1 cup beef or Rich Chicken Stock (see page 203)

1 cup Dark Lager

2 teaspoons caraway seeds

1 bay leaf

½ teaspoon dried marjoram

¼ cup tomato purée

1 pound sauerkraut, drained

1 cup sour cream

Brown the sausages over medium heat in a large Dutch oven or casserole for 5 minutes. Remove with a slotted spoon and reserve. Add the meats to the fat in the pot. Sprinkle with salt and pepper, and brown the chunks on all sides for 5 minutes. Remove and reserve. Add the onions, cover the pot, and cook until the onions brown, about 20 minutes, stirring frequently. Put in the garlic, red bell pepper, and the carrot. Cook for 2 minutes. Stir in the paprika until the vegetables are well coated. Add the stock, lager, caraway seeds, bay leaf, marjoram, tomato purée, and sauerkraut. Bring everything to a boil. Reduce to a simmer, and add the meats and one quarter of the sausage for flavor. Simmer, uncovered, for 1¾ hours, until the meat is tender. Add the remaining sausage, and cook 15 minutes more. Degrease the sauce. Remove solids, boil it down if necessary until it is syrupy. Remove the pot from the heat, add back solids, and stir in the sour cream. Serve at once with homemade spaetzle or noodles.

SERVES 8.

Red Cabbage Braised in Cider and Beer

This sweet-and-sour red cabbage is peppier than the usual version of the classic Eastern European accompaniment to roast goose, pork, or venison. The combination of beer and cider provides a wonderful balance to the cabbage, onions, and apples. A malty Octoberfest beer would be a good match: Try August Schell Oktoberfest or Kemper Festbier from Washington. This easy-to-make dish is best prepared a day ahead and rewarmed before serving.

4 tablespoons (½ stick) butter
2½ pounds red cabbage,
  shredded or thinly sliced
½ medium onion, sliced
2 cups grated Granny Smith
  apples
1 tablespoon sugar
2 tablespoons cider vinegar
⅓ cup chicken stock

3 bay leaves
½ teaspoon freshly ground
  black pepper
½ teaspoon whole caraway
  seeds
½ bottle Dark Lager
½ cup apple cider
Salt

Melt the butter in a large pot or Dutch oven over medium heat. Add the cabbage and onion, cover, and cook until the cabbage has wilted, stirring occasionally. Stir in all the remaining ingredients, and cook, uncovered, until the cabbage is quite tender, about 30 minutes, stirring from time to time. Remove the bay leaves. Taste for salt and serve.

SERVES 6 AS A SIDE DISH.

Brussels Sprouts with Bacon and Beer

Don't turn your nose up. Brussels sprouts can be wonderful! They just have to be fresh and not overcooked. Most stores keep sprouts until they are too old, stinky, and bitter. The best time of year to buy sprouts is in the early fall, when they are at their freshest, and, if you are lucky, you might be able to find them still on the stem.

This is a very nice side dish with turkey, roast pork, or grilled chicken. Oktoberfest-style lagers are terrific with Brussels sprouts; the sweet malt and bitter hop undertones meld nicely with the earthy tang of the sprouts.

¼ pound thinly sliced bacon,
   cut into shreds
1 tablespoon olive oil
1 small onion, thinly sliced

1 pound Brussels sprouts,
   trimmed and thinly sliced
¼ cup beer
Salt and pepper

Cook the bacon in a large skillet over medium high heat until it begins to crisp. Pour off all but 1 tablespoon of the fat. Add the olive oil and onion, and cook for 5 minutes. Put in the sprouts and the beer, and cook for 2–3 minutes, until most of the beer is absorbed.

SERVES 4–6.

Wild Rice and Corn Crepes

These crepes make a great side dish with roast chicken or duck, braised meats and stews, and just about anything with mushrooms in it. The nutty flavors of wild rice go beautifully with dark beers like Samuel Adams Winter Lager or Coors Winterfest. If you're lucky enough to live close to Madison, Wisconsin, Capital Brewery's Gartenbrau Wild Rice lager is a rare treat and perfect with any wild rice dish.

This recipe comes from Nancy Oakes, Bruce's wife, and chef-owner of L'Avenue Restaurant in San Francisco.

6 eggs, beaten
6 tablespoons butter, melted
1 cup or more milk
½ cup cornmeal
½ cup flour
1 cup cooked wild rice (directions follow)

4 green onions or scallions, thinly sliced
1 cup fresh or frozen corn kernels
Salt and pepper
Peanut or olive oil

Mix together the eggs, 4 tablespoons of the melted butter, and the milk. Gradually stir in the cornmeal and flour. Stir in the cooked wild rice. Sauté the green onions and corn in the remaining 2 tablespoons of butter over medium heat for 2 minutes. Add to the batter, which should have the consistency of thin pancake batter. Add more milk if needed. Heat a 7-inch nonstick pan over medium-high heat, and brush with the oil. Pour in enough of the batter to cover the bottom of the pan. Cook 2–3 minutes until the bottom is lightly browned. Turn the crepe over and cook 1 minute more. Serve at once.

MAKES 12–15 CREPES, SERVING 6–8.

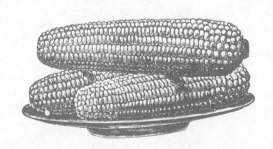

TO COOK WILD RICE

The California Wild Rice Program recommends the following method for cooking wild rice:

Add 1 cup wild rice and a pinch of salt to 3 cups boiling water. Return to a boil, reduce to a simmer, cover the pot, and cook 35–45 minutes until the kernels have burst and the rice is tender. Minnesota wild rice might require longer cooking: 50–60 minutes.

MAKES 3–4 CUPS COOKED RICE.

Spinach Torte

By itself, this flavorful spinach casserole makes a satisfying lunch with a salad and a Dark Lager like Sprecher Winterbrew. The raisins provide a hint of sweetness, which balances nicely with the light bitterness and malty flavors of a full-bodied lager. Cut into serving pieces, the torte makes an excellent side dish with lamb, game, or veal.

4–5 bunches spinach (3–4 pounds), washed well, cooked, and squeezed dry, or 3 boxes (10 ounces each) frozen spinach, thawed and squeezed dry
2 cups finely chopped onion
2 garlic cloves, minced
½ cup chopped raisins
½ teaspoon dried sage
¼ teaspoon nutmeg
½ teaspoon dried marjoram
1 teaspoon black pepper
1 teaspoon salt
¾ cup olive oil
6 eggs, beaten
1½ cups plain bread crumbs
½ cup freshly grated Parmesan cheese
¼ cup pine nuts (optional)

Preheat the oven to 325° F. In a large bowl combine the first 11 ingredients with 1 cup of the bread crumbs. Place in a greased 9- × 13-inch baking dish. Sprinkle with the remaining ½ cup bread crumbs, the Parmesan cheese, and optional pine nuts. Bake for 1 hour until the spinach is firm and a knife inserted comes out clean. Cut into 3-inch squares.

SERVES 8–10 AS A SIDE DISH; 4–6 AS A LUNCHEON DISH.

Curried Cauliflower

Curry and beer go particularly well together, especially crisp, light lagers such as Augsburger or Erlanger. This spicy cauliflower dish is an excellent accompaniment to roast or barbecued lamb and is a delicious stand-alone vegetarian main course.

3 tablespoons butter
1 large onion, thinly sliced
2 medium carrots, sliced into rounds
4 garlic cloves, chopped
1 2½–3-pound cauliflower, separated into florets
2 tablespoons paprika
2 teaspoons whole cumin seeds
1 teaspoon coriander
1 teaspoon powdered ginger
1 teaspoon turmeric
4 fresh or canned tomatoes, peeled, seeded, and chopped
1 cup plain yogurt
Salt and pepper
Tabasco
Cilantro sprigs for garnish (optional)

Heat the butter in a large high-sided skillet or Dutch oven over medium heat. Put in the onion and carrots, and cook, covered, for 5 minutes. Stir in the garlic, cauliflower, and spices. Cover and cook for about 10 minutes. Stir in the tomatoes and yogurt along with a pinch of salt and pepper. Cover and cook 15 more minutes until the cauliflower is quite tender. (The yogurt will curdle, but that is okay.) If the sauce is a bit watery, remove the solids with a slotted spoon and boil the sauce until it just thickens. Put back the solids, and cook a minute to rewarm. Taste for salt and pepper; if you'd like a bit more heat, add Tabasco. Serve with rice, and garnish with the optional cilantro.

SERVES 6–8.

SAUERKRAUT

Most of us aren't lucky enough to live in a neighborhood where homemade sauerkraut can be found in German, Polish, or other East European delis. And even though canned or bottled sauerkraut is sold in the supermarket, it just isn't the same as the homemade version. Sauerkraut packed in jars or canned is good enough in its own way, but lacks the richness and flavor of the home-fermented product.

And maybe that's the key—fermentation. Homemade sauerkraut is naturally fermented cabbage with no vinegar or preservatives other than salt added. It is the product of a lactic acid fermentation and is pleasingly tart but not mouth-puckeringly sour, as some of the commercial products are.

Sauerkraut is a wonderful food to have with beer. Its slightly sour flavors balance the malt sweetness and pick up the bitterness of the hops, making both the beer and the food taste better. Sauerkraut and beer enhance the flavors of the other elements of a meal. Smoked meats, poultry, winter vegetables, potatoes—all seem to perk up when cooked and eaten with sauerkraut and beer.

Making sauerkraut at home in small quantities is a relatively simple process, and if you store the finished kraut in the refrigerator, you needn't worry about getting involved in canning or preserving. On the other hand, if you are a home gardener with lots of cabbage ready for harvesting or would like to put up larger quantities of homemade kraut, *The Joy of Cooking* gives detailed instructions for making and canning sauerkraut.

Sauerkraut is simply salted cabbage that produces its own brine. The salt draws some of the sugars out of the cabbage, which friendly bacteria use to produce lactic acid, carbon dioxide, and other flavorful by-products. The result of the fermentation is the tart cabbage we call sauerkraut, which means "sour cabbage" in German.

Sauerkraut has many uses. Briefly heated, it is the ideal accompaniment to sausages or smoked meats; cold, it can be used to make innovative salads. For a mild flavor, cook sauerkraut for an hour or so, adding a little beer to the pot as it cooks. Even without any other flavorings, this makes an excellent side dish.

Cooked with pork, smoked or fresh (see Country Spareribs

and Sausages Braised with Sauerkraut and Dark Lager*),
sauerkraut becomes a true beer feast, and cooked together with
fresh cabbage in beer (see Sauerkraut and Cabbage in Amber
Lager*), it makes an interesting and unusual vegetable dish to
accompany grilled or roast meat or poultry.

The best container to make small quantities of sauerkraut in
is a 3- to 5-gallon plastic tub with a lid. You can find these in
hardware stores, restaurant supply houses, or your local deli (ask
if you can buy the tubs foods like pickles and olives are sold in
wholesale). If you do use a recycled tub or bucket, be sure it was
used before for food, and not glue, paint, putty, or other non-
food products.

The key to successful sauerkraut, as in all fermentations, is to
make sure everything is very clean. If you have a dishwasher, run
the bowls, tubs, spoons, and other utensils you are going to use
through a full cycle or wash them by hand with lots of soap and
hot water before starting.

Cabbage picked late in the season is preferred by kraut-mak-
ers for its higher sugar content, but you can make excellent
sauerkraut any time with cabbage bought from the supermarket.

*See Index.

Homemade Sauerkraut

12½ pounds (about 5–6 heads)   ½ cup kosher or pickling salt
fresh cabbage

Trim away the outer leaves of the cabbage, and wash the cabbage thoroughly. Cut each head into quarters and cut away the core. Using a
large sharp knife, kraut shredding board (available at hardware stores
in German or Polish neighborhoods), or food processor fitted with the
thinnest slicing blade, cut the cabbage into thin shreds about the thickness of a penny, or thicker if you desire.

In a large stainless steel bowl or plastic dish tub sprinkle half the cabbage with ¼ cup of the salt, and mix well with your hands. Let the cabbage stand for 5 minutes; juices will begin to come out of the salted

kraut. Pack and press the cabbage into the fermenting tub; more juices will form as you pack the cabbage firmly down in the tub. Repeat the same process for the remaining cabbage and salt. The packed cabbage should be 4 or 5 inches from the top of the tub.

The cabbage must be covered by juice to prevent mold or spoilage. If there is not enough juice to cover, make up some additional brine by dissolving 3 tablespoons of salt in 8 cups of tap water. Pour in just enough to cover the cabbage, and save any leftover brine.

To keep the cabbage submerged in the brine during fermentation, it must be weighted down. The easiest way to do this is to fill a large Ziploc bag with brine to use as a weight. The bag must fit tightly against the inside of the tub to keep air from the surface of the kraut. If one bag is not enough, use two or three. Place plastic wrap over the top of the tub, and put a clean terry cloth towel over the wrap. Secure the towel with twine or elastic around the top of the tub, and don't open until the fermentation is almost over (see below).

Ideal temperatures for fermentation are between 65° or 75° F. The warmer the temperature in the area where you place the tub, the sooner the fermentation will be completed. Don't let the temperature get above 75° F., however, as warmer temperatures can encourage spoilage. This is why making sauerkraut has always been a fall activity—a way to preserve the summer's harvest for the oncoming winter at a time when the temperature is just right for fermentation.

At 65° F., the fermentation should take 5 weeks; at 70° F. about 4 weeks, and at 75° F. about 3 weeks. Remove the towel and plastic wrap. There should be no bubbles of CO_2 evident in the brine, even when the tub is gently tapped. If fermentation is still going on, cover, and check again in a day or two. The best procedure is to start checking the kraut after 3 weeks or so, depending on the ambient temperature of the storage area.

The sauerkraut should have a yellow-white appearance with no white spots. White spots, unpleasant or off odors, a brown or pink color, or a very soft texture indicate improper fermentation. Discard the kraut, clean everything thoroughly, and start over. This doesn't happen very often, however, and is usually a result of improper sanitation and/or too much heat.

The sauerkraut can be packed into small containers or jars, and stored in the refrigerator. Refrigerated it will keep for at least 6 months. For instructions on canning kraut, consult *The Joy of Cooking*. Our recipe makes about 4–6 quarts sauerkraut.

Pineapple Sauerkraut

A traditional sweet-and-sour side dish with ham, this easy-to-make recipe is also splendid with roast duck or chicken.

2 pounds sauerkraut, prefer-
    ably homemade
4 cups unsweetened pineapple
    juice
½ teaspoon black pepper

2 whole cloves
1 2-pound ripe pineapple,
    peeled, cored, and cut into
    ¾-inch cubes

Drain the kraut, and taste it. If it is too sour, wash it under cold running water, and squeeze dry. In a heavy nonreactive pot mix the kraut with the pineapple juice, pepper, and cloves, and bring to a boil. Stir with a fork to separate individual shreds. Reduce the heat to a simmer, cover, and cook for 1½ hours. Most of the liquid should be absorbed by the cabbage. Check the pot from time to time to time. If the liquid is gone, add more pineapple juice or water. Stir in the fresh pineapple cubes, and cook for 2–3 minutes until heated through. Drain and serve.

SERVES 6–8 AS A SIDE DISH.

Sauerkraut and Apple Salad

Serve this nippy salad as a side dish for a barbecue or picnic.

1 pound sauerkraut, preferably
    homemade
1 cup peeled diced tart apple
1 cup grated carrots (about 2
    carrots)
¼ cup finely sliced green
    onions or scallions

¼ cup salad oil
1 teaspoon caraway seeds
1 teaspoon sugar
Salt and pepper

Drain the kraut and taste it. If it is too tart, wash it under cold running water and squeeze it dry. Mix together the kraut, apple, carrots, and green onions. Toss well with the oil, caraway seeds, and sugar until completely mixed. Season to taste with salt and pepper, and serve.

SERVES 4-6.

Beer and Horseradish Mustard

Beer and mustard seem made for each other, especially when you use beer as the main liquid to blend with the pungent seeds. If the horseradish in this recipe makes the mustard too hot for your taste, just leave it out. If, on the other hand, like us you prefer your mustard on the fiery side, load it up with more. This coarse-grained mustard is particularly good on corned beef or smoky sausages like our Fresh Beer Sausage.*

¼ cup whole brown mustard seeds

¼ cup whole yellow mustard seeds

1 cup lager

⅔ cup red wine vinegar

¼ teaspoon ground allspice

1 teaspoon coarsely ground black pepper

1 teaspoon minced garlic

4 tablespoons prepared horseradish

2 teaspoons sugar

1 teaspoon salt

Mix both mustard seeds, ½ cup of the lager, and the red wine vinegar in a small bowl, and let stand at room temperature for at least 3 hours. Put the mixture in a blender, and add the remaining ingredients. Process to a coarse consistency. Scrape the mixture into the top of a double boiler. Stir the mustard over simmering water for 5–10 minutes until it begins to thicken, but is not quite as thick as commercial prepared mustard. Scrape the mustard into a jar, and let cool. It will thicken as it cools. If the mustard seems too thick after cooling, thin it down with a teaspoon or so of additional beer or vinegar. Cap the jar, and store the mustard in the refrigerator where it will last indefinitely.
MAKES 2 CUPS.

*See Index.

Gingerbread Stout Cake

Rick Rodgers, an accomplished baker and New York food writer, gave us this recipe for some of the most delightful gingerbread we've ever tried. It's great cold and keeps well, but if you can be organized enough to serve it warm, it rises to new heights. Try it with a bit of whipped cream flavored with a little Stout (about 1 tablespoon per 1 cup whipping cream with sugar to taste) and some crushed candied ginger (about 1 teaspoon). Serve it with some of the Stout used in the recipe: Sierra Nevada Stout or Hart Sphinx Stout from Washington.

Butter and flour for the baking pan

2½ cups all-purpose flour

2 teaspoons powdered ginger

2 teaspoons cinnamon

2 teaspoons baking soda

½ teaspoon cloves

½ teaspoon salt

1 cup (2 sticks) unsalted butter at room temperature

1¼ cups packed light brown sugar

2 large eggs at room temperature

1 cup molasses

¾ cup Stout, flat, at room temperature

Confectioners' sugar for garnish

Preheat the oven to 350° F. Butter and flour well a 12-cup fluted cake pan, such as a Bundt pan. Sift together all the dry ingredients.

Using a hand-held mixer set at high, beat the butter and sugar in a large bowl until light in texture, about 1 minute. Beat in the eggs, one at a time. Beat in the molasses (the batter may look curdled at this stage—don't worry). Lower the mixer speed to medium. Beat in the flour mixture, one third at a time, scraping down the sides of the bowl often. Beat in the Stout.

Scrape the batter into the prepared pan, and smooth the top. Bake until a toothpick inserted in the center comes out clean, 50–60 minutes. Cool in the pan on a wire cake rack for 10 minutes, then unmold onto the rack. Eat warm or cool completely. Dust with confectioners' sugar before serving.

SERVES 8–12.

The Northeast: Neighbor-hood Bars, Blind Pigs, and the Friday Fish Fry

Caponata

Crostini

Good Chopped Chicken Liver

Broccoli Soup

Leek and Cabbage Soup

Ziti and Smoked Sausage Salad

Fried Oysters I

Fried Oysters II

Fried Shrimp

Fried Calamari (Squid)

Fried Clams

Edy's Fried Fish (With Beer Batter I)

Fried Fish (With Thin Beer Batter II)

Tempura (With Beer Batter III)

Onion Rings

Audrey's New Hampshire Codfish Cakes

Lobster Rolls

Marinated Mussels

Clams or Mussels Steamed in Beer

Sicilian Stuffed Peppers

Maria's Pasta and Eggplant in Beer

Italian Chicken with Pasta, Anchovies, and Tomatoes

Bollito Misto

Salsa Verde

Cotechino Sausage with White Beans

Corned Beef or Pastrami Boiled in Beer

Corned Beef or Pastrami Hash

Nancy's Spicy Meat Loaf with Beer Gravy

Spicy Beer 'N Beef Gravy

Braised Lamb with Leeks and Ale

You can still see them in old Polish and Irish neighborhoods in Brooklyn and Philly, South Boston and Buffalo. Their neon signs gleam on dark streets, define the street corners. The name of the owner comes first: Ryan's, Pete's Place, Flo's, George & Eddie's. Sometimes another line offers a specialty: Dancing, Fish Fry, Fried Shrimp, Good Eats, Hofbrau. In some cities you find one every block or so. In others, urban renewal, the flight to the suburbs, and gentrification have left just one or two for old neighborhood regulars.

The neighborhood bar has been one of the centers of social life in Eastern cities from the early 1900's down to the present day. Bar owners offered liberal credit (even though the signs said otherwise), cashed paychecks, organized Friday-night fish fries, weekend clambakes, Memorial Day picnics, softball teams, and parties for weddings, wakes, and first communions. Tavern owners were substantial citizens, pillars of the church, important people with an in at City Hall, connections with the local alderman, the union, and the neighborhood precinct house.

Neighborhood bars provided local beer on tap, hard liquor, good food cooked by the proprietor or his wife, and a meeting place where people could come together for enjoyment, relaxation, and to transact much of the business of everyday life. If you needed a plumber or electrician, most of the time you didn't consult the Yellow Pages. You simply asked at the bar or left word you needed some work done. If you

World Series fans in 1952.

wanted to get your nephew on the cops or needed somebody to talk to the rent board, you asked the publican to have a word with Alderman Reilly or Councilor Winczeski. In a well-run establishment, the beer was cold and the taps clean, the bar well polished, the liquor unwatered, the patrons relatively sedate, and the advice generally sound.

Verlyn Klinkenborg has chronicled such a neighborhood tavern in Buffalo in his warm and evocative book *The Last Fine Time* (Knopf, 1991). He traces the history of George & Eddie's, the bar owned by his father-in-law Eddie Wenzek and Eddie's Polish-born father and mother. Filled with rich social history and minute details of life in the Polish neighborhoods of Buffalo, the book describes the evolution of the urban bar from the early blind pigs, illegal joints that served moonshine and needled beer in back rooms, to the upscale leatherette and Formica night spots of the late 40's and early 50's.

Klinkenborg also gives us a picture of how beer and food were an integral part of everyday life in urban America. The first thing that strikes you is the sheer number of local beers available. In the old days every city had many different local breweries, some providing beer for only one neighborhood or ethnic group. Deliveries of kegs and bottles were made every day, and the rumble of the beer trucks each morning was a part of

New York saloon scene.

the waking-up ritual along with milk trucks, the iceman, and wagons hawking produce through the streets.

Beer drinkers had real choices in the days before the big nationals consolidated American brewing in the huge Midwestern brewing centers. Klinkenborg, who delights in lists of long-gone products and their slogans, tells us that in Buffalo alone the thirsty tavern-goer could find: Simon Pure Beer from the William Simon Brewery ("To be sure, drink Simon Pure"), Duquesne Pilsner ("Have a Duke"), Phoenix Imported Danish Yeast Beer, Iroquois Beer, Ballantine's Ale, Schreiber's Manru Beer, and brews from the Christian Weyand Brewing Company, George Rochevot Lion Brewery, Gerhard Lang's Park Brewery, Magnus Beck Brewing Company, Schreiber's Brewery, Ziegele Brewing Company, George F. Stein Brewery, Schusler Brewery, Gilbert Klinck Brewery, the Mohawk Brewery, The Great Lakes Brewery, the Broadway Brewing Company, and the Consumer's Brewery.

For kids and those ladies and gents who wanted something lighter, there was Vernor's Ginger Ale, Birch Beer on draft (a Cincinnati was a popular mix of birch beer and lager), O-So Grape Drink, Upper 10 Lime Lemon Soda, and Doctor Swett's Early American Root Beer ("Rich in Dextrose").

The food was hearty: soups (see our Leek and Cabbage Soup*), meat

*See Index.

and potatoes (see our Corned Beef or Pastrami Boiled in Beer*), and homemade sauerkraut (see Sauerkraut*) cooked in the back kitchen by Mrs. Wenzek in the early days; then there were grilled steaks (see Marinating and Grilling, page 155) and fried shrimp (see Deep Frying Seafood and Vegetables, page 240) after the bar and restaurant were redone in gleaming Naugahyde by young Eddie in 1947 or so.

The Friday-night fish fry has long been a tavern tradition in Catholic neighborhoods all up and down the Eastern Seaboard. The happy combination of the weekly paycheck and the prohibition against eating meat on Friday led many a family to spend the evening feasting on batter-fried fresh fish, shrimp, clams, and oysters at the neighborhood tavern. (see our Three Beer Batters*). Washed down with mugs of local beer or soft drinks, the crunchy seafood was usually accompanied by cole slaw (see Peanut Slaw*), potato salad (see Warm Potato Salad with Beer Dressing*), or crisp fried potatoes (see Bay Wolf BBQ Potato Chips*). Each tavern had its own special sauce such as our Spicy Tartar Sauce* or Creamy Horseradish Cocktail Sauce* to accompany the fried foods.

Certain taverns and neighborhoods developed other specialties. One of the most famous, Buffalo chicken wings, was invented in a neighborhood tavern in Buffalo in the late 1940's or early 1950's. For this popular bar snack, chicken wings are liberally sprinkled with hot pepper sauce, deep fried, and served with celery sticks and blue cheese dressing on the side. Fried chicken wings are quintessential beer food, spicy and easy to eat with one hand while holding a beer mug in the other (see our Adobo Chicken Wings*). Other flavorful bar snacks include Beer and Blue Cheese Croutons,* Popcorn with Parmesan and Garlic,* and Sweet and Spicy Nuts.*

In Italian neighborhoods, bars often provided food for picnics, festivals, and saint's days, offering appetizers like Crostini,* Sicilian Stuffed Peppers,* and more substantial

*See Index.

"Beer boy" carrying pails of draft beer in New York in the early 1900's.

D. G. Yuengling & Son Brewery, Pottsville, Pennsylvania—America's oldest continuously operating brewery.

dishes like Italian Chicken with Pasta, Anchovies and Tomatoes,* or Maria's Pasta and Eggplant in Beer* with kegs of local beer.

While most neighborhood taverns today serve only national brands on tap or in bottles, a great many are taking advantage of the microbrewery revolution and expanding their selection of draft and bottled beers. Virtually every big city has at least two or three small breweries producing handcrafted beers and ales, and the spread of contract brewing (see Introduction), has widened the choice of beers considerably. In addition, a few of the old regional breweries have survived, and, like Anchor in the West, they are finding a new market of sophisticated, knowledgeable beer drinkers interested in quality.

One regional brewery with a great talent for survival is D. G. Yuengling & Son of Pottsville, Pennsylvania. Founded in 1829, Yuengling is the oldest continuously operating brewery in the United States and is still controlled by the family of the original founder, David Yuengling. At first the brewery made ale and "common beer," but it was one of the first American breweries to switch over to lager making in the 1840's.

Yuengling survived Prohibition and the virtual elimination of small regional breweries, and now produces about 200,000 barrels of premium beer. Its most popular beer is Yuengling Premium, a full-bodied malty lager with a light gold color, a nice touch of hops, and fresh, clean flavors. This crisp lager complements flavorful pasta dishes like our Ziti and Smoked Sausage Salad* or Spicy Italian Chicken with Pasta.*

Yuengling Porter with its deep amber/brown color, undertones of

*See Index.

coffee and roasted malt, and pleasant lingering bitterness is one of the better American dark beers. We especially like it with richly flavored dishes such as Chopped Chicken Liver Sandwich* or Cornish Hens in Stout.* The brewery's Lord Chesterfield Ale is a pale gold light ale with fruity malt aromas nicely balanced by a good bite of hops. It makes a fine match with Fried Clams* and Fried Oysters,* especially when they are dipped in a zesty sauce like our Creamy Horseradish Cocktail Sauce* or Spicy Tartar Sauce.* Yuengling's beers are fairly priced and can be found throughout the East and in many national markets.

Another survivor of the great twentieth-century consolidation of breweries is Straub Brewery of St. Mary's, Pennsylvania. Producing today about 40,000 barrels, the brewery was founded in 1872 and makes two beers—a medium-bodied light lager, Straub Beer, and Straub Light. The pale gold lager is brewed from barley malt and untoasted cornflakes and undergoes a long, slow fermentation (six to seven weeks), which produces a relatively high alcohol level and a very dry finish. Try a light fresh lager like this with our spicy Marinated Mussels* or Fried Clams.* The brewery also produces an excellent Light Beer with more character and flavor than most; its delicate taste goes nicely with Tempura* and other lightly fried foods.

Jones Brewing Company of Smithton, Pennsylvania, twenty-five

*See Index.

Delivery wagons at Yuengling & Son, late nineteenth century.

miles south of Pittsburgh, was founded by William B. "Stoney" Jones, a Welsh immigrant, in 1907. Originally his beer was called Eureka Gold Crown beer, but immigrant miners had trouble pronouncing it—they simply asked for "Stoney's Beer." Today the brewery's best-selling beer is called Stoney's, a light-bodied, malty lager popular in the Pittsburgh area. Jones Brewing also makes Stoney's Light Beer and Esquire Extra Dry Beer, recently rated the top domestic dry beer by *The New York Times*. Both are well made, crisp, and smooth, with more flavor than most national light and dry brews.

The Pennsylvania Brewing Company, founded in 1986, was one of the first microbreweries in the state and produces a popular amber lager, Penn Pilsner, full bodied, malty, with delicate hop flavors. German brewmaster Alexander Deml is a graduate of the Brewing Institute at Weihenstephen and concentrates on Bavarian-style lagers. He also makes a light, Helles-style beer, Penn Light Lager, along with Penn Dark and Kaiser Pils, pale gold and crisp, with plenty of hop bitterness in the finish. These malty, German-style lagers are especially good with complex flavorful dishes like our Braised Lamb with Leeks and Beer.*

The Philadelphia Brewing Company/Samuel Adams Brewhouse is a small brewery/brew-pub in the center of Philadelphia that specializes in English- and colonial American-style ales. It features Ben Franklin's Golden Ale, crisp, light, and floral, Poor Richard's Amber Ale in the English style, and George Washington Porter, modeled on the dark ale brewed in Philadelphia that was Washington's favorite tipple. Traditional ales like these are delicious with colonial favorites, such as Pickled Oysters* or Lobsters Boiled in Light Ale.*

An excellent Amber Ale is offered by Dock Street Brewing Company of Bala-Cynwyd, Pennsylvania, a contract brewery that distributes nationwide. The copper-colored ale, made at F. X. Matt in upper New York State, is full bodied and creamy, with rich malt flavors pleasantly balanced by light hops. Amber ale provides a pleasing undertone of flavor to piquant seafood dishes like our Marinated Mussels.*

Stoudt Brewery of Adamstown, Pennsylvania, produces lagers in the German tradition: Golden Lager, made with five different roasted barley malts and a blend of German hops; Octoberfest Marzen, a malty, red-dish-amber lager; Weizen, an unfiltered, refreshing wheat

*See Index.

West End Brewing Company, Utica, New York.

beer; Raspberry Weizen, the same beer fermented with fresh red raspberries; and Adamstown Amber Ale, a full-flavored Bitter-style ale.

The largest family-operated regional brewery in America is Genesee Brewing Company of Rochester, New York. Founded in 1878, the 2½ million-barrel brewery distributes its beers in twenty-six states and is available in most national markets. Genesee Beer is a full-bodied, pale malty lager with light hop flavors and a pleasant finish. Genesee Bock is a dark version of this beer, medium amber in color with round, roasted malt aromas. Genesee Cream Ale is a light, smooth ale, slightly sweet, with hints of hops and a pleasant balance overall. Genesee Twelve-Horse Ale has a deep gold color, rich flavors, and a good blend of hops and malt—one of the better ales made by a large production brewery in the United States. Cream ales are a true American creation: light ales that are particularly good with piquant appetizers such as Crostini* spread with Caponata,* or a Tuna Caponata Sandwich.*

F. X. Matt of Utica is another regional brewery that has survived in upstate New York. Originally named the West End Brewery (because it served Utica's West End) in 1888, it now brews a wide range of beers under its Utica Club and Matt's labels. Saranac Adirondack Lager is an all-malt lager made exclusively with two-row barley malt and American Cascade and German Hallertau hops. It is lagered longer than most American beers, and carbonation is achieved naturally by *kräusening,*

*See Index.

the addition of freshly fermenting beer rather than the common CO_2 injection method in American breweries. The lager is pleasantly balanced with malt sweetness offset by lightly bitter hop flavors. We think this excellent American lager makes a fine match for that favorite tavern fare: Corned Beef or Pastrami Boiled in Beer* with pungent Horseradish Mustard.*

Matt's Premium was voted the top Pilsner-style lager at the 1984 Great American Beer Festival and is brewed in small quantities to ensure freshness and flavor. Matt's Light is a clean Light Beer, pleasant and easy to drink, and Utica Club Pilsener is a dry, light-bodied lager, smooth and mildly hopped. Utica Club Cream Ale is a light ale with characteristic fruity ale flavors balanced by moderate hop bitterness.

F. X. Matt also produces beer and ale for many of the region's contract brewers, making each brew according to the formula created by the individual proprietors. Some of the contract brews made at Matt include Brooklyn Lager and Brown Ale, Dock Street Amber Ale, Cleveland's Erin Brew, Harpoon Lager and Ale, Manhattan Gold, Montauk Light, Albany Amber, New Amsterdam Beer and Ale, Old Heurich, and Portland Lager. F. X. Matt's beers are generally available all over the region, and its contract brews can be found in many Eastern markets.

The Manhattan Brewing Company is a thriving brew-pub that opened in 1984 in Manhattan's SoHo section. It serves freshly brewed ales and lagers in its restaurant/brewery gleaming with copper kettles and polished oak. In addition to draft beers served in the pub, it distributes Manhattan Gold Lager in bottles throughout the greater New

York area. Manhattan Gold Lager is a pale gold Pilsner-style lager, malty, full in body, and refreshingly dry. Like the best European Pilsners, the beer has a pronounced fragrance from Czechoslovakian Saaz hops, with enough malt to balance significant hop bitterness. Its rich, dry flavors make it a natural to accompany Clams or Mussels Steamed in Beer.*

Located in the historic Park Slope neighborhood, Brooklyn Brewery aims to revive a long tradition of brewing in the borough. Currently offering two beers

*See Index.

Early New York breweries. The old Schaeffer's Brewery is below.

made according to pre-Prohibition recipes at F. X. Matt, the owners plan to open their own brewery soon. Brooklyn Lager is a deep gold beer with a hoppy, yeasty aroma, rich body, and creamy head and mouth feel. It has just enough flavor to stand up to Sicilian Stuffed Peppers.* Brooklyn Brown Ale blends two-row crystal, chocolate, and black malts for a complex, satisfying malt flavor. It is one of the few American ales that are dry hopped, resulting in a full-blown hoppy bouquet balanced by malt aromas. Try this full-flavored Dark Ale with Nancy's Spicy Meat Loaf* and Spicy Beer 'N Beef Gravy.* Both beers are naturally *kräusened* for a pleasantly creamy feel in the mouth.

Old New York Brewing Company was the first contract brewer in America and has its New Amsterdam Amber Lager and New Amsterdam Ale made to its specifications at F. X. Matt of Utica. Brewed at a high original specific gravity of 1.050 (see Appendix I, How Beer Is Made) the Amber Lager has rich malty flavors and great balance. New Amsterdam Ale is dry hopped for an intense floral aroma with Cascade

*See Index.

hops, the hop flavors marrying nicely with malt. A hoppy ale like this is a pleasant match for that favorite bar snack, Fried Onions Rings.*

Long Island Brewing's Montauk Light is a premium Light Beer with only 105 calories per bottle, but with the taste of a traditionally brewed beer. Made at F. X. Matt the light lager is smooth and dry, lightly hopped and very drinkable—a pleasant beer to have with crisp Fried Shrimp* with Rémoulade Sauce.*

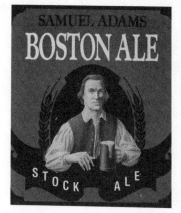

Brewing in New England goes back to colonial days, and microbreweries, contract brewers, and brew-pubs are thriving throughout the region these days. One of the most successful small breweries in the country is the Boston Beer Company that produces Samuel Adams lagers and ales. Founded by Jim Koch in 1985 as a contract brewery, Boston Beer now has its own production facility in the old Haffenreffer Brewery in Boston, and also has beers made at other locations around the country to ensure freshness and timely delivery.

Samuel Adams beers are widely available all over the United States and represent a real revolution in brewing and marketing in this country. They offer excellent quality at good prices and provide beer lovers with a line of distinctive American beers that can compete successfully with most imports. In fact, Samuel Adams Boston Lager was the first American beer to pass the Bavarian Purity Law (*Reinheitsgebot*) that allows beer to be sold in Germany.

Koch comes from a long line of brewers and makes his flagship beer, Samuel Adams Boston Lager, using one of his great-grandfather's recipes. The full-bodied Amber Lager employs a traditional German decoction mash (see Appendix I, How Beer Is Made) for full malt flavors and is dry hopped with German hops for added fragrance. It is a high-gravity brew similar in character to Pilsner Urquell, the great Bohemian lager. We think it makes a fine companion to that New England Friday night special, codfish cakes (see Audrey's New Hampshire Codfish Cakes*).

Samuel Adams Double Bock is brewed only once a year in the spring and is a full-bodied, medium Dark Lager in the Munich-Maerzen tradition. Very rich in the mouth, it is quite strong (7.2 percent alcohol) and heady, with great depth and a lingering malty finish. Samuel

*See Index.

Adams Octoberfest is brewed only in late summer and is aged for two months before release. Reddish-amber in color from the large amounts of roasted crystal and caramel malt, it is full bodied, malty, and powerful. Samuel Adams Winter Lager is a dark wheat Bock with full body and spicy flavors, while Boston Lightship is a light lager with a refreshing mild malt and hop character.

Samuel Adams Boston Stock Ale is a high-gravity, strong Amber Ale with extra malt providing body and sweetness, and English ale hops (Fuggles and Kentish Goldings) giving it a pleasantly bitter undertone. It is one of the best American ales made in the English style available in national markets.

Harpoon Ale is Massachusetts Bay Brewing Company's main product, bottled and sold throughout New England. The brewery also offers Golden Harpoon Lager, Harpoon Oktoberfest Ale, and Harpoon Winter Warmer Ale in its brew-pub. Commonwealth Brewing produces 4,000 barrels of ale, available on draft and bottled, in English and traditional New England styles. The light ale, called Blonde Ale, is very popular at the Boston brew-pub, where they also offer Boston's Best Burton Bitter made in the English Bitter style along with Amber Ale, Gold Ale, and Special Old Ale.

Catamount Brewing of White River Junction, Vermont, was one of the first microbreweries in New England and produces ales based on classic American and British styles. Its Catamount Gold Ale is based on the traditional ales of old New England, pale in color with lightly roasted malts and a crisp hoppy finish. An old-fashioned light ale like this complements the delicate flavors of New England Lobster Rolls.* Catamount Amber is modeled on British India Pale Ale, using roasted crystal malt for color and flavor and with a high hop level. Catamount Porter, in the style of early British and American Porters, uses heavily roasted malts to achieve its dark color and hearty flavors. Dark beers like this are excellent paired with robust dishes like our Cotechino with White Beans* or Bollito Misto.*

Catamount is expanding its production to 10,000 barrels this year, and contract brews for two small New England breweries. It makes Old Post Road Real Ale for the Old Marlborough Brewing Company

*See Index.

of Massachusetts and Frank Jones India Pale Ale for D. Jones Limited in New Hampshire.

Post Road Real Ale is described by the brewery as a "classic tavern ale," and is a copper-colored, well-balanced ale with generous hop flavors and a good malty finish. Frank Jones India Pale Ale is amber in color with a crisp, hoppy character balanced by smooth malt flavors. These hearty ales are just the thing to have with a spicy Meat Loaf and Pickled Onion Sandwich.*

Other Eastern breweries include New Haven Brewing, specializing in English-style ales, Connecticut Brewing with its Nathan Hale Golden Lager, and New England Brewing, which produces a unique amber colored beer, Atlantic Amber. Hope Brewing in Rhode Island, Mountain Brewers, and D. L. Geary in Vermont, and Clement Brewing in New Jersey are also making first-rate, small-production ales and lagers.

The scene in the eastern United States is one of creative ferment with micros, brew-pubs, and many contract brewers reviving traditional American ales and lagers and making exciting beers in the English and Continental styles. If you don't find the exact beer described in your area, try a similar type. You should be able to find plenty of beers with real character in a wide range of styles just about anywhere along the Eastern Seaboard these days.

*See Index.

Caponata

This spicy Sicilian eggplant and caper relish is traditionally served with crostini, toasted Italian bread rounds (recipe follows), but it is equally delicious layered with fontina or provolone, Italian cold cuts, and thinly sliced onions on French bread in a fantastic hero sandwich. Caponata also can be used to make a piquant tuna sandwich (see page 282) or pasta salad.

With this zesty appetizer we like a hoppy ale such as Old New York Brewing Company's New Amsterdam Ale or Samuel Adams Boston Stock Ale. This recipe was provided by Marlene Levinson, Bay Area cooking teacher.

1 medium eggplant, about
   1 pound, unpeeled and cut
   into ¾-inch cubes
Salt
¾ cup olive oil or more,
   if needed
2 cups diced celery
2 cups chopped onions
⅓ cup red wine vinegar
1 teaspoon sugar
2 large tomatoes, peeled,
   seeded, and diced (about
   2 cups)

2 tablespoons capers, drained
½ cup sliced pimiento-stuffed
   green olives (4-ounce
   bottle)
2 anchovy fillets, chopped
   (optional)
3 tablespoons finely chopped
   parsley
1 teaspoon fennel seeds
Pepper

Toss the eggplant cubes generously with salt, and drain in a colander in the sink for at least 30 minutes. In a large frying pan heat ¼ cup of the olive oil over medium heat. Put in the celery and onions, and, stirring frequently, cook until the vegetables soften, about 10 minutes. Remove the onion/celery mixture from the pan and set aside.

Wash the eggplant well under running water, and pat dry with paper towels. Reheat the skillet over medium heat, add the remaining olive oil, and cook the eggplant, stirring occasionally, until it is lightly browned and each piece is quite soft, about 10–15 minutes.

While the eggplant is cooking, mix together the vinegar, sugar, and tomatoes in a small saucepan. Bring to a boil, and simmer until a smooth sauce forms. If the sauce seems too thick, add a little water. Add the cooked onion/celery mixture to the eggplant. Pour the tomato sauce over all, and add the capers, olives, optional anchovies, parsley, and fennel seeds. Simmer over low heat for 20 minutes, adding more water if the caponata begins to dry out. Season with salt and pepper to taste, and refrigerate until cool. Caponata is best made a day ahead, and will keep, covered, in the refrigerator for 5–6 days.

SERVES 4–6 AS AN APPETIZER.

Crostini

Crostini are often found at Italian-American parties and picnics. They are basically toasted French or Italian bread rounds with savory toppings. Crostini are spicy and flavorful, and great snacks with light beers like Utica Club or Genesee Cream Ale.

The recipe below is for basic crostini. To make garlic crostini, add 1 clove minced garlic to the oil. For cheese crostini, sprinkle each bread round with grated Parmesan. You can also add chopped herbs to the oil or some finely chopped Greek or Sicilian olives. Plain or garlic-flavored crostini can be topped, after toasting, with anchovies, freshly grilled or salted, roasted peppers, Caponata (see preceding recipe), or fresh goat cheese.

1 25-inch baguette   Pinch salt
½ cup olive oil

Preheat the oven to 375° F. Using a serrated knife, cut the bread into ¼-inch rounds or diagonal slices. Brush each slice liberally with olive oil, sprinkle with salt, and place on a baking sheet. Bake until golden brown and crisp, about 10 minutes. Let cool before adding toppings.

MAKES ABOUT 40 ROUNDS.

Good Chopped Chicken Liver

Chopped chicken liver is simple and delicious—it's a fine match for a flavorful Pale Ale like Ballantine India Pale Ale.

The key to great chopped liver is to use impeccably fresh chicken livers and to pay close attention to the cooking of the onions. We used the traditional schmaltz *(rendered chicken fat, available in the kosher food sections of most urban supermarkets), but corn oil margarine also works well if you want to tone down the cholesterol.*

¾ cup rendered chicken fat (*schmaltz*) or corn oil margarine
1½ pounds onions, roughly chopped

Salt and pepper
1 pound fresh chicken livers
Griebenes (chicken skin cracklings left over after rendering *schmaltz*) (optional)

Heat ¼ cup of the *schmaltz* or margarine in a heavy skillet over medium heat. Add the onions, and sprinkle lightly with salt and freshly ground pepper. Cover the pan. Cook the onions, stirring frequently, until they develop a rich brown color, about 20 minutes. Regulate the heat so the onions don't burn. Transfer to a large bowl. Adjust the heat under the pan to medium, and add ¼ cup of the *schmaltz* or margarine. After any sputtering subsides, put in the chicken livers, and sprinkle lightly with salt and pepper. Cook for about 5 minutes, or until they begin to brown. Turn the livers, and cook them until they are just firm to the touch, and are still slightly pink on the inside. Add the livers, along with any pan juices and the optional *griebenes* to the onions. When they are cool, add the remaining ¼ cup *schmaltz* or margarine, and grind everything through the medium (¼- or ⅛-inch) plate of a food grinder. Mix well, and season with salt and pepper to taste. Pack tightly into a bowl just large enough to hold the chopped liver, cover with plastic wrap, and refrigerate until firm. Serve as an hors d'oeuvre with dark rye rounds or as a sandwich.

To make sandwiches: Spread the chopped liver on rye bread, cover with thinly sliced red onions, and serve with kosher-style dill pickles. Whatever you do, don't put any mayonnaise on your chopped liver sandwich: That is sacrilege and would call down the wrath and derision of any self-respecting Second Avenue deli counterman.

SERVES 8 AS AN HORS D'OEUVRE; ENOUGH FOR 6 SANDWICHES.

Broccoli Soup

Italian cooks take broccoli to great heights, using this flavorful (and healthful) vegetable in a mind-boggling variety of ways from soup to pasta, pizza to salad. Here is a simple and delicious soup that combines broccoli's earthy taste with aromatic Italian sausage, tomatoes, and pasta. Try this with garlic bread or bruschetta and a full-bodied lager, such as Yuengling Premium. The soup makes a rich and filling meal, with only a small amount of meat.

½ pound mild Italian sausage removed from casing
¼ cup diced smoked ham or prosciutto
1 tablespoon olive oil
4 tablespoons chopped garlic
4 cups Rich Chicken Stock (see page 203)
2 fresh tomatoes, peeled, seeded, and chopped
3 cups coarsely chopped broccoli, with tough part of stems removed
2 cups elbow macaroni
Pinch nutmeg
Salt and pepper
Freshly grated Parmesan cheese

Brown the sausage and ham or prosciutto in the olive oil over medium heat in a Dutch oven or heavy pot for about 5 minutes, crumbling the sausage meat with a fork. Put in the garlic, and cook for 1 minute. Add the chicken stock and chopped tomatoes. Bring to a boil, reduce the heat, and simmer for 5 minutes. Put in the broccoli, macaroni, nutmeg, salt and pepper, and cook 10 minutes until the macaroni is done to your taste. Taste for seasonings. Degrease the soup, and serve immediately with freshly grated Parmesan cheese.

SERVES 4–6.

Leek and Cabbage Soup

This satisfying soup is great for brunch, lunch, or dinner. Use a good-quality smoked kielbasa or other full-flavored smoked sausage. A robust ale will underline this hearty soup's smoky, earthy flavors. Try Brooklyn Brown Ale or Old Post Road Ale.

1½ quarts beef stock or Rich Chicken Stock (see page 203)

1 12-ounce bottle ale

1½ pounds beef stew meat, cut into 1-inch cubes

1 ham hock

3 sprigs fresh thyme or 1 teaspoon dried

¼ pound salt pork, diced

1 large onion, thinly sliced

3 medium leeks, split, well rinsed, and thinly sliced

2 carrots, coarsely chopped

4 medium red potatoes, cut into 1-inch dice

2 pounds quartered and sliced cabbage

1 bunch Swiss chard, leaves only, sliced

¾ pound smoked kielbasa, cut into ½-inch rounds

Salt and pepper

Sour cream

2 tablespoons chopped fresh thyme or parsley

Bring the stock and ale to a boil in a large soup pot. Add the stew meat, ham hock, and thyme. Reduce the heat to a simmer, and cook for 1½ hours. Meanwhile, render the fat from the salt pork in a heavy skillet over medium heat. Add the onion and leeks, and cook them, covered, for 10 minutes, stirring occasionally. Add the onions, leeks and salt pork to the soup pot, along with the carrots, potatoes, cabbage, and chard. Cook for 15 minutes. Remove the meat from the ham hock, chop it, and return it to the soup. Fry the sausage in a heavy skillet for 5 minutes to render some of the fat. Transfer the sausage to the soup, and cook everything for 10 minutes more. Test the vegetables to make sure all are tender. Adjust seasonings. Serve the soup garnished with sour cream and the chopped fresh thyme or parsley.

SERVES 8–10.

Ziti and Smoked Sausage Salad

This zesty, easy-to-prepare salad makes a great lunch or light dinner with an assertively flavored ale like Dock Street Amber or Frank Jones Ale.

1 pound smoked sausage,
  such as kielbasa, linguiça,
  or andouille, sliced
1 pound ziti or other tubular
  pasta cooked *al dente*
1 red bell pepper, fire-roasted,
  peeled, and chopped (see
  page 251) or 1 cup
  chopped jarred pimiento
4 tomatoes, cut into wedges

½ pound small zucchini,
  thinly sliced
1 cup chopped parsley
¼ cup freshly grated Parmesan
  cheese
1 teaspoon each of chopped
  fresh rosemary, oregano,
  and basil
1 cup Mustard Vinaigrette
  (see page 271)

Sauté the sausage in a frying pan, using a little oil if necessary, over medium-high heat for 5 minutes to render the fat. Drain, and combine in a large bowl with the remaining ingredients. Toss well with the vinaigrette, and serve at room temperature.

SERVES 6.

DEEP FRYING SEAFOOD AND VEGETABLES

Beer has always been the preferred beverage to drink with fried food. Tavern-owners have long been aware of this and frequently offer an array of deep-fried bar snacks. They also often host Friday-night fish fries. Buffalo chicken wings, fried eggplant and zucchini, fried seafood (shrimp, oysters, and clams), and various types of fried potatoes are all common items on tavern and brew-pub menus all over America.

And deep-fried food is very popular, even with today's health-conscious diners. Fried food does not have to be heavy, greasy, and high in cholesterol. If done well, deep-fried foods are light and virtually greaseless, and the use of pure vegetable oils largely eliminates saturated fats and cholesterol.

With the proper care and preparation, deep-fried beer-battered seafood, fish, onion rings, potatoes, and other fresh vegetables can be feather-light, crisp, and delicious. The key to great deep frying is using fresh high-quality vegetable oil and maintaining the proper temperature at all times. For those who wish to do a lot of frying, a wise purchase might be one of the many home-style electric deep fryers. Some models have covers to reduce spattering, filters to keep down odors, and thermostats for maintaining a constant temperature.

Frankly, though, most of the best fried foods we've eaten were cooked in stove-top pots fitted with makeshift baskets. All you need is a good-sized heavy skillet, a basket or Chinese strainer, and a candy thermometer to monitor the temperature of the oil.

The ideal temperature range for deep frying is 350°–375° F. If the oil gets much below this range, it will penetrate the coating and make the food greasy and heavy. If it goes much higher, the food will burn on the outside but remain raw inside. Food fried within the correct range will come out crisp, light, and not at all greasy.

In order to keep the temperature of the oil from dropping drastically when food is added, you need to have plenty of oil, enough to completely submerge the food. On the average, the oil should be about 3–4 inches deep. Cook the food in small batches so the temperature is not affected radically, and always adjust the heat to maintain the right temperature range. Here the candy thermometer becomes indispensable.

Use oils that are low in saturated fats and cholesterol, such as canola, peanut, corn, or safflower oil. And don't reuse oil. The high heats required for deep frying break the oil down, leading to off flavors.

Deep frying is a last-minute process. In order that the coating doesn't become gummy, food should be battered or breaded right before frying. And fried food does not reheat well or taste very good when allowed to cool.

Most fried foods are coated with flour, bread crumbs, or batter, which acts as a barrier between the oil and the food and adds the crispy exterior that makes fried food so desirable.

Another reason fried foods are so popular is that they lend themselves to a tremendous variety of dipping sauces. We provide some with our recipes and make suggestions for other sauces you may wish to improvise.

Fried Oysters

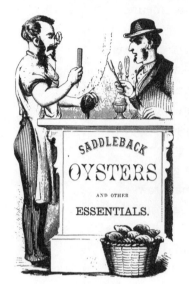

Some of the greatest beer and food combinations involve fried oysters: oyster loaves and Dixie Beer in the bars near the Irish Channel in New Orleans; fried oysters with tartar sauce and Anchor Steam Beer on the docks by San Francisco Bay; batter-fried oysters and hot cocktail sauce with cold mugs of Shaeffer's lager at Brooklyn's Sheepshead Bay; baskets of crisp fried Wallapa Bay oysters and Ballard Bitter in Seattle's Pike Place Market.

Many regions of the country have their own favorite ways to fry oysters, but all the best methods seem to involve finely ground cornmeal called corn flour (called Fish Fry in Louisiana), a fine flour made from dried corn. Corn flour can often be found in health food stores or from Cajun and Creole food suppliers (see Appendix IV, Mail Order Sources).

Here are a couple of our favorite recipes for fried oysters.

Fried Oysters I

⅓ cup cornmeal
⅓ cup flour
⅓ cup cornstarch
½ teaspoon salt
1 teaspoon finely ground black
  pepper

1 teaspoon paprika
½ teaspoon cayenne
2 dozen medium shucked
  oysters
1 cup buttermilk
Vegetable oil for deep frying

In a shallow bowl or on a plate mix together all the ingredients, except the buttermilk, oysters, and oil. Put the buttermilk in a bowl and dip each oyster in it, then in the seasoned flour mixture. Shake off the excess. Heat vegetable oil to a depth of 3–4 inches to 360°–375° F. In it fry 6 oysters at a time for 3–4 minutes, or until golden. Drain on paper towels.

SERVES 4 AS A BAR SNACK OR APPETIZER.

Fried Oysters II

1½ cups corn flour (see head-
    note above), or 1 cup flour
    plus ½ cup cornmeal
½ teaspoon salt
1 teaspoon finely ground black
    pepper

½ teaspoon cayenne
2 dozen medium shucked
    oysters

Mix the flour and spices together, and dredge each oyster in the mixture to coat. Shake off excess, and fry as above.

SERVES 4 AS A BAR SNACK OR APPETIZER.

Fried Shrimp

*Like oysters, shrimp take well to cornmeal-based coatings. Try the coating
in Fried Oysters I (see page 242) or this one.*

1 egg
1 cup milk
2 cups corn flour (see head-
    note above), or 1 cup flour
    plus 1 cup corn meal
2 teaspoons paprika
1 teaspoon salt

1 teaspoon finely ground black
    pepper
1 teaspoon dried thyme
2 pounds peeled large raw
    shrimp
Oil for deep frying

Beat the egg and milk together in a bowl. In a separate bowl mix the
corn flour or cornmeal/flour combination with the spices and thyme.
Heat the oil to a depth of 3–4 inches to 360°–375° F. Dip each shrimp
into the egg/milk mixture, then dredge it in the seasoned flour. Shake
off any excess, and fry 12 or so shrimp at a time about 5 minutes, until
golden brown, taking care to maintain the temperature of the oil.
Remove the shrimp and drain on paper towels. Serve with our Creamy
Horseradish Cocktail Sauce (see page 50) or Spicy Tartar Sauce (see
page 128).

SERVES 6–8 AS A BAR SNACK OR APPETIZER.

Fried Calamari (Squid)

Squid cut into rings or strips is best simply coated with flour and corn-starch, then fried, although you may want to experiment with either our Fried Oyster I coating (see page 242) or one of the Beer Batter recipes (see pages 246 and 247).

We like fried squid best with just some fresh lemon juice squeezed over it, but tomato-based marinara sauces, garlic fried in olive oil with lemon, and, of course, Spicy Tartar Sauce (see page 128) are all delicious. Nancy Oakes, San Francisco chef and Bruce's wife, likes to toss fried squid in a mixture of grated orange rind, orange juice, chopped jalapeño peppers, and cilantro for a Southwestern touch.

Light lagers seem to go best with fried squid, especially if you are serving a picante dipping sauce. Try Berghoff-Huber Light or Yuengling Premium Light.

2 pounds medium squid
1 quart vegetable oil, such
    as canola, corn, or peanut,
    for deep frying
1 cup flour
1 cup cornstarch

1 teaspoon salt
2 teaspoons finely ground
    black pepper
½ teaspoon cayenne
Lemon wedges
Dipping sauce

To clean squid, separate the body from the head and tentacles. Cut the tentacles just below the eye, and discard the heads. Make sure the beak is removed and discarded. Pull off the fins and purple film from the outside of the body. Pull out the quill and the milky film from inside the body sack. Wash thoroughly inside and out under cold running water. Cut the body into ½-inch rings or ¼-inch strips and dry quite well on paper towels.

Heat 1 bottle (25–32 ounces) of vegetable oil (to a depth of 3–4 inches) in a 4-quart heavy pot or deep skillet. Bring the temperature of the oil to 360° F. In a bowl or on a plate mix the flour and cornstarch with the salt and spices. Roll a handfull of the squid in the seasoned flour, shake off any excess, and lower a batch of squid into the oil in the pot. Adjust the heat if the temperature of the oil goes to either side of 360° F. Fry for 1–2 minutes, until the squid pieces are lightly golden. Squid should be crisp and only slightly chewy. Fry the squid in batches, removing it as it is done with a slotted spoon or Chinese strainer. The squid is best served immediately, but you can keep batches warm on a paper towels on a platter in a 200° F. oven until the cooking is completely done. Serve with the lemon wedges or a dipping sauce.

SERVES 4–6 AS BAR SNACK OR APPETIZER.

Fried Clams

If you are fortunate enough to live in a part of the country where freshly shucked frying clams are available, you already know how great they are fried. In New England, you'll want to purchase freshly shucked soft-shell clams. In the Northwest, try razor clams. Don't use frozen clams, cherrystones, or pismo clams, as they get too tough when fried.

You can fry the clams using the Fried Shrimp recipe (see page 243) or Fried Oysters I (see page 242), or you can use the following method, popular in New England. Serve with our Spicy Tartar Sauce,* lemon wedges, and cold light lager or Wheat Beer with a lemon slice added.

2 pounds shucked frying clams, picked over for shells	1 teaspoon salt
2 cups milk	2 teaspoons finely ground black pepper
2 cups corn flour, or 1 cup flour plus 1 cup johnnycake meal or other cornmeal	½ teaspoon cayenne
	Vegetable oil for deep frying

Soak the clams in the milk. Mix together the corn flour or the flour and cornmeal and spices in a shallow bowl. Drain the clams, and toss a handful into the seasoned flour. Shake off any excess. Heat oil to a depth of 3–4 inches to 360°–375° F. and in it fry the clams for 12 minutes, until lightly golden. Drain on paper towels and eat at once, or keep warm in a 200° F. oven until ready to serve.

SERVES 6–8 AS APPETIZER OR BAR SNACK.

*See Index.

Fried Fish

For small thin pieces of fish—catfish fillets or sole strips—we suggest using the batter for Fried Oysters I (see page 242) or the one for Fried Shrimp (see page 243). For larger pieces of fish suitable for the classic accompaniment to English-style ales, fish-and-chips, try one of the beer batters listed below.

For best results, use skinless fillets. Good varieties for frying are cod, rock cod, halibut, tilefish, hake, haddock, thresher shark, or grouper. Serve fish-and-chips with Spicy Tartar Sauce (see page 128) and malt vinegar.

Edy's Fried Fish (With Beer Batter I)

2 pounds skinless fish fillets	1 teaspoon finely ground black pepper
1 egg	1 teaspoon salt
1 cup lager	½ teaspoon cayenne
2 tablespoons vegetable oil	Vegetable oil for deep frying
1¼ cups flour	

Cut the fish into pieces about 4 inches long by 2 inches wide. In a bowl mix together the egg, lager, and the 2 tablespoons oil. Stir in the flour and spices until smooth. The batter should be a little runny.

Heat 3–4 inches of vegetable oil in a heavy pot to 350°–360° F. Drop each piece of fish into the batter and pick it up with your fingers or with a slotted spoon, allowing any excess batter to drip back into the bowl. Gently place each piece of fish in the hot oil. Do not overcrowd; cook the fish in batches. Turn the fish as it cooks, so that it browns evenly on all sides. Remove when the fish is golden brown, about 5–7 minutes. Drain on paper towels.

SERVES 4, WITH 2–3 PIECES PER SERVING.

Fried Fish
(With Thin Beer Batter II)

This batter is also great for onion rings. It makes enough for 3 large onions, cut into ¼-inch rings.

2 pounds skinless fish fillets
1 egg
2 tablespoons vegetable oil
1 cup lager
1 cup flour
1 teaspoon baking powder

1 teaspoon finely ground black pepper
½ teaspoon cayenne
½ teaspoon salt
Vegetable oil for deep frying

Prepare the fish and beer batter as directed in the above recipe. This batter is a bit more runny than the first one and gives a lighter result. Cook as directed above.

SERVES 4.

Tempura (With Beer Batter III)

This eggless batter renders the lightest and crispiest results on fried shrimp, shellfish, mushrooms, eggplant, asparagus, zucchini, and other firm vegetables. The secret, as with pancake batter, is not to overmix it. To see lumps of flour is okay, and you should use the batter immediately after mixing the wet and dry ingredients together lightly.

The following recipe makes enough batter for 3 pounds of shrimp, and 2–3 pounds of vegetables, enough to feed 6 hungry beer drinkers as a snack or appetizer.

1¼ cups flour
1 teaspoon salt
1 tablespoon finely ground black pepper

½ teaspoon cayenne
1 12-ounce bottle lager beer, cold
Vegetable oil for deep frying

In a bowl mix together the flour, salt, pepper, and cayenne. Quickly whisk in the beer until the ingredients are just barely blended. Lumps of flour are not to be worried about. Heat the oil to 360° F. Dip seafood or vegetable pieces into the batter and fry a few at a time until golden brown.

SERVES 6.

Onion Rings

This simple recipe makes some of the best onion rings we've ever tasted. The key is to soak the raw onion rings in yogurt before breading and frying. Some people use buttermilk to soak the rings, but yogurt works even better because it is thicker and makes the flour stick better.

½ pint plain lowfat yogurt
2 cups flour
1 teaspoon salt
1 teaspoon finely ground black pepper

½ teaspoon cayenne
1 teaspoon paprika
3 large onions, cut and separated into ¼-inch rings
Vegetable oil for deep frying

Spoon the yogurt into a medium bowl. If it seems too thick, stir in a little water. Combine the flour and spices in another bowl. In batches soak the onion rings in the yogurt. Remove and shake off any excess. Dredge the rings in the seasoned flour, shaking off any excess before frying. Heat vegetable oil to a depth of 3–4 inches to 360°–375° F. and in it fry the rings in batches, until golden brown, about 2–3 minutes. Drain on towels and eat at once.

SERVES 6–8 AS BAR SNACK OR APPETIZER.

Audrey's New Hampshire Codfish Cakes

Audrey Oakes grew up in rural New Hampshire and learned this simple but popular family recipe from her mother. Audrey passed it on to her daughter, Bruce's wife, Nancy, who showed us how make these savory codfish cakes.

In Audrey's family, they always ate codfish cakes with poached eggs as a brunch or simple supper. With a Spicy Tartar Sauce (see page 128) and some sliced lemons, these cakes also make a delicious appetizer or bar snack with a hoppy ale such as Catamount Gold Ale or Yuengling Lord Chesterfield Ale.

Audrey says the secret to her codfish cakes is that she cooks the cod and potatoes together and that she rolls the cakes in packaged pancake mix. Crumbled saltine crackers also make an excellent coating.

1 pound boneless skinless salt cod fillets

½ pound Russet or other baking potatoes, peeled and quartered

1 cup finely chopped onion

4 tablespoons butter, softened

½ cup finely chopped parsley

1 egg

2 egg yolks

Salt and pepper

Vegetable oil for frying

Packaged pancake mix or fine saltine cracker crumbs

To prepare the salt cod: Put the codfish fillets in a bowl and wash them under cold running water for 10 minutes. Cover with cold water and place in the refrigerator overnight. Pour off the water and add new water to cover 3 or 4 times. The fish should be soft, with most of the salt removed. Drain and dry, and cut the fillets into 1-inch chunks.

Bring 2 quarts water to a boil in a saucepan. Add the salt cod, potatoes, and onion, and reduce to a simmer. Cook until the potatoes are tender, about 20–25 minutes. Drain off the liquid, and put the fish, potatoes, and onion in a bowl. Add the butter, and mash with a fork. The mixture should not be smooth, but should have a somewhat coarse texture. Stir in the egg and egg yolks until thoroughly blended. Taste, and season with salt and pepper. Form the mixture into small disk-shaped cakes about ¾ inch thick and 2–3 inches in diameter (or smaller for bar snacks). You may refrigerate them at this point for up to 5 hours in advance.

When ready to serve, heat about ¼ inch of vegetable oil in a heavy skillet. Roll the cakes in the pancake flour or fine cracker crumbs, and fry over medium heat 2–3 minutes per side or until nicely golden brown. Serve at once.

SERVES 4 FOR LUNCH; 6–8 AS AN APPETIZER OR SNACK.

Lobster Rolls

Traditionally in New England, where lobster is plentiful, leftover lobster is dressed with mayonnaise and stuffed into lightly toasted hot dog buns. Sometimes green onions, celery, and other ingredients are added, but the key here is to keep the flavorings simple, so the rich taste of the seafood shows through.

If you're not lucky enough to have lobster leftovers, you can easily substitute shrimp or cold poached scallops. With this delicious and elegant sandwich drink Massachusetts Bay Brewing's Golden Harpoon Lager or Samuel Adams Lightship Light Pilsner.

2 cups diced cooked lobster
meat, or 2 cups chopped
diced cooked shrimp or
scallops
2 tablespoons chopped parsley
1 rib celery, cut into ¼-inch
dice (optional)
1 green onion or scallion,
thinly sliced (optional)

⅓ cup mayonnaise
2 teaspoons fresh lemon juice,
or to taste
A few drops Tabasco, or to
taste
Salt and pepper
4 fresh hot dog buns

Mix together the lobster or other seafood with the parsley, optional celery and scallion, and the mayonnaise. Season with the lemon juice, Tabasco, and salt and pepper. Open each hot dog bun up, without completely separating the halves, and lightly toast it. Divide the lobster salad among the rolls and serve.

SERVES 4.

Marinated Mussels

Marinating mussels in their shells creates a dish that looks spectacular on the table, and also makes diners remove the mussels from the shells themselves, thus slowing down consumption, which can get out of hand with this delightful seafood.

The mussels make a wonderful appetizer or party snack when served with a full-flavored ale.

1 recipe Mussels Steamed in Beer (recipe follows)
½ cup diced jarred pimientos or fire-roasted red bell peppers (see below)
1 cup finely chopped red onion
1 cup diced tomatoes
¼ cup roughly chopped capers
½ cup chopped parsley
½ cup chopped fresh basil
2 teaspoons minced garlic
1 teaspoon dried red pepper flakes
¼ cup red wine vinegar
½ teaspoon salt
½ teaspoon freshly ground pepper
½ cup olive oil

Place the cooked mussels in their shells in a large bowl. Toss in all the chopped vegetables and herbs, except the garlic. In a small bowl mix together the garlic, red pepper flakes, vinegar, salt, and pepper. Gradually stir in the olive oil. Pour the vinaigrette over the mussels, and toss well until the mussels are well coated, and the vegetables are well distributed throughout. Transfer to a large platter, and serve at once.

SERVES 6–8 AS AN APPETIZER.

FIRE-ROASTING AND PEELING PEPPERS

To fire-roast and peel fresh peppers (bell peppers, pimientos, chiles), roast the peppers under a broiler or over an open flame until the skin is blistered and charred. Put the peppers into a plastic or paper bag for 15 minutes to steam. Scrape the skin off under running water. To prepare dried chiles, soak in hot water until soft and puree in a food processor with enough water to make a thick sauce.

Clams or Mussels Steamed in Beer

Both clams and mussels taste great when steamed briefly in beer with seasonings like garlic, herbs, and peppers. You can also use this method to steam small oysters. The key to success is cleaning the shellfish well and purging them of any sand.

To prepare clams or mussels, scrub them thoroughly with a stiff brush under cold running water. Remove the beards from mussels. Place the shellfish in a large bowl, cover with cold water, and throw in 2–3 handfuls of flour or cornmeal. Refrigerate for at least 4 hours or overnight. The shellfish will filter-feed on the flour, purging themselves of sand and excess salt in the process. Before cooking, drain and rinse the shellfish under fresh cold running water. Discard any clams, mussels, or oysters that open before cooking.

Clams good for steaming are cherrystones, littlenecks, soft shells, or steamers. Serve with plenty of bread for sopping up the juice, and full-bodied lagers like Nathan Hale Golden Lager or Samuel Adams Boston Lager.

Save any leftover mussels to make Marinated Mussels (see preceding recipe).

1 bottle lager
4 garlic cloves, chopped
1 onion, coarsely chopped
2 bay leaves
½ teaspoon dried red pepper flakes
1 tablespoon whole black peppercorns
2 tablespoons chopped fresh herbs, such as thyme, basil, or chervil, or 2 tablespoons chopped fresh parsley
2 tablespoons fresh lemon juice, or more to taste
4 pounds mussels; 8 pounds littleneck or cherrystone clams; or 6 pounds small oysters, cleaned (see directions above)
4 tablespoons butter

In a large pot or Dutch oven with a tight-fitting lid mix the beer with the garlic, onion, spices, herbs, and lemon juice. Bring to a boil, add the shellfish, being careful not to break the shells, and cover tightly. After 5 minutes over high heat, check the shellfish. They should all be completely open and cooked through. If not, cover, and cook 1–2 minutes more. Clams like cherrystones with thicker shells will take longer than thin-shelled littlenecks or mussels.

Remove the shellfish and carefully strain the broth, taking care that any sand remains in the pot. Stir the butter into the broth until melted and taste for lemon. Heap the shellfish in a large bowl or deep platter, and serve the broth on the side for dipping, sopping up bread, or drinking.

SERVES 6–8 AS AN APPETIZER; 4 AS A MAIN COURSE.

Sicilian Stuffed Peppers

The sweet and salty taste of these peppers is great with a full-flavored ale such New Haven Brewing's Elm City Golden Ale. The peppers are ideal as a side dish or as a main course for lunch or a light dinner with an onion/orange salad and focaccia. *The stuffing also works well with small fish, such as sardines, herrings, or smelts.*

6 red or green bell peppers	½ cup raisins
2 cups croutons, preferably homemade (see page 198)	¼ cup chopped parsley
	1 tablespoon ale
2 garlic cloves, minced	Salt and pepper
12 anchovy fillets, minced	6 tablespoons olive oil
½ cup pine nuts	

Preheat the oven to 350° F. Halve the peppers lengthwise and seed them. Bring a large pot of lightly salted water to a rolling boil, and add the peppers. Reduce the heat, and simmer for 5 minutes. Drain and pat dry. Lay the peppers in an oiled baking pan, cut sides up. Mix together the croutons, garlic, anchovies, pine nuts, raisins, parsley, and ale, and season to taste with salt and pepper. Stuff the peppers with the mixture, and sprinkle the top of each with some of the olive oil. Bake for 30 minutes. The peppers are wonderful hot out of the oven or cooled to room temperature, but they don't refrigerate well. You can, however, prepare them the day before up to the baking stage, refrigerate, and bake them before serving.

SERVES 12 AS APPETIZER; 6 AS A MAIN COURSE.

Maria's Pasta and Eggplant in Beer

This family favorite comes to us from Italian cooking teacher Maria Cecchini. The easy-to-make dish provides a quick and satisfying dinner when served with a salad and a glass of lager.

½ cup olive oil
1 medium eggplant, about
   1 pound, peeled and diced
Salt and pepper
6 ounces smoked ham, cubed
1 cup lager
1 teaspoon chopped fresh rosemary or ½ teaspoon dried

1 cup fresh or frozen peas
1 pound large tubular pasta
   such as *penne* cooked
   according to the directions
   on the package
Freshly grated Parmesan
   cheese

In a large skillet heat the olive oil over medium heat. Put in the egg-plant, and season with salt and pepper. Cook, stirring, for about 10 minutes, until it becomes soft. Stir in the ham, and fry 2 minutes. Add the lager and rosemary, and bring to a boil. Reduce the liquid by half. Put in the peas, reduce to a simmer, cover, and cook for 2 minutes. Stir the cooked pasta into the sauce, and cook for 30 seconds to heat through. Transfer to a serving bowl, sprinkle with plenty of Parmesan cheese, and serve.

SERVES 4–6.

Italian Chicken with Pasta, Anchovies, and Tomatoes

Contrary to the image of the ubiquitous glass of red wine, beer is a popular drink in Italy and at Italian-American gatherings. Try this zesty chicken over your favorite pasta, along with a green salad with marinated onions, plenty of crusty French bread, and a lively lager like Utica Club Pilsener.

1 can (2 ounces) anchovy
  fillets
2 ounces pancetta or Italian
  bacon, chopped
2 cups diced onion
3 garlic cloves, chopped
½ pound mushrooms, sliced
2 cups canned crushed
  tomatoes in puree
1 cup Rich Chicken Stock
  (see page 203)
1 cup dry white wine

½ cup oil-cured pitted
  black olives
1 teaspoon dried basil or
  1 tablespoon chopped fresh
3 cups cooked chicken, cut
  into 2-inch pieces, or
  1½ pounds chicken livers,
  cleaned and separated
  into lobes
¾ pound dried pasta of
  choice, cooked to taste

Drain the oil from the anchovies into a large deep skillet or heavy Dutch oven. Add the pancetta and cook over medium heat until the fat has rendered, about 5 minutes. Pour off all but about 2 tablespoons of the fat. Add the onion, garlic, and mushrooms, and cook 5 minutes. Add the tomatoes, stock, wine, olives, and basil. Bring to a boil, and reduce the heat to a simmer. Cook, uncovered, for 20 minutes, stirring occasionally. Chop the anchovy fillets finely, and add them to the sauce, which should be getting slightly syrupy. If not, turn up the heat to reduce some of the liquid. Add the chicken meat. (If you are using chicken livers, sauté them first in olive oil until firm but still pink, then add them to the sauce.) Cook for 5 minutes. Serve the sauce over the pasta.

SERVES 4–6.

Bollito Misto

This wonderfully hearty dish is similar to pot-au-feu, *New England boiled dinner,* feijoada completa, *corned beef and cabbage, and other boiled mixtures of vegetables and various meats. It's a great dish to serve to a large group of hungry grape pickers, barn raisers, deck builders, or just plain friends. There's something heartening about sitting down to a huge platter of meats and vegetables, surrounded by good company, talk, and laughter. A big, full-bodied Amber Ale goes best here: Try Sierra Nevada Pale Ale or Canada's Black Horse Ale.*

You will have to pay some attention to the preparation, since the cooking times provided are only estimates. The basic idea is that you cook the meats together, removing each as it becomes tender and covering it to keep it warm and moist. Once all the various meats are removed, you cook vegetables in the same stock, adding those with the longest cooking time first. The vegetables are then removed, and the meats are added back to the pot to reheat briefly. The meat and vegetables are arranged on separate platters and should be accompanied by salt and pepper and a spicy aromatic Salsa Verde (recipe follows).

4 pounds short ribs
4 2-inch pieces veal shanks
   (about 2½ pounds total)
2 large cotechino sausages
   (about 1½ pounds total)
1 4-pound roasting chicken,
   trussed
3–4 quarts Rich Chicken Stock
   (see page 203) or beef stock
2 cups amber ale
4 garlic cloves, unpeeled

1 rib celery
1 onion stuck with 1 whole clove
1 carrot
1 whole leek, split and washed
2 teaspoons dried thyme or
   6 sprigs fresh
1 teaspoon dried rosemary or
   2 sprigs fresh
2 bay leaves
10 peppercorns
Salt

Vegetables

12 small red potatoes, washed
   (about 1½ pounds total)
12 boiling onions, peeled
1 small Savoy cabbage, quartered
2 carrots, cut into ¾-inch
   chunks
1 bunch baby turnips

1 parsnip, cut into ¾-inch
   chunks
¼ pound green beans, cut into
   2-inch pieces
6 small zucchini or pattypan
   squash, cut in half

Put the short ribs, veal shanks, sausage, and chicken in a 3-gallon stockpot with the stock and ale and bring to a boil. Make sure the meats are covered by the liquid. If not, add more. Skim off any scum that rises to the surface. Put in the garlic, celery, onion, carrot, leek, herbs, peppercorns, and a pinch of salt. Reduce heat to a simmer. Cook until the meats become tender, then remove them to a large covered bowl. The chicken, veal, and sausage will take about 1–1½ hours. The short ribs about 2–2½ hours.

Strain the stock, and discard the aromatic vegetables. Skim off as much of the surface fat as you can before adding the vegetables. Put in the potatoes and onions. Cook for 5 minutes, then add the cabbage, carrots, turnips, and parsnip. Cook for 10 minutes, then add the green beans and squash. Cook 5 minutes. All the vegetables should be tender. If not, cook them a few minutes more. Remove the vegetables to a warm serving platter. Return all the meats to the pot and reheat for 5 minutes. Slice the sausage into thick rounds, cut up the chicken, and arrange all the meats on a serving platter. You may serve the stock separately, or you can use it at another time as the base for lentil, bean, or vegetable soup.

SERVES 10–12 WITH SPLENDID AND VARIED LEFTOVERS.

Salsa Verde

Serve this piquant Italian sauce with Bollito Misto (see page 256), or Cotechino Sausage with White Beans (see page 258), or boiled beef, chicken, or veal.

3 garlic cloves
1 2-ounce can anchovy fillets
6 sun-dried tomatoes packed
   in olive oil
2 bunches Italian flat-leaf or regular parsley (about 1 pound)

1½ cups extra-virgin olive oil
¼ cup balsamic vinegar
Salt and pepper to taste

In a food processor, process the garlic, anchovies, and sun-dried tomatoes for 30 seconds. Add the parsley and pulse to chop roughly. Pour in the olive oil and balsamic vinegar and pulse to blend in, but don't puree the sauce. Taste for salt and pepper. Sauce will keep for 5–7 days refrigerated in a closed jar.

MAKES 2–3 CUPS.

Cotechino Sausage with White Beans

Cotechino sausages are large aromatic boiling sausages found in the many Italian delicatessens and butcher shops of the Northeast. They go particularly well with beans, especially the flavorful Italian cannellini beans. If you can't find these, navy or Great Northern beans will do almost as well. New Amsterdam Amber Lager would be a nice match with this Italian neighborhood favorite.

2 cotechino sausages ($1\frac{1}{2}$–2 pounds total), left whole
5 cups Rich Chicken Stock (see page 203) or beef stock
1 cup dry white wine
1 pound dried white beans, soaked overnight in cold water to cover and drained
2 cups canned Italian-style tomatoes, chopped

2 bay leaves
2–3 sprigs fresh rosemary or 2 teaspoons dried
2 medium onions, chopped
1 carrot, chopped
1 rib celery, chopped
1 tablespoon chopped garlic
$\frac{1}{2}$ cup chopped parsley
Salt and pepper

Place the sausages, stock, and wine in a large pot or Dutch oven. Bring to a boil. Add the presoaked beans, tomatoes, bay leaves, and rosemary. Simmer, uncovered, for 1 hour. Add the vegetables, and continue to simmer until the beans are tender, about 1 hour more. Taste for salt and pepper. Remove and discard the rosemary sprigs and bay leaves. Remove the cotechino, and cut into $\frac{1}{4}$-inch slices. Place the bean mixture in a shallow serving bowl, and mix in the cotechino, arranging a few slices of it on top.

SERVES 6–8.

Corned Beef or Pastrami Boiled in Beer

This flavorful version of the traditional boiled dinner is enhanced by Dark Ale in the pot and on the table. Try it with Commonwealth Brewing Company's Amber Ale from Boston or Catamount Porter from Vermont.

1 piece corned beef or pastrami
  (2–3 pounds total)
1 whole head garlic, unpeeled
24 ounces ale
10–12 small red potatoes

4 onions, quartered
1 head cabbage, quartered
2 carrots, peeled cut into 2-
  inch pieces

Put the meat in a large pot with the garlic, ale, and enough water to cover the meat by 1 inch. Bring to a boil, lower heat, and simmer for 1½ hours. Put in the potatoes and cook 15 minutes. Add the remaining vegetables and more water if necessary, and cook 15 minutes. Remove the vegetables and taste the meat to be sure it is done. If not, cook it 15 minutes more, or until tender. Remove the meat, slice, and serve with the vegetables. Save any leftover meat, vegetables, and stock for Corned Beef or Pastrami Hash (recipe follows).

SERVES 4, WITH LEFTOVERS FOR HASH.

Corned Beef or Pastrami Hash

Freshly made corned beef or pastrami hash is a far cry from the canned product. It's great fried and served for brunch with poached or fried eggs, or as a substantial lunch with a mug of Frank Jones Ale from New Hampshire or Hope Red Rooster Ale from Rhode Island.

¼ cup fat trimmed from
  cooked corned beef or pastrami (see preceding recipe)
3–4 cups chopped leftover
  vegetables, including potatoes (see preceding recipe),
  or chopped cooked new
  potatoes

2–3 cups (about 1 pound)
  coarsely chopped leftover
  cooked corned beef or
  pastrami (see preceding
  recipe)
½ cup leftover stock (see
  preceding recipe) or chicken
  stock

Chop the fat finely, and render in a large frying pan over medium-high heat. Add the chopped vegetables or potatoes to the rendered fat (add a little butter if necessary), and sauté for 10 minutes. Add the chopped meat and the stock, and cook 10 minutes until the stock evaporates and the hash is nicely browned on the bottom. Turn onto a platter, and serve with poached or fried eggs.

SERVES 4.

Nancy's Spicy Meat Loaf with Beer Gravy

Bruce's wife, Nancy Oakes, says that the key to the juiciness of this spicy meat loaf is the "milk sop." She cooks fresh or, even better, slightly stale bread in liquid to make a panade, *a thickener often used by French cooks.*

This recipe makes enough for 2 loaves. It's so good as leftovers and for sandwiches (see page 286) that you'll want that extra loaf the next day. Nancy likes to cook meat loaf in bread pans like pâté. She says this makes them moister. But you can free-form the loaves in a roasting pan, if you wish.

Drink the same beer you use in the tangy gravy with this dish—an Amber Ale such as Old Post Road Ale from Old Marlborough Brewing.

3 tablespoons olive oil	1 cup milk
1½ cups chopped onions	8 slices fresh or day-old French
½ cup finely chopped celery	bread
½ cup chopped red bell pepper	4 pounds ground chuck
¼ cup chopped green	3 eggs
bell pepper	4 teaspoons salt
½ cup thinly sliced green	2 teaspoons black pepper
onions or scallions	1 teaspoon dried red pepper
3 tablespoons minced garlic	flakes
½ cup chili sauce or catsup	1 teaspoon cumin
1 tablespoon Worcestershire	1 teaspoon dried thyme
sauce	½ cup chopped parsley
2 teaspoons Tabasco	Spicy Beer 'N Beef Gravy
4 tablespoons Dijon mustard	(recipe follows)

In a quart saucepan heat the olive oil over medium-high heat. Add the onions, celery, bell peppers, green onions or scallions, and garlic. Cover and cook for 5 minutes, stirring frequently. Stir in the chili sauce, Worcestershire, Tabasco, mustard, and milk. Bring to a boil, and reduce to a simmer. Stir in the bread, and continue to stir until the mixture has the consistency of oatmeal. Spoon the mixture into a large bowl, and cool in the refrigerator for 20 minutes.

Preheat the oven to 350° F. Remove the bowl from the refrigerator, and add the ground chuck and eggs. Mix together all the remaining spices and parsley in a small bowl, and sprinkle over the meat. Squeeze and knead the mixture with your hands until all the elements are well blended. Do not overmix or the meat loaf will have a mealy texture.

Divide the mixture into 2 equal parts, and place each in a 9 × 5 × 3-

inch loaf pan. Tap the pans several times on the work surface to pack the meat and eliminate air bubbles. Place the pans on a cookie sheet to catch any juices that spill over, and bake for 1 hour until the internal temperature on a meat thermometer is 150° F. Alternatively, you can shape the 2 loaves free hand in a large baking pan to measure 2 inches high, 5–6 inches wide, and 10–12 inches long. Bake for 1 hour as above. Remove the loaves, place on a platter, slice, and serve with the gravy.

SERVES 8–10, WITH LEFTOVERS.

Spicy Beer 'N Beef Gravy

Great on the preceding Spicy Meat Loaf, this gravy is also delicious on roast beef or pork.

1 tablespoon olive oil	1 bay leaf
2 large onions, coarsely sliced	½ teaspoon dried thyme
6 garlic cloves	3 whole fresh jalapeño chiles
½ carrot, coarsely sliced	(whooee!—or fewer if you
½ rib celery, coarsely sliced	don't like it hot)
½ bottle Amber Ale	Defatted pan juices, if any
1½ cups beef stock (you can	1 tablespoon flour
use canned)	Salt and pepper

In a large heavy pan heat the olive oil over medium heat. Add the onions, garlic, carrot, and celery. Cover, and cook 15–20 minutes, stirring occasionally, until the vegetables begin to brown. Add the beer and boil until the liquid is reduced by half. Add the stock, bay leaf, thyme, and chiles. Reduce to a simmer, cover, and cook for 30 minutes.

Pour off all the pan juices from the meat loaves or roast meats into a glass measuring cup. Spoon off 1 tablespoon of the fat on top into a saucepan. Remove the rest of the fat, and discard. Add these juices to the stock mixture in the large pan.

Heat the fat in the saucepan over medium heat, and stir in the flour. Continue to stir until the fat and flour are blended into a roux. Cook a minute more, and stir the roux into the gravy. Bring to a boil, and cook to thicken it for 5 minutes. The gravy should have the consistency of heavy cream. Remove the chiles and bay leaf, and serve the gravy over the meat with a side dish of mashed potatoes.

MAKES 1–1½ CUPS.

Braised Lamb with Leeks and Ale

This dish can be made with an inexpensive cut of meat like lamb shoulder, stew, or neck, and it can also serve as an enjoyable centerpiece for a dinner party. There's plenty of flavorful sauce, so accompany the braised lamb with egg noodles or fresh fettuccine. A full-bodied, malty Scottish- or Irish-type ale brings out the rich flavor of the leeks and the piquant undertones of garlic, mustard, and Worcestershire sauce. Grant's Scottish Ale is a good choice.

3 pounds lamb shoulder, leg, or neck, boned and trimmed of fat, cut into 2-inch chunks
Salt and pepper
2 teaspoons dried tarragon
2 teaspoons fresh chopped rosemary or 1 teaspoon dried
2 tablespoons olive oil
4–5 leeks, cleaned, halved, and thinly sliced (about 6 cups)

6 garlic cloves, minced
1 cup ale
4 cups beef stock
2 tablespoons coarse-grained mustard
2 teaspoons Worcestershire sauce
4–6 tablespoons sour cream
Sprigs of fresh rosemary or parsley for garnish

Season the lamb with salt, pepper, and half the tarragon and rosemary. Brown it in a large high-sided skillet or Dutch oven in the olive oil over high heat for about 10 minutes, stirring and turning the meat so it browns evenly. Remove from the pot with a slotted spoon. Add the sliced leeks to the fat remaining in the pan, cover, and cook over medium heat, stirring occasionally, until they are quite soft, about 10 minutes. Put in the garlic, and the remaining tarragon and rosemary. Mix in the lamb, and add the ale and stock. Cover the pot and cook at a simmer for about 1 hour or until the lamb is quite tender.

Transfer the lamb to a heated platter. Degrease the cooking liquid, add the mustard and Worcestershire sauce to the pot, bring to a boil, and cook until juices thicken. Remove the pot from the heat, and stir in the sour cream. Season with salt and pepper. Pour some of the sauce over the lamb, and serve the rest in a serving bowl. Garnish the lamb with the sprigs of fresh rosemary or parsley.

SERVES 4–6.

Southern Cooking: Sweet and Spicy with Growlin' Gator, Wild Boar Amber, Blackened Voodoo Lager

Sweet and Spicy Nuts

Peanut Slaw

Muffuletta Salad

Asparagus Wrapped in Country Ham in Mustard Vinaigrette

Curried Fish Chowder

Shrimp Boiled in Beer and Spices

Barbecued Shrimp New Orleans Style

Shrimp Rémoulade

Cajun Mirliton and Seafood Ragout

Baked Oysters in Garlic Bread Crumbs

Red Bell Peppers Stuffed with Seafood and Chicken

Chicken Breasts Stuffed with Eggplant, Shrimp, and Ham

New Orleans Hot Pot

Bourbon Stout Yam Waffles

Tuna Caponata Sandwich

Oyster or Shrimp Loaf

Oyster or Shrimp Po'Boy

Fried Eggplant Muffuletta

Mexican Grilled Chicken Torta

Meat Loaf Sandwich

Smoked Chicken, Brie, and Roasted Red Pepper Sandwich

Limburger and Raw Onion Sandwich

Burgers

Beer has always been a popular beverage in the American South from Virginia's Old Dominion to the Louisiana bayous. The weather ranges from warm to hot to off-the-scale, people spend a lot of time eating and drinking outdoors, and the cuisine emphasizes the spicy and sweet/sour flavors that go so well with beer.

A frosty bottle of cold lager is definitely what you want to have in your hand at a summer afternoon barbecue in Alabama or a Saturday night shrimp boil on Bayou Teche. Whether you're eating fried catfish in Atlanta or an oyster po'boy in an oyster bar in the French Quarter, cold beer is the drink of choice.

Beer in the American South goes back to George Washington, Thomas Jefferson, and other gentleman home brewers, but brewing as an industry never really took hold in a big way south of the Mason-Dixon line. The weather was just too warm for effective brewing in the days before refrigeration, and the lack of ice and the relative scarcity of German immigrants kept a large part of the region from joining in the Lager Revolution of the nineteenth century. Hard times after the Civil War and religious attitudes also hindered the development of large-

scale brewing in much of the South: Mississippi, for example, is the one state in the country that has never had a commercial brewery.

In the early days most of the South's beer was shipped down from Philadelphia, but two brewing centers grew up in the nineteenth century: New Orleans and Louisville. Both had ample water, German immigrants with brewing skills (Louisville had nearby Cincinnati's German population to draw on; New Orleans its *cote des Allemandes* just outside the city), and a trade and shipping network connected by the Mississippi and Ohio rivers.

New Orleans had over twenty breweries at

one time, but these days only Dixie Brewing Company and Abita Brewing survive. Dixie was founded in 1907 and has hung on over the years since Prohibition, selling its popular light lager, Dixie Beer, to diners in Creole and Cajun restaurants, and revellers in the bustling bars and nightclubs of the French Quarter.

In recent years the 200,000-barrel regional brewery has expanded its repertoire, and now also makes a pleasantly malty Dixie Amber Light Lager, Blackened Voodoo Lager, a "bewitching" dark all-malt lager, and small batch special brews that include a Bitter Brown Ale, a Dortmunder-style Lager, an Altbier, and a special beechwood-smoked Rauchbeer offered to patrons of a few New Orleans brew-pubs.

Abita Brewing Company in Abita Springs on the north shore of Lake Pontchartrain was founded in 1986 and is Louisiana's only microbrewery. The all-malt lagers produced at the 6,000-barrel a year brewery are distributed in New Orleans, Baton Rouge, and other Louisiana markets. The most popular is an Amber Lager, copper colored, with rich malt flavors. The brewery also makes Abita Gold, a crisp, full-bodied light lager, and Abita Fallfest, brewed using pale, caramel, and chocolate malts, with complex, malty flavors and pleasant hop balance.

Both breweries are doing quite well and are popular with food and beer lovers who flock to the thriving Cajun and Creole restaurants in New Orleans and the surrounding countryside. Beer is definitely the right thing to drink with this exciting and sometimes incandescent cuisine. We prefer the light lagers like Dixie Beer and Abita Gold with spicy seafood dishes such as Barbecued Shrimp New Orleans Style,* Shrimp Rémoulade,* Baked Oysters in Garlic Bread Crumbs,* and Cajun Mirliton and Seafood Ragout.*

More complex and sophisticated Creole combinations of seafood, chicken, and aromatic vegetables such as our Red Bell Peppers Stuffed with Seafood and Chicken* lend themselves to malty amber lagers like Dixie Amber Light Lager and Abita Amber. Robust and intensely flavored New Orleans specialties like New Orleans Hot Pot,* a favorite of

*See Index.

neighborhood tavern-goers, go best with full, dark beers like Dixie's Blackened Voodoo Lager and Abita Fallfest.

Kentucky's Oldenberg Brewery is the only one that remains of the state's once thriving breweries. The 12,500-barrel microbrewery founded in 1987 in Fort Mitchell just across the river from Cincinnati boasts

the largest microbrewery/brew-pub entertainment center in the United States. It has a 700-seat Great Hall, an English-style brew-pub that can serve 250, a large outdoor beer garden, a gift shop, and a Breweriana display with over 750,000 items.

Oldenberg Blonde is a crisp, dry American Pilsner-style lager, and Premium Verum is a dark German-style lager with malty flavors from Munich and black malts balanced by lightly bitter Czechoslovakian Saaz hops.

Bohannon Brewing Company of Nashville, Tennessee, a microbrewery founded in 1989, makes a wide range of beers in its 5,000-barrel brewhouse, including Market Street Light and Pilsner Draft lagers, Bock, Munich Amber, and Oktoberfest Dark Lagers, and Holiday Ale.

Maryland's two microbreweries, British Brewing of Glen Burnie and Wild Goose Brewing Company of Cambridge, both make ales in the English and old colonial style. British Brewing's Oxford Class Ale is medium bodied with full flavors and a finely balanced bitterness, while Wild Goose offers three ales: Wild Goose Amber, a robust and full-bodied English-style Pale Ale, Thomas Point Light Golden Ale, a pleasant light ale with dry, crisp flavors, and Samuel Middleton's Pale Ale, golden amber in color and pleasantly hoppy.

Carrying on the tradition of Virginia plantation owners like Washington, Jefferson, and Madison who brewed their own beers from locally grown grains are two microbreweries, Old Dominion Brewing of Ashburn near Washington, D.C., and Virginia Brewing Company of Virginia Beach. Dominion Lager is a fresh, golden lager, smooth, full bodied, and complex. It is sold in the Washington, D.C., area and in northern Virginia markets. Virginia Brewing Company specializes in lagers and offers Clyde's Lager, Dark Horse Winter Lager, Gold Cup Pilsener, and People's Choice Amber Lager. Another

D.C. area beer is Olde Heurich Maerzen, marketed by contract brewer Christian Heurich Brewing Company, an all-malt lager with full malt flavors and a pleasantly bitter finish.

These English- and colonial-style ales and malty lagers match very nicely with traditional plantation "made dishes" like our Asparagus Wrapped in Country Ham in Mustard Vinaigrette* and Chicken Breasts Stuffed with Eggplant, Shrimp, and Ham.*

Contract breweries thrive in the South, often with attention-getting names and wild labels that translate into popular T-shirts, good-ole-boy caps, and other breweriana. One of the most striking labels and better beers is Wild Boar Amber Lager offered by the Georgia Brewing Company of Atlanta. The label features the Georgia razorback in all its bristling glory: The front of the T-shirt shows the boar's head while the back gives us a close-up view of the pig's other end. The beer itself is quite good: a smooth amber lager using caramel malt with Washington Cascade and German Tettnanger hops with sweet malty flavors and a pleasing light bitterness. It's a very nice match for that other Georgia product—pecans—especially when spiced up and lightly sweetened as in our recipe for Sweet and Spicy Nuts.*

T-shirts and other beer-related items are an important part of both profit and advertising for small breweries and contract breweries. In fact, Growlin' Gator Lager Beer had a T-shirt even before there was a beer. Owner Bill Burrer came up with a snappy T-shirt design featuring a grinning alligator in sunglasses holding up a bottle of beer with Everglade palm trees and a full moon in the background. The motto on the shirt reads: Growlin' Gator Lager Beer/ The Beer with a Bite/Favorite of Lounge Lizards Everywhere. The T-shirt was an instant success with college students on spring break, but then everybody started asking for the beer. So Burrer went into the beer business to supply the growing demand and created Gator Lager, a pleasant, deep-gold lager in the American Pilsner style. It's a nice light lager to go with spicy dishes like Alice's Ceviche* or Mexican Grilled Chicken Torta,* and is available in Florida and other southern markets.

*See Index.

Sweet and Spicy Nuts

This recipe produces crisp and virtually addictive walnuts or pecans that are slightly sweet and mildly spicy. It works just about as well with unsalted peanuts and almonds. The nuts make fantastic beer snacks, and bowls of them will disappear while you and your friends watch the home team on TV and sample local beers. So be sure to make plenty of nuts; you can always store them in jars if there are any left after the game. They also make an excellent garnish for salads, and go very nicely with cheese and fruit as an aperitif or party snack.

1 pound shelled whole walnuts or pecans	½ teaspoon cayenne
4 tablespoons sugar	2½ teaspoons kosher salt
1 teaspoon freshly ground black pepper	4 teaspoons peanut oil

Preheat the oven to 375° F.

For walnuts only: Bring 3 quarts water to a boil, add the walnuts, remove from the heat, and let the nuts soak for 1–2 minutes. Drain and spread the walnuts on a large cookie sheet. Bake 5–6 minutes or until dry. This process removes some of the bitter tannic taste of the walnut skins.

For all nuts (walnuts, pecans, peanuts, almonds): Mix together the sugar, spices, and salt in a small bowl. Put the nuts in a large bowl, and toss with the peanut oil until well coated. Sprinkle in the seasoning mix, and toss well until all the nuts are coated. Spread the nuts on cookie sheets and roast 15–20 minutes, until brown, shiny, and crisp, and they have a wonderful nutty aroma. Remove the nuts from the oven and let cool. Eat at once, or pack into jars.

MAKES 1 POUND.

Peanut Slaw

The crunchy, sweet-and-sour slaw goes nicely with most beers. How about Oldenberg Blonde or Bohannon Pilsener? This recipe came from Pam Student and Pam Barnett, two budding chefs from Bruce's wife's restaurant, L'Avenue.

1 medium green cabbage, about 2 pounds, cored and shredded

½ medium red cabbage, about 1 pound, cored and shredded

2 carrots, shredded

1 red bell pepper, quartered, seeded, and thinly sliced

4 green onions, thinly sliced

1 cup finely chopped red onion

1 tart green apple, such as Granny Smith, cored and shredded

2 garlic cloves, minced

1–2 teaspoons dried red pepper flakes

1 cup mayonnaise

¼ cup sour cream

¼ cup beer

¼ cup brown sugar

2 tablespoons lemon juice

1 tablespoon malt, cider, or distilled white vinegar plus additional to taste

1 cup dry roasted peanuts

Salt and pepper

Lemon juice to taste

In a large bowl toss together all the vegetables and the apple with the garlic and red pepper flakes. In another bowl mix the mayonnaise, sour cream, beer, brown sugar, lemon juice, and vinegar. Mix the dressing into the salad along with the peanuts. Taste for salt and pepper, lemon juice, and vinegar, and add to taste.

SERVES 8–10.

Muffuletta Salad

This colorful salad features a richly flavored olive dressing that tastes great on the classic Italian sandwich of meat, cheese, and olives—muffuletta. Over fresh vegetables and cheese, it makes a nice light entrée or first course. The versatile dressing is also very good on sandwiches, classic or otherwise, all kinds of salads and cold vegetables, and cold grilled or poached fish, seafood, or chicken. Ales seem to go best with the dressing's spicy flavors; try British Brewing's Oxford Class Ale or Wild Goose Amber Ale.

Muffuletta Olive Dressing

1½ cups chopped pitted
    Kalamata olives
1 cup chopped Italian green
    olives with pimientos
½ cup olive oil
½ cup chopped parsley
4 anchovy fillets, finely
    chopped

2 tablespoons capers
1 teaspoon chopped fresh
    oregano or ½ teaspoon
    dried
4 garlic cloves, finely chopped
½ red onion, finely chopped
½ cup red wine vinegar
Freshly ground black pepper

To make the olive dressing: Mix together all the ingredients for the dressing and let sit, refrigerated, for at least 2 hours or overnight. The dressing keeps, covered, for more than a week in the refrigerator.
MAKES 4–5 CUPS.

Salad

3 pounds zucchini, cut into
    2 × ½-inch spears
½ pound carrots, cut into
    2 × ½-inch spears

½ pound Swiss cheese, cut into
    ¼-inch-thick julienne strips
¼ pound Italian salami, cut
    into strips

To make the salad: Blanch the zucchini spears in boiling water for 45 seconds, and refresh them under cold water. Blanch the carrots in boiling water for 6 minutes, and refresh them similarly. In a large bowl mix the vegetables, cheese, salami, and the olive dressing. Chill and serve.
SERVES 8.

Asparagus Wrapped in Country Ham in Mustard Vinaigrette

Earthy asparagus, smoky ham, and piquant mustard/vinegar flavors make this springtime dish a great match for a malty Amber Lager such as Wild Boar Amber from Georgia.

1 pound large asparagus,
   trimmed
½ pound thinly sliced country, Smithfield, or
   Westphalian ham

Mustard Vinaigrette

1 tablespoon Dijon mustard
1 tablespoon chopped shallots
½ teaspoon minced garlic
2 tablespoons chopped fresh
   parsley

2 tablespoons red wine vinegar
   or raspberry vinegar
6 tablespoons olive oil

Steam or boil the asparagus until tender, about 6 minutes. Let cool and wrap the crisp spears in slices of the ham. Arrange on a platter.
To make the vinaigrette: In a food processor or mixing bowl mix together the mustard, shallots, garlic, parsley, and vinegar. Gradually blend in the olive oil.

Pour the dressing over the wrapped asparagus spears, and serve.
SERVES 4.

Curried Fish Chowder

Many types of fish can be used in this hearty chowder. The important thing in choosing any variety is to make sure that the flesh is firm enough so it doesn't fall apart during cooking. If you live on the Atlantic Coast, you can use haddock or sea bass. On the Gulf Coast, redfish, red drum, or speckled trout work well. In other parts of the country, try sea bass, halibut, swordfish, shark, or other firm-fleshed fish. Once you add the fish and shrimp, serve the chowder without delay to keep them from overcooking. This recipe is from Boston chef Steve Armbruster, an expert on Creole and Southern cooking.

A crisp light lager like Abita Gold or tart Wheat Beer like Bohannon Weizzen would make a good match with this spicy chowder.

1 tablespoon peanut oil
½ tablespoon butter
1½ tablespoons unbleached flour
1 small red onion, finely chopped
1 medium yellow onion, finely chopped
2 ribs celery, finely chopped
½ red bell pepper, chopped
4 garlic cloves, minced
2 serrano or jalapeño peppers, seeded and finely chopped
1 large red potato, cut into ½-inch dice
1 large red yam, cut into ½-inch dice

3 cups fish stock or bottled clam juice
1 cup light lager or Wheat Beer
1 tablespoon curry powder
½ teaspoon cayenne
1 teaspoon dried thyme
½ pound shrimp, peeled, rinsed, and deveined
¾ pound firm fish, cut into 1-inch cubes
2 tablespoons lemon juice, or more to taste
Salt and pepper
Tabasco

Heat the oil and butter over medium heat in a heavy 4- to 6-quart pot or Dutch oven. Add the flour, stirring steadily over low heat until light brown in color, 10–12 minutes. Add the onions and celery to the roux and cook for 10 minutes, until the vegetables are soft. Put in the bell pepper, garlic, and hot peppers and cook for 2 minutes. Add the potato and yam, and cook everything for 5 minutes, stirring well. Whisk in the fish stock and lager, and add the curry powder, cayenne, and thyme.

Bring the soup to a boil, and reduce to a simmer. Cook gently for 10 minutes. Then add the shrimp and fish, along with enough lemon juice to give the soup a piquant taste, and cook for only about 3 minutes more, until fish is just done. Taste for salt and pepper. Serve immediately, with Tabasco on the side for those who want more heat.

SERVES 8.

Shrimp Boiled in Beer and Spices

In bayou fishing camps and at Cajun get-togethers, shrimp boiled in beer and spices is the universal snack. The shrimp are usually washed down with goodly amounts of light lager like Dixie Beer or Abita Gold.

The shrimp taste best if they are cooked in the shells and, anyway, the tradition of peeling shrimp while everyone shoots the breeze and drinks beer is all part of a shrimp boil. Serve the shrimp at room temperature, or cold with small bowls of catsup, lemon quarters, and horseradish, and a big bottle of Tabasco. Guests can make their own dipping sauce as hot as they want, so don't stint on the napkins (or the beer).

2 pounds large shrimp (15–20 count), preferably in the shells	1 teaspoon cayenne
	4 tablespoons pickling spice
	6 drops Tabasco
2 cups water	1 head garlic, left whole
2 12-ounce bottles light lager	Juice of 2 lemons
2 bay leaves	

Wash the shrimp and set aside. Put all the remaining ingredients in a 6-quart stockpot, and bring to a boil. Boil for 10 minutes, and then add the shrimp. After the liquid returns to a boil, cook the shrimp for 5–7 minutes until they are pink and firm. Remove the shrimp and let them cool to room temperature or refrigerate. Serve on platters and encourage your guests to make their own dipping sauce.

SERVES 6–8.

Barbecued Shrimp
New Orleans Style

These spicy shrimp aren't really barbecued but are cooked in a hot oven in a sauce laced with herbs, Tabasco, and beer. Most likely the dish was created by the Italians who settled in New Orleans, making use of local spicy ingredients and lots of garlic.

Be sure to provide plenty of crusty bread to sop up the delicious sauce. It's best to leave the shrimp in the shells, and let guests peel them as they eat. The shrimp retain more flavor this way, and it slows down consumption, which can be prodigious.

The traditional accompaniment to this flavorful appetizer is lots of Dixie Beer and plenty of napkins. Just about any light lager tastes great here, and the napkins are essential.

2 cups olive oil
1 head garlic, peeled and
    minced
Juice of 2 lemons
1 teaspoon dried rosemary or
    1 tablespoon chopped fresh
1 teaspoon dried basil or 1
    tablespoon chopped fresh
1 teaspoon dried oregano or
    ½ tablespoon chopped fresh
1 teaspoon cayenne
1 teaspoon Tabasco

1 tablespoon sweet Hungarian
    paprika
4 bay leaves, crushed
2 teaspoons crushed black
    pepper
1 teaspoon salt
2 tablespoons Worcestershire
    sauce
1 cup light lager
2 pounds large unshelled
    shrimp (20–26 count, per
    pound)

Preheat the oven to 450° F. In a large heavy ovenproof pan heat the olive oil on top of the stove, and add all the other ingredients, except the beer and shrimp. Cook over medium heat for 5 minutes, stirring frequently. Add the shrimp, tossing well with the spices. Stir in the beer. Place the pan, uncovered, in the hot oven for about 10 minutes, or until the shrimp are pink and the sauce bubbly. Transfer to a platter and serve immediately.

SERVES 8–10 AS AN APPETIZER.

Shrimp Rémoulade

Rémoulade is a spicy, mayonnaise-based sauce that is a classic accompaniment to shrimp in Creole cuisine. It's also delicious with hard-boiled eggs, cold poached fish, chicken, or cold meats. Try a full-bodied lager such as Old Dominion Lager with this lively dish.

4 quarts water	1 pound medium unshelled
2 tablespoons salt	shrimp (30–35 per pound)

Rémoulade Sauce

1½ cups coarsely chopped celery	¼ cup prepared horseradish
1 cup sliced green onions or scallions	1 cup mayonnaise
½ cup chopped parsley	2 tablespoons olive oil
½ cup coarsely chopped pimiento	¼ cup tarragon vinegar
½ cup Creole or Dijon mustard	2 tablespoons paprika
	½ teaspoon cayenne
	Salt and pepper
	¼ head iceberg lettuce, shredded (optional)

Bring the water and salt to a boil in a large pot. Add the shrimp and cook uncovered 5–7 minutes or until they are pink and firm. Drain in a colander, and cool under cold running water. Peel and refrigerate the shrimp until ready to serve.

To make the rémoulade sauce: In a food processor fitted with the metal blade chop the celery, green onions, and parsley. Do not overprocess; the pieces should be about ⅛ inch in size. Place the chopped vegetables in a bowl. Process the pimiento to a puree in the food processor, and add the mustard, horseradish, and mayonnaise. With the processor running, gradually add the olive oil and tarragon vinegar. Turn off the processor, and put in the previously chopped vegetables, paprika, and cayenne. Pulse 2 or 3 times, one or two seconds, to mix everything thoroughly. Taste for salt and pepper. The sauce can be made ahead, and kept in the refrigerator for 3–4 days.

To serve, place 6 or 7 shrimp on a plate with or without the optional lettuce, and spoon generous amounts of the sauce over them. This recipe makes extra sauce.

SERVES 4–6.

Cajun Mirliton and Seafood Ragout

Mirliton, a delicate squash-flavored vegetable, is actually a member of the cucumber family. It provides a nice complement to spicy seafood in this flavorful ragout from Louisiana. Wild Goose Brewing's Thomas Point Light Golden Ale would make a tasty accompaniment.

This recipe is a favorite at the Bay Wolf Restaurant in Oakland, California, and was developed by Michael Wild, owner/chef, and Carole Bredlinger, former chef at the restaurant, who is now a Bay Area–based food writer.

2 mirlitons (chayotes), pattypan squash, or seedless cucumbers, split in half lengthwise
3 ripe tomatoes
2 tablespoons olive oil
½ onion, diced
½ rib celery, diced
2 garlic cloves, minced
½ red bell pepper, diced
½ green bell pepper, diced
¼ pound andouille or other spicy smoked sausage, diced
2 ounces tasso or smoked ham, diced
2 sprigs fresh thyme or 1 teaspoon dried

1 tablespoon paprika
¼ teaspoon cayenne
¼ cup dry white wine
1 cup fish or Rich Chicken Stock (see page 203)
½ cup heavy cream
⅔ pound firm white fish, diced into 1-inch pieces
8 large shrimp (20–25 per pound), shelled and deveined
¼ pound crabmeat
8 oysters, shucked
Salt and pepper to taste
Tabasco to taste
8 cooked crawfish (optional)

Put the 4 mirliton halves in a single layer in a saucepan and cover with salted water. Cover, and simmer on medium heat 30–45 minutes, or until the flesh of the squash is tender. Remove from the water, scoop out the seeds, and keep the squash warm until ready to serve. (If you are using pattypan squash or cucumber, parboil the halves until done, about 10 minutes for squash, 7 minutes for cucumber.)

Preheat the oven to 350° F. Place the unpeeled whole tomatoes on an oiled pan, and bake for about 30 minutes, until the skin is quite wrinkled. (Baking the tomatoes helps to concentrate the flavor and makes the skin easier to remove.) Peel the tomatoes, and remove any seeds. Chop fine, and set aside.

Put 2 tablespoons of the olive oil in a large frying pan over medium-high heat. In it sauté the onion, celery, garlic, bell peppers, andouille or smoked sausage, and tasso or ham for 5 minutes. Add the thyme, paprika, and cayenne, stir, and sauté for 1 minute. Put in the tomatoes, wine, stock, and cream, increase the heat, and boil rapidly, stirring occasionally, until the sauce is thickened, about 10 to 15 minutes. Reduce the heat. Add the fish and shrimp, and simmer for 3–4 minutes. Put in the crab and oysters, bring everything to a boil, and then turn off the heat. Taste for salt and pepper and Tabasco.

Slice each mirliton half lengthwise into 8 slices, and make a fan arrangement on each plate. Spoon the seafood mixture over each fan. Accompany the dish with buttered rice, and if you desire, garnish with whole cooked crawfish.

SERVES 4.

Baked Oysters in Garlic Bread Crumbs

Herbs, bread crumbs, and plenty of garlic take oysters to new heights in this piquant dish. Serve with a crisp light lager such as Oldenberg Premium Verum or Growlin' Gator Lager.

½ cup butter
½ cup olive oil
4 cups bread crumbs
8 garlic cloves, minced
1 teaspoon dried rosemary
1 teaspoon dried oregano

1 teaspoon dried basil
1 cup freshly grated Parmesan cheese
24 shucked medium-sized oysters (about 1 pint)

Preheat the oven to 450° F. In a large skillet melt the butter with the olive oil over medium heat. Add the bread crumbs, and stir until they are well coated and lightly browned. Put in the garlic, herbs, and cheese, and cook for 1 minute. Spread the bread crumbs ½-inch thick in a 9- or 10-inch cake pan or baking dish. Arrange the oysters on top, and cover with the remaining crumbs. Bake for 20 minutes. Serve immediately.

SERVES 8 AS AN APPETIZER.

Red Bell Peppers Stuffed with Seafood and Chicken

Louisiana cooks, both Cajun and Creole, just love to stuff peppers with seafood, and the addition of chicken makes the stuffing even more interesting. This recipe works equally well with shrimp, crab meat, or crawfish tails (available mail order from Louisiana specialty seafood packers; see Appendix IV, Mail Order Sources). Wild Goose Brewing's English-style Pale Ale, Samuel Middleton's Pale Ale, would be a good choice with this dish.

½ cup finely chopped onion
¼ cup finely chopped celery
4 tablespoons butter
½ pound raw shrimp, shelled and coarsely chopped, or ½ pound picked-over lump crab meat, or ½ pound peeled crawfish tails and fat, coarsely chopped
¼ cup finely chopped green onions or scallions
½ pound cooked chicken, finely chopped

1 cup bread crumbs
1 egg, beaten lightly
½ teaspoon dried thyme
½ teaspoon cayenne
1 teaspoon Worcestershire sauce
½ cup beer
Salt and pepper
4 large red bell peppers, halved, seeded, and ribs removed

Preheat the oven to 350° F. In a pan cook the onion and celery in the butter for 5 minutes over medium heat. Remove to a large bowl, and add the shrimp, green onions, chicken, bread crumbs, egg, thyme, cayenne, and Worcestershire sauce. Moisten with the beer, and mix well. Taste for salt and pepper.

Stuff the mixture into each pepper half, and place the peppers, stuffed sides up, in a roasting pan. Cover with foil and bake for 15 minutes. Remove the foil, and continue to bake for 5 minutes more to brown the tops lightly.

SERVES 4–6 AS A MAIN COURSE; 12–16 AS AN APPETIZER WHEN CUT INTO QUARTERS.

Chicken Breasts Stuffed with Eggplant, Shrimp, and Ham

This Creole dish seems complicated, but it is actually easy to make, and can serve as a delectable centerpiece for a buffet or elegant picnic. It is wonderful served hot from the oven, but just as good refrigerated and eaten the next day at room temperature. Serve it with Abita Amber Lager from Louisiana.

1 medium eggplant, cut in 1½-inch dice

¾ cup olive oil

½ pound smoked ham or Cajun tasso, finely chopped

½ green bell pepper, finely chopped

1 rib celery, finely chopped

2 cloves garlic, minced

½ cup finely chopped green onions or scallion

½ pound shrimp, shelled and chopped

2 cups day-old bread crumbs

½ teaspoon cayenne

1 teaspoon Worcestershire sauce

2 eggs, lightly beaten

½ cup ricotta cheese

Salt and pepper

8 chicken breasts (about 3 pounds), boned, with skin left intact

2 tablespoons melted butter

Preheat the oven to 350° F. In a baking pan rub the eggplant cubes with ½ cup of the olive oil and bake for 20 minutes, until quite soft. Set aside. Heat the remaining ¼ cup oil in a pan over medium-high heat. Add the chopped ham or tasso and vegetables, and cook for 10 minutes, stirring occasionally. Put in the shrimp, and cook 3 minutes. In a large bowl mix the eggplant with the ham and shrimp mixture and all the remaining ingredients, except the chicken. Cut a pocket in each breast and stuff generously with the filling. Brush with melted butter and season the chicken with salt and pepper. Bake for 30 minutes or until the breasts have an internal temperature of 160° F. on a meat thermometer. Serve hot or at room temperature.

SERVES 8.

New Orleans Hot Pot

This hearty soup-stew is a favorite with the regulars at Sam's Pool Hall, a neighborhood joint in New Orleans that serves fiery and hearty soups, stews, and gumbos across a scarred and much-used bar. At Sam's they call this Vegetable Beef Soup, but we've renamed it New Orleans Hot Pot because it can get up to the incandescent level, depending on how much cayenne goes in. This soup-stew is a far cry from any vegetable beef soup that ever came out of a can.

Our version is really more stew than soup and should be served in large bowls, with hot cornbread. At Sam's, the soups are always served with hot sauce on the side, just in case they're not flammable enough for some of those iron palates at the bar.

The beverage of choice at Sam's is Dixie Beer, a crisp light lager made in New Orleans. Light lager is refreshing, especially if you have a heavy hand with the red pepper. We think, though, that a full-bodied dark beer tastes even better with this spicy stew. Try Dixie's Blackened Voodoo Lager for a real N'Awlins neighborhood experience.

1½ pounds beef stew meat or ham, cut into 1-inch cubes
1 cup dark beer
1 cup tomato puree
1 quart homemade beef or Rich Chicken Stock (see page 203)
2 bay leaves
1 teaspoon dried thyme
2 teaspoons dried sage
1 teaspoon cayenne (more if you like it hot)
½ teaspoon salt
1 teaspoon freshly ground pepper
¾ pound carrots (3 medium), diced

1 pound turnips (3 medium), diced
1 pound red potatoes (3 medium), diced
¼ cup salad oil
¼ cup flour
1 medium onion, coarsely chopped
2 ribs celery, coarsely chopped
1 red bell pepper, diced
Salt and pepper
Tabasco to taste
4 green onions or scallions, finely chopped, for garnish

Put the meat, beer, tomato puree, and stock in a stockpot or Dutch oven. Bring to a boil, and add the bay leaves, thyme, sage, cayenne, salt, and pepper. Reduce the heat to a simmer, cover, and cook for 45 minutes. Put in the diced vegetables, and cook for 15 minutes.

While the meat and vegetables are cooking, make a brown roux by heating the oil in a large heavy skillet, stirring in the flour, and cooking over medium heat for 15–30 minutes, stirring constantly so the roux doesn't burn. When the roux has a rich brown color, add the onion, celery, and red bell pepper. Cook, uncovered, over medium heat, stirring occasionally, until the vegetables are soft, about 5 minutes. Now stir this mixture into the large pot, cover, and continue to cook an additional 20 minutes, or until the meats and vegetables are tender. Taste for salt and pepper, and Tabasco. Garnish with the chopped green onions. Ladle into large soup bowls, and offer hot pepper sauce on the side.

SERVES 8–10.

Bourbon Stout Yam Waffles

These thick, puffy waffles are wonderful for Sunday brunch or a light lunch, accompanied with Stout or a Dark Lager, such as Virginia Brewing's Dark Horse Winter Lager. This is a good dish to make when you have leftover yams.

1½ cups flour
1 tablespoon baking powder
½ teaspoon salt
3 eggs, separated
½ cup milk
½ cup Stout

2 tablespoons bourbon
1 cup mashed cooked yams, cooled
2 tablespoons melted butter
Pinch each nutmeg, cardamom, and ginger

Sift together the flour, baking powder, and salt. Beat the egg yolks and mix them with the milk, Stout, bourbon, yams, melted butter, and spices. Beat the egg whites until they form soft peaks and fold them into the batter. Cook like ordinary waffles, following your waffle iron instructions. Pour on plenty of good-quality maple syrup.

MAKES 6 WAFFLES WITH ENOUGH FOR SECONDS.

SANDWICHES

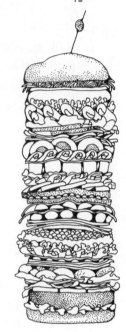

Sandwiches and beer seem made for each other. A pastrami on rye, a Reuben sandwich with corned beef and sauerkraut, a juicy burger, or an Italian sub, all taste better with beer.

The key to making great sandwiches is to use good fresh breads, flavorful fillings, and an array of mouth-tingling condiments. With spicy and interesting condiments even the simplest sandwich can become a hand-held meal oozing with delight: ham and Swiss on rye dressed with Horseradish Beer Mustard* and some Red Onions Pickled in Lime Juice*; roast beef on a fresh onion roll spread with Rémoulade Sauce*; smoked turkey or ham with a little Peanut Slaw* on top and some Russian dressing—mayonnaise blended with catsup and a little mustard—on the bread.

In our beer tour across America, we came across some very special sandwiches, all of which were washed down with fine examples of the local brew. Here are a few of the most memorable.

*See Index.

Tuna Caponata Sandwich

2 6½-ounce cans tuna, packed in water, drained

½ cup Caponata (see page 235)

2 ripe tomatoes, sliced

4 leaves lettuce, washed and dried

4 crusty Italian or French rolls, halved, or baguettes, cut into 6-inch pieces

Break the tuna up into large chunks. Spread caponata on both sides of the rolls. Sprinkle tuna generously over one side of each roll. Top it with sliced tomato and lettuce. Assemble the sandwiches and enjoy with a light lager or Wheat Beer.

SERVES 4.

Oyster or Shrimp Loaf

This is the great "peace maker" of New Orleans, so called because an errant husband coming back late from a night in the French Quarter would bring one home to appease his long-suffering wife. A "loaf" is made by hollowing out the last 8 inches or so of the butt end of a French bread. This is filled with freshly fried oysters or shrimp and a little tartar sauce, mayonnaise, or homemade aioli. The sandwich is then wrapped in foil, and quickly warmed in a hot oven before serving.

1 dozen freshly fried oysters or shrimp (see Fried Oysters I, page 242, Fried Oysters II, page 243, or Fried Shrimp, page 243)
1 8-inch piece French bread

Spicy Tartar Sauce (see page 128), or mayonnaise
Tabasco to taste

Preheat the oven to 450° F. Prepare the loaf by removing the crumb from the piece of French bread, leaving a hollow center large enough to put the seafood into. With a knife or narrow spatula, spread the tartar sauce or mayonnaise over the interior of the bread, and stuff the bread with the oysters or shrimp, completely filling it. Wrap in foil, and bake 5–10 minutes to heat thoroughly. Serve with Tabasco.

SERVES 1.

Oyster or Shrimp Po'boy

A po'boy, another favorite New Orleans sandwich, is similar to the oyster or shrimp loaf above except that the bread is cut in half, brushed with butter, and grilled. It is then spread with sliced dill pickle, shredded cabbage, sliced tomatoes, and a generous layer of fried seafood. The seafood is then dressed with tartar sauce or mayonnaise, and the two halves are jammed together. The big challenge with eating a po'boy is to do it without everything ending up in your lap.

Fried Eggplant Muffuletta

This Italian-inspired sandwich is another New Orleans tradition. Normally muffuletta is made with layers of Italian cold cuts and cheese with an olive salad generously spread on split loaves of Italian bread. This spicy (and salty) sandwich is popular in French Quarter taverns, and always seems to require the consumption of a couple of bottles of Dixie Beer.

The key to a good muffuletta lies in the olive salad used as a dressing. Instead of cold cuts and cheese, we suggest a sandwich of fried eggplant. Other tasty fillings could be grilled boneless and skinless chicken breasts or sliced turkey.

1 medium eggplant, cut lengthwise into ¼-inch slices	2 cups milk
	Flour
Salt and pepper	1 loaf French or Italian bread, cut in half lengthwise
Olive oil	
2 eggs	1 cup Muffuletta Olive Dressing (see page 270)

Sprinkle each eggplant slice on both sides with salt and pepper. Heat ¼ inch of the olive oil to medium hot in a heavy frying pan. In a bowl lightly beat the eggs with the milk. Dredge each eggplant slice in flour, then dip it in the egg/milk mixture. Fry several slices of eggplant at a time until soft and golden brown on both sides. Drain on paper towels.

To assemble the sandwich, spread both sides of the bread generously with the muffuletta dressing. Cover the bread with fried eggplant, making more than one layer if you want. Reassemble the loaf, and slice into 4-inch pieces.

SERVES 4–6.

Mexican Grilled Chicken Torta

Tortas are wonderful Mexican sandwiches that feature meat or chicken on a lightly crusted roll with a soft interior. The sandwich is dressed with plenty of spicy condiments or garnishes: Guacamole,* Salsa Cruda,* or Red Onions Pickled in Lime Juice.* You can also make tortas with left-over roast pork, thinly sliced grilled steak, grilled fish, or grilled boneless chicken breast. If you live near a Mexican bakery, get the soft rolls called bolillos. If not, use fresh Italian or French rolls.

Marinade

1 tablespoon olive oil

3 tablespoons lemon juice

1 garlic clove

1 teaspoon chile powder

½ teaspoon salt

4 skinless boneless chicken
   breasts

4 rolls, each 5–6 inches long
   (Mexican *bolillos*, French,
   or Italian)

Mayonnaise

4 slices Swiss or Jack cheese

Guacamole (optional)

Salsa Cruda (see page 308)

Sliced tomato (optional)

Red Onions Pickled in Lime
   Juice (see page 309)

2 cups shredded lettuce

Mix together all the marinade ingredients. Marinate the chicken breasts in a bowl covered with plastic wrap at room temperature for 1–2 hours or overnight in the refrigerator. Turn the chicken from time to time. Broil or grill the chicken breasts for at least 5 minutes per side, or until the meat is firm.

To assemble the sandwich, cut each roll in half. Pull some bread out of the center, and spread each half with mayonnaise. Cover with sliced cheese, and place a grilled breast on the cheese. Spread some optional guacamole on the chicken, followed by salsa cruda or sliced tomato. On the other half of the roll, arrange some pickled red onions and shredded lettuce. Press the two halves of the roll together and serve. Make sandwiches with the remaining ingredients in the same manner.

MAKES 4 SANDWICHES.

*See Index.

Meat Loaf Sandwich

To us the best thing about meat loaf is the great sandwiches it makes. Meat loaf is delicious cold the next day. This is not so surprising as it is nothing more than pâté with a different name. See Nancy's Spicy Meat Loaf (page 260) for a tasty version.

Our favorite way to eat meat loaf is on toasted whole-grain bread. Dress the bread with Honey Beer Mustard* and some mayonnaise. Pile the sliced meat loaf high and garnish with Tavern Pickled Onions.*

Smoked Chicken, Brie, and Roasted Red Pepper Sandwich

1 5-inch piece of baguette, split horizontally
Brie cheese

4 slices smoked chicken breast
Roasted sweet red peppers

Spread one side of the baguette with Brie. Top with slices of smoked chicken. Cover with some of roasted red peppers. Top with the remaining bread and eat with a bib and plenty of napkins.

MAKES 1 SANDWICH.

Limburger and Raw Onion Sandwich

Limburger is a wonderfully pungent cheese made in Wisconsin, and particularly suited to beer. To make these sandwiches, simply place thick slices of the cheese and rounds of raw mild onion between two slices of good German- or Jewish-style rye bread. If you wish, you can also add thin slices of Wisconsin summer sausage. Then spread on some coarse-grained mustard, and enjoy with a glass of lager.

*See Index.

Unusual Garnishes and Condiments

Chutney on lamb or pork burgers

Pickled onions and sharp Cheddar cheese

Welsh Rarebit (see page 53) over a beef burger

Roast Peppers

Chopped Greek olives

Feta cheese

Caponata (see page 235)

Rémoulade Sauce (see page 275)

Burgers

Burgers and beer are a natural combination—a burger in one hand and a cold beer in the other is the original American balancing act.

It's pretty hard to improve on the classic hamburger: chopped lean chuck cooked rare and served on a toasted sesame bun with mayonnaise, red pepper relish, slices of red onion and beefsteak tomato, and crunchy lettuce. But there are variations that can spice up even this sublime experience.

Burger Variations

1. Mix 2 parts ground turkey with 1 part finely chopped smoked sausage, such as Cajun andouille or Portuguese linguiça. Grill as usual. Serve with mayonnaise, barbecue sauce, and Peanut Slaw (see page 269) on the burger. (Leave the peanuts out, if you prefer.)

2. Ground lamb can be made easily in a food processor. Trim shoulder or leg meat of fat, dice, and then coarsely chop with the metal blade. Season the meat with chopped garlic, a little cumin, curry powder or ground coriander, and turmeric. Form into patties, grill, and serve in

warm pita bread with Red Onions Pickled in Lime Juice (see page 309), yogurt, chopped fresh cilantro, and lemon wedges.

3. To make a Japanese-flavored burger, mix lean beef with a little soy sauce, chopped fresh ginger, chopped green onion, and mirin (sweet sake). Serve with shredded daikon (white radish) and mayonnaise mixed with a little wasabi, Japanese powdered horseradish.

4. For a Chinese-accented burger, make patties from lean ground pork flavored with chopped garlic, ginger, soy sauce, Chinese bean paste, a little sugar, and sesame oil. Serve with shredded iceberg lettuce, thinly sliced onions, and rice vinegar blended with sesame oil.

5. For a Mexican-inspired variation, mix lean ground beef with chopped garlic, a pinch of cumin, and a little chile powder. Serve burgers with melted Monterey Jack cheese, a generous layer of Guacamole (see page 309), and thinly sliced tomato.

NORTH OF THE BORDER: HOT CHILES AND COLD BEER

Alice's Ceviche

Fish, Cucumber, and Avocado Salad

Basque Chorizo, Red Pepper, and Garbanzo Salad

Adobo Chicken Wings

Gorditas

Tamales with Chorizo and Sweet Potato Filling

Tacos, Burritos, Tostadas, and Quesadillas

Salsa Cruda

Guacamole

Red Onions Pickled in Lime Juice

Chicken in Green Mole Nut Sauce

Sonoran Lamb Stew (Birria)

Lamb Shanks Braised in Beer and Cilantro

O'Shea's Black Beans

Early saloons in the Old West were primitive at best, usually only an adobe hut or false front cabin with planks laid between a couple of barrels of Taos Lightning or trade whiskey. Miners and cowboys tossed back whatever was served with little consideration for flavor. What they looked for in those early days, we are told by Richard Erdoes in *Saloons of the Old West* (Knopf, 1979), was power and effect, as nick-

Calamity Jane enjoying a beer with a cowboy at what looks like the start of a lively afternoon in Montana.

names for the local hooch attest: Red Dynamite, Skullbender, White Mule, Who Shot John, Tangle Leg, Tarantula Juice, Scorpion Bible, Tiger Spit, Panther Piss, and the Miner's Friend. The arrival of beer, in these circumstances, was a relief.

The coming of beer to Western saloons was seen as a civilizing influence, and breweries quickly grew up in San Antonio, Denver, Helena, and other large towns and growing cities across the West. A brewery, like a church or library, was a sign that a town was on the way up, and was often one of the first businesses established by local entrepreneurs (after the saloon and cathouse, of course). Beer spoiled easily in the hot climate, it was bulky to ship, and usually sold for a nickel a glass, so just about any town of any consequence boasted a local brewery or two. Tombstone, Arizona, for example, had its own Golden Eagle Brewery before the population was much over 300.

German brewers came West after the Civil War, producing lager beer wherever ice (and later refrigeration) was available. Most saloons in the larger towns offered patrons a selection of draft ales from small beer at 3 percent alcohol to XXX strong ale at 10 percent, and often lager. In cities with significant immigrant populations, beer halls in the German tradition sprang up, providing customers with light lagers,

Bocks, and even Dopplebocks, along with entertainment, good food, and *Gemütlichkeit.*

Beer went well with the typical German food of these new settlers and also complemented the spicy barbecue and Mexican dishes of the Southwest, such as Quesadillas,* flour or corn tortillas with cheese and savory fillings, and Tamales,* masa cornmeal stuffed with spicy meat or chicken and steamed in corn husks. As commercial beer became more available, it became the favorite table beverage of many in the West, replacing *pulque,* the fermented juice of the maguey cactus, *tiswin,* an Apache corn-based beer, or water with just enough whiskey added to cut the flavors of alkali and mud.

San Antonio, Texas, and the surrounding countryside near New Braunfels attracted many German and Czech immigrants in the nineteenth century, and the state's first brewery was founded there in 1855 by William Menger. San Antonio rapidly became an active brewing center, and the home of Lone Star and Pearl beers. These are the two quintessentially Texan beers; when Willy Nelson and the boys were

*See Index.

The Rifle Saloon, Colorado.

Czech brewers (above) made flavorful lagers at Spoetzl Brewery (right) in Shiner, Texas.

whooping it up in Texas saloons, odds are they were putting away more than a few long-necks of Lone Star or Pearl.

Lone Star Brewing was started by Adolphus Busch, owner of Budweiser, in the 1880's, and the label was finally sold to Heileman, a huge national brewer, a hundred years later. Today Lone Star is a standard American Pilsner, vaguely malty with a light touch of hops and mildly pleasant flavors. Pearl Brewing opened in 1885 and got its name from the tiny pearl-like bubbles (in German *perle*) in the clear light lager. Pearl survived Prohibition by selling ice and soft drinks and today produces a variety of beers at its San Antonio plant. Its best-known product is Pearl Premium Lager Beer, a bright gold lager with fresh, clean flavors and a pleasant bite of hops, and Pearl Cream Ale, a golden ale with a sweet malt character and good hoppy finish.

These light, American Pilsner-style beers are a good match for the spicy Mexican-inspired food that is so popular all over the West. Gorditas,* patties of fried masa dough with spicy fillings, and Tacos,* tortillas folded around piquant chopped meat or chicken, are just two Mexican specialties that are complemented by the clean, refreshing taste of these light lagers, especially when they are served with chile-laced Salsa Cruda* or Guacamole.*

Spoetzl Brewery was founded in 1909 in Shiner, Texas, and is one of the few small regional breweries to survive in the West. It produces 60,000 barrels of Shiner Premium and Shiner Bock Beer. Shiner Premium is a high-quality, hoppy light lager with full, malty flavors and excellent balance. Shiner Bock is an Amber Lager with roasted malt flavors and mild hop character.

West End Brewing Company of Dallas produces 6,000 barrels of its popular West End Lager for the city's taverns and the exciting Dallas restaurants that offer new interpretations of Southwest cuisine (see our Fish, Cucumber, and Avocado Salad* and Alice's Ceviche*). Old City Brewing, a contract brewer, markets Pecan Street Lager in the university town of Austin, where it is much appreciated in student pubs along with tangy bar snacks like Popcorn with Parmesan and Garlic* or Adobo Chicken Wings* in a fiery sauce.

Denver, Colorado, became one of the brewing centers of the West with the establishment of the Rocky Mountain Brewery in 1859, which was quickly followed by a host of other lager breweries, almost all founded by German immigrants. Only one survived Prohibition and the demise of regional breweries—Adolph Coors.

Founded in Golden, a few miles west of Denver, in 1873, the lager brewery produced 500 barrels the next year. By 1880, output was at 3,500 barrels, and in 1902 Coors made 62,000 barrels of lager. Production today exceeds 20 million barrels of Coors, Coors Light, and Coors Extra Gold, along with specialty beers, Coors Winterfest, George Killian's Irish Red Ale, and Herman Joseph's 1868. Coors has always been unpasteurized, and until recently was shipped under refrigeration to Western markets only. During the 1950's and 1960's it became a cult beer in the East, with Secret Service agents smuggling cases on board Air Force One for Kennedy clambakes, and New York beer lovers buying contraband six-packs at high prices. Another production facility was built on the East Coast a few years ago, and now the beer can be found nationwide.

*See Index.

Coors is a fresh, clean lager in the American Pilsner style with light, sweet flavors. Coors Extra Gold, the brewery's premium beer, is similar in its freshness, with a bit more malt and some hop flavor. Coors Light, the immensely popular and heavily promoted "Silver Bullet," is clean and light, with very little malt flavor and character.

Coors specialty beers are interesting developments in a brewery this size and reflect the influence of European and microbrewery styles. Winterfest is an Amber Lager in the Octoberfest style, pleasantly malty, slightly sweet, and lightly hopped. George Killian's Irish Red Ale is brewed to a formula from an Irish ale brewery; it is a reddish Amber Ale with malty flavors and a light touch of hops to balance.

Denver and Boulder, the university town in the mountains above the city, are hotbeds of home brewing and beer fanaticism. The Association of Brewers of Boulder, founded by beer guru Charlie Papazian, is a rich resource for information about beer and brewing in America. The association's Institute for Brewing Studies publishes *The New Brewer: The Magazine for Micro and Pub-Brewers, zymurgy Magazine* for home brewers and beer lovers, and the annual *Microbrewers Resource Directory*. Its Brewer's Publications offers books on beer and brewing.

The Association of Brewers also sponsors the Great American Beer Festival each year where brewers of every ilk from all over the country come together to taste beer and compete for national awards. This festival is *the* event of the beer lover's year and is not to be missed by anyone who loves beer and wants to find out what's going on in American brewing. At last year's tenth annual festival, festival-goers were offered tastes of over 500 beers from 159 breweries in 37 different styles. The festival is held at the Denver Merchandise Mart, a huge hall that fills up quickly with avid beer tasters. Happily for all, accommodations are available within easy walking distance of the mart.

Boulder Brewing, founded in a goat shed outside Boulder in 1979 by three local home brewers, is the oldest microbrewery still operating in America. It has since moved to more spacious and hygenic quarters in Boulder and recently went public to raise capital for expansion. The brewery makes ales in the English tradition, and is having much success in the national marketplace with its excellent Boulder Extra Pale Ale.

The Extra Pale Ale is a warm amber color with a firm caramel-

Delivery wagon of Kessler Brewing Company, Helena, Montana.

colored head and lovely hop/malt bouquet. It shows excellent balance between lightly sweet malt and dry hop flavors, and is a satisfying and full-flavored ale. Boulder Red Ale is a copper-colored ale with rich malt flavors and a delicate touch of hops, while the Amber Ale is a bright amber color with pleasantly hoppy aromas and characteristic ale fruitiness. Boulder Porter is a chocolate brown ale with complex flavors of roasted dark malts and light hops. Boulder Stout, judged the Best Stout in America at the Great American Beer Festival, is almost black in color, with intense flavors of roasted barley and dark malt; it is high in alcohol, only for the "stout-hearted," say the brewers.

These deeply flavored ales are good accompaniments to complex chile-accented dishes like Chicken in Green Mole Nut Sauce,* Sonoran Lamb Stew (*Birria*),* Lamb Shanks Braised in Beer and Cilantro,* and O'Shea's Black Beans.*

Odell Brewing Company is another Colorado brewer, making small batches of ale in a converted grain elevator in Fort Collins. Its Golden Ale is a medium-bodied light ale, mildly hoppy and malty, Ninety Shilling Ale is an Amber Ale in the full-bodied Scottish style, and Riley's Red Ale is a deep-copper-colored ale—strong, malty, and bitter.

*See Index.

Another Fort Collins brewery, Old Colorado Brewing, makes Ft. Collins Pride, a pleasant Pale Ale, and Oktoberfest, an amber malty lager.

Montana Beverages of Helena carries on a Western brewing tradition that began in 1865 when immigrant gold miner Nicholas Kessler began brewing beer for fellow miners in Last Chance Gulch, later renamed Helena. Kessler prospered and turned Kessler Brewing Company into one of the most successful and technologically advanced breweries in the West, importing icemaking and later refrigeration machinery to brew the fresh, clean lagers that became so popular in the late nineteenth century. The brewery closed in 1957, but the label was revived in 1982 by the founders of Montana Beverage, a microbrewery producing lagers in the European style. Their most popular beer is Kessler Lager, a Dortmunder-style light Amber Lager with sweet malty flavors and a hoppy aftertaste. Lorelei Extra Pale Lager is a light lager that includes wheat malt in the brew. The brewery also produces seasonal beers: a spring Bock, summer Amber Wheat Beer, Oktoberfest, and a special beer for the winter holidays.

Brew-pubs and small microbreweries are springing up all over the West these days. To mention just a few: HOPS!, a popular restaurant and brewery in Scottsdale, Arizona, ties its flavorful beers in with creative and interesting beer cuisine; Crazy Ed's Black Mountain Brewing in Cave Creek, Arizona, serves Crazy Ed's Arizona Pilsner, crisp and hoppy; Electric Dave Brewery of South Bisbee, Arizona, turns patrons on with Electric Light and Electric Dark; Cooper Smith's Pub and Brewing in Fort Collins, Colorado, makes quite a bang with a powerful Black Powder Barley Wine; and Coeur d'Alene Brewing in Idaho distributes robust, English-style T.W. Fisher's ales throughout Idaho, Washington, Oregon, and Montana. One of the most successful brew-pubs in the West is Denver's Wynkoop Brewing, Colorado's first brew-pub, which does a land-office business with its Sagebrush Stout and Wilderness Wheat beer.

Perhaps the most memorable beer made in the West can be found at tiny Preston Brewing of

Embudo Station, New Mexico: Green Chili Beer. Made with New Mexican green chiles, the beer is described by beer writer William Brand in the Oakland (California) *Tribune* as "heavenly—especially if you're partial to chili flavors anyway. It has a smooth, lightly malted taste and is well-hopped, but the predominant flavor comes from the chilies. The taste is so thick you can almost chew it. It's also *muy picante*—that is, spicy."

This beer is a good example of the interesting, and often delicious, experimental beers being made by small U.S. brewers these days. Other chile-flavored beers can be found: We sampled a red chile beer at a Mexican restaurant in Seattle, many Western brew-pubs have made them, and one contract brewer from Michigan markets a chile-laced Cajun beer. Any of these chile-flavored beers would go well with dishes that use chiles, such as our Chicken in Green Mole Nut Sauce,* or Mexican favorites like Tacos,* Tamales,* and Quesadillas.*

Contract brewers are jumping on the Western wagon with special brews that have a rough and ready appeal and a cowboy image: Roughrider Premium Beer, which the Dakota Brewing Company tells us has a "true western flavor," is a light-bodied American-style Pilsner; Kershsenstine Diamond makes Rattlesnake Beer, a light lager with hoppy aromas and a touch of sweetness.

Beer and food in the West are a hot combination, with chefs at exciting restaurants such as the Rattlesnake Club in Denver, the Mansion at Turtle Creek in Dallas, and Mark Miller's Coyote Cafe in Santa Fe creating their own new versions of Southwest cuisine and matching them with beer. The spicy foods are naturally suited to beer, and microbreweries, brew-pubs, and beer-oriented restaurants can be found in many Western cities and towns.

*See Index.

Alice's Ceviche

Ceviche, fish or seafood marinated in lime or lemon juice and chiles, is popular along the Pacific Coast from Puerto Vallarta to L.A. It's a great dish to have with beer, and is especially good as a snack or appetizer when served with fried tortilla chips. It makes a fine filling for Tacos* or topping for Tostadas.*

The fish used for ceviche must be impeccably fresh, although high-quality frozen Mexican prawns can also be used. This recipe comes from Alice Peterson, an accomplished Southwestern cook from Santa Cruz, California.

Light lager goes best with this picante dish: Shiner Premium or Pete's Pacific Dry Lager.

1 pound fresh fish fillets, such as rock cod or red snapper, finely chopped, or 1 pound raw prawns, shelled, deveined, and finely chopped
1 cup fresh lime juice
4 Roma tomatoes, seeded, juice squeezed out, and chopped
¾ cup chopped white onion

2 jalapeño chiles, seeded and finely chopped
½ cup finely chopped carrot
½ cup chopped fresh cilantro
1 tablespoon dried oregano
6 tablespoons olive oil
½ cup frozen peas, thawed
Salt
1 avocado, peeled and sliced
Tortilla chips

Marinate the fish or prawns in the lime juice until opaque, about 1 hour. Strain the fish and discard the juice. Mix the fish with the remaining ingredients, except the avocado and tortilla chips. Taste for salt. Spoon the ceviche into cocktail glasses or small bowls. Garnish with the avocado slices and serve with the tortilla chips or crackers.

SERVES 4–6 AS AN APPETIZER.

*See Index.

Fish, Cucumber, and Avocado Salad

This quick salad is a great way to use leftover poached or grilled fish. It makes a light and refreshing lunch when paired with a hot baguette and Brie. Serve a light lager like Pecan Street Lager from Old City Brewing Company.

½ pound firm-fleshed cooked fish, such as halibut, swordfish, or tuna, diced

2 cucumbers, peeled, seeded, and cut into ½-inch cubes

1 avocado, peeled, pitted, sliced lengthwise

10 cherry tomatoes, cut in half

Dressing

1 tablespoon Dijon mustard

1 teaspoon soy sauce

¾ cup homemade or high-quality commercial mayonnaise

1 teaspoon lemon juice, or to taste

Place the fish in a large bowl. Add the cucumber to the bowl. In a small bowl mix together the dressing ingredients.

Stir the dressing into the fish and cucumber mixture, tossing gently to coat well. Spoon the mixture into a shallow serving bowl or deep platter, and arrange the sliced avocados and cherry tomatoes artfully on top and around the edges. Serve at once. This salad does not keep well since the cucumber can get watery and the avocado slices will turn brown.

SERVES 4.

Basque Chorizo, Red Pepper, and Garbanzo Salad

Garbanzos, or chick peas, are usually a part of the salad and tapas trays in Basque restaurants. Often they are mixed with chorizo and red peppers. This cold salad makes a delicious appetizer or side dish for a buffet. We prefer home-cooked garbanzos, but you can use canned ones as long as you wash them well to get rid of the briny taste. This recipe was adapted

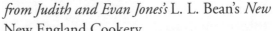

from Judith and Evan Jones's L. L. Bean's *New New England Cookery.*

Use a spicy dried sausage like Italian pepperoni, salami, Basque or Spanish chorizo, or linguiça with the garbanzos. It's a good idea to make this salad up a day or so in advance of serving so that the flavors have a chance to mellow.

Match with a full-bodied Amber Ale—Odell Ninety Shilling Ale or Boulder Amber Ale.

2 cups cooked garbanzos (about ½ cup dried), preferably home cooked

5 tablespoons fruity olive oil

3 tablespoons red wine vinegar

1 teaspoon minced garlic

1 medium red or golden bell pepper, thinly sliced

2 teaspoons chopped fresh oregano or marjoram or ½ teaspoon dried

½ cup finely chopped sweet red or Walla Walla onion

1 tablespoon capers

¼ pound very thinly sliced dried Basque or Spanish chorizo, or other spicy dried sausage

¼ cup chopped parsley

Salt and pepper

¼ cup small black olives for garnish

Mix all the ingredients together in a bowl and marinate at room temperature for 1 hour or refrigerate, covered, overnight. Taste for salt and pepper. Place in a shallow serving bowl, garnish with the black olives, and serve with plenty of good sourdough French bread.

SERVES 4–6.

Adobo Chicken Wings

Buffalo chicken wings have received a lot of attention over the past few years as the ultimate bar food. They are a great snack, but there are other tasty ways to make chicken wings that go well with beer (see Tandoori Marinade*).

Adobo, a Spanish word, describes a blend of spices and vinegar that is used to marinate and coat food, and each Spanish-speaking country has its own interpretation of the piquant sauce. Our version comes from Anzonini, a Spanish gypsy chef and flamenco musician, who originally used it as a coating for chunks of shark. We think it is very good with chicken wings and even better with chicken livers. Use either in the following recipe, but cook the livers for 8–10 minutes only.

A Pilsner-style lager will go well with this spicy chicken: Crazy Ed's Black Mountain Gold or Electric Dave's Electric Light, for example.

10–12 chicken wings, or 1½ pounds chicken livers	¼ cup Hungarian or Spanish paprika
4 garlic cloves, peeled	½ cup red wine vinegar
1 teaspoon dried oregano	2 tablespoons olive oil
1 teaspoon salt	2 cups flour
1 teaspoon black pepper	Vegetable oil for deep frying

Cut off the wing tips and discard. Cut each wing at the joint into 2 pieces. Chop the garlic in a food processor. Add all the remaining ingredients, except the flour and vegetable oil. Process for 10 seconds or so to make a smooth red paste.

Heat 3–4 inches of vegetable oil to 350° F. in a deep fryer. Generously rub each wing piece in the paste, then dredge in flour. Shake off any excess. Fry all the larger wing sections, the first joints, for 10–12 minutes until deep brown. Fry the smaller second joints for 8–10 minutes. Fry chicken livers for 8–10 minutes. Drain on paper towels. Serve warm or at room temperature.

SERVES 4–6 AS A BAR SNACK OR APPETIZER.

*See Index.

Gorditas

These thick fried patties topped with an assortment of savory garnishes are just right for an informal weekend gathering. All you have to do is lay out a big platter of gorditas and an array of garnishes and let your guests do the rest. Gorditas make a superb lunch or first course, and combine well with a light ale like Santa Fe Pale Ale.

If you are fortunate enough to live near a Mexican market, you can buy the dough already prepared. Otherwise, make your own with masa flour, increasingly available in supermarkets around the country. Use any or all of the garnishes listed, or try out some new ones.

Masa Dough

¼ cup vegetable shortening or lard (don't use butter; it will burn)

½ teaspoon salt

2 cups masa harina (Mexican hominy flour)

1¼ cups warm water

Vegetable oil for deep frying

1 cup shredded Jack cheese

1 pound Mexican-style chorizo, removed from casings

To make the dough: Cream the shortening and salt in a mixing bowl. Alternating, add small amounts of masa harina and water until the mixture is well blended. This will form a soft dough. Wrap well in plastic wrap and refrigerate at least 30 minutes. Well wrapped, the dough should keep 3–5 days.

Divide the dough into 6–8 equal portions. Moisten your hands with water, and form the dough into thick cakes, about ¼-inch thick and 3–4 inches in diameter. Cook the gorditas on an ungreased griddle, on a *comal*, or in a heavy frying pan over medium-high heat. Turn the cakes occasionally, and cook them until the masa is set and no longer has a doughy look. Remove the cakes from the heat, and when they are cool enough to handle, pinch up the edges to form a ⅜- to ½-inch rim to hold the filling. This part of the recipe can be done ahead of time.

When you are ready to finish the gorditas, place about ½ inch of oil in a heavy skillet and heat over medium-high heat to about 400° F. Fry the gorditas until they are light brown. Don't turn them over, but brown the tops by spooning hot oil over them. As they brown, remove and drain on paper towels. Serve hot with the Jack cheese on top, sprinkled with fried chorizo. Let your guests add other garnishes.

To make the chorizo garnish: In a heavy skillet fry the chorizo over medium-high heat, crumbling it with a fork, for 5–7 minutes. Drain off excess fat.

MAKES 6–8 GORDITAS.

Other Garnishes

Red Onion Pickled in Lime Juice (see page 309)
Salsa Cruda (see page 308)
Guacamole (see page 309)
Sliced radishes
Thinly sliced green onions or scallions

Diced cold cooked chicken
Chopped cilantro
Sliced pimiento-filled olives
Finely chopped red onion
Sliced jalapeños *en escabeche*
Chopped chipotle chiles *en adobo*

Tamales with Chorizo and Sweet Potato Filling

Tamale-making takes some doing, but it is a pleasant activity and fun to do with friends. A tamale-making party offers an enjoyable time, a delicious meal, and a great opportunity to taste a selection of fine beers. Tamales freeze very well, so be sure to make plenty.

1 recipe Masa Dough (preceding recipe)

Chorizo and Sweet Potato Filling

1½ pounds Mexican-style chorizo, removed from casings
6 medium tomatoes, peeled and seeded or canned Italian-type style tomatoes

1½ cups diced sweet potatoes or red boiling potatoes
Corn husks (available at Latin markets)

Fry the chorizo in a heavy skillet over medium heat for 5 minutes. Pour off the grease, and add the tomatoes and potatoes. Cover, and cook until the potatoes are tender and most of the liquid has been absorbed.

*Tamales
with
Chorizo
and Sweet
Potato
Filling
(continued)*

If the pan dries out, add a little chicken stock or water. Degrease the pan and refrigerate the filling before using.

To make the tamales: Soak the corn husks in warm water until pliable. Remove and discard any corn silk, and wash the husks thoroughly. Keep the husks damp, but not dripping wet, until ready to use. Don't be alarmed if some of the husks tear during handling; you can always use another piece of husk to overlap the tear.

Lay the damp husk out on your work surface. Place 2–3 tablespoons of the dough in the center of the husk, and spread it with a spoon or spatula to form a thin rectangular layer. Allow a 1-inch border on one side of the husk, and spread the masa to the edge of the other. Allow at least a 3-inch border of husk exposed at each end. The rectangle of dough should measure about 4 × 5 inches. If the husk is not large enough, patch with another piece to make the area larger, using a little masa to glue the pieces together.

Spoon 1–2 tablespoons of the filling over the center of the dough, leaving a small border of masa around the filling. To form the tamale, fold the side of the husk with masa all the way to the edge over the filling. Then fold the other over so that the uncovered husk wraps around the other side. Fold both ends in over the filled center to make a rectangular package. Lay the tamales on the work surface folded side down to keep them closed, or tie with a strip of husk or string.

Set up a covered steamer or improvise a rack above 2–3 inches of boiling water. Layer the tamales, folded sides down, leaving enough space around them so that steam can circulate freely. Cover the pot, and adjust the heat so that the water boils gently throughout the cooking period. Cooking times will vary, depending on the size of the pot and how many tamales you are steaming. A single recipe of 24 tamales takes about 1 hour. The best way to tell if a tamale is cooked is to pluck one from the pot, unwrap it, and take a bite. It is done if the dough is cooked through, doesn't stick to the husk, and no longer has a raw doughy taste.

Cooked tamales can be frozen and then reheated without thawing. Simply steam them for 20–30 minutes, or until they are hot all the way through. To reheat unfrozen tamales, steam them for 10 minutes, or until thoroughly heated. Or you can warm them in a heavy frying pan or on a griddle or *comal,* turning them frequently for about 5–10 minutes, until the husks are brown. Serve hot with a salsa of choice.

MAKES ABOUT 24 TAMALES.

Tacos, Burritos, Tostadas, and Quesadillas

The national taco chains may have given some of us a narrow vision of the taco: a crisp fake tortilla shell filled with ersatz ground beef, bland sauce, lettuce, and grated imitation cheese. Not very appetizing, to say the least.

Think, however, of a fresh corn tortilla warm from the griddle, filled with chunks of spicy meat, fish, seafood, or chicken, garnished with freshly made salsa, guacamole, and chopped ripe tomatoes. That's a taco worth eating, and with almost any filling, great with beer.

Tacos are a delicious and quick way to use leftovers or to eat freshly stewed or grilled food. They also make great party food: Just heat up a dozen or so tortillas and wrap them in towels. Spread a table with an array of grilled meats, fish, or chicken. Serve some Salsa Cruda (see page 308), chopped tomatoes, Red Onions Pickled in Lime Juice (see page 309), sour cream, Guacamole (see page 309), and grated cheese. And let your guests make their own. Serve with a light lager like Pete's Pacific Dry or Eureka.

An easy way to fill tacos is with grilled marinated meat or fish (see Marinating and Grilling, page 155).

An excellent book with many tips on tacos is Victoria Wise and Susanna Hoffman's *The Well-Filled Tortilla Cookbook,* published in 1990 by Workman Publishing.

Beef Taco

Marinate flank steak in Ale Marinade for Steak (see page 156). Grill to your taste, slice thin on the diagonal, and wrap in warm corn tortillas with Guacamole (see page 309), diced tomatoes, and Red Onions Pickled in Lime Juice (see page 309).

Fish Taco

Marinate albacore, red snapper, or shark in our Lemon and Lager Marinade for Fish (see page 155). Grill until done, cut into chunks, and eat in warm corn tortillas with lime juice, Salsa Cruda (see page 308), shredded lettuce or cabbage, and Red Onions Pickled in Lime Juice (see page 309).

Chicken Taco

Marinate chicken breasts in Bourbon Stout Marinade (see page 157). Bone, chop chicken coarsely, and toss with Salsa Cruda (see page 308). Serve in warm corn tortillas with shredded lettuce and Guacamole (see page 309).

Easy Leftovers Taco

Make this quick and easy taco with any leftover grilled or roast meat, poultry, or fish. Heat a heavy frying pan over medium-high heat. Put in a fresh corn tortilla, and turn after 10–15 seconds. Sprinkle grated cheese over the tortilla, and add strips or chunks of cooked meat, chicken, or fish. Cover the pan a good 20 seconds or so. Slide the tortilla onto a plate, and add Salsa Cruda (see page 308), shredded lettuce, chopped onions, Guacamole (see page 309), or your favorite garnish. Roll or fold the tortilla, and bite down.

Burritos

A burrito is a rolled version of the taco, usually made with a flour tortilla. Often burritos contain beans or rice, in addition to the meat or vegetable filling. To make a burrito, heat a flour tortilla until soft and pliable, add a filling such as those described above along with cooked pinto beans or rice, roll, and tuck ends in. Any filling that works in a taco will do just fine for a burrito, too.

Many of our recipes also make excellent fillings for tacos, burritos, and tostadas: Chicken in Green Mole Nut Sauce,* Lamb Shanks Braised in Beer and Cilantro,* Beef Brisket with Lemons and Chiles,* Alice's Ceviche,* Great Goulash,* and Sonoran Lamb Stew (*Birria*).*

You can use the leftovers of any of these by removing the meat from the bones, if any, and cutting it into ½-inch chunks. Gently rewarm in the sauce. Heat tortillas on a *comal,* dry frying pan, or griddle, wrap the meat, fish, or poultry pieces in the tortillas, and garnish with grated cheese, salsa, onions, lettuce, and so on.

*See Index.

Tostadas

Tostadas are essentially salads piled on top of a fried tortilla (usually corn, but sometimes flour). To fry the tortilla, heat ½ inch oil in a heavy frying pan to just below the smoke point. Add a tortilla, and cook for 1 minute. Turn and cook 1–1½ minutes more until the tortilla is crisp and light brown. Drain on a paper towel.

Some people like to coat the tortilla with a layer of refried beans before piling on the salad, but this is not essential and in our opinion makes a rather heavy tostada. To build a tostada: Heap the fried tortilla with shredded lettuce or cabbage lightly tossed with oil and vinegar. Add shredded or diced grilled meat, fish, seafood, or chicken, grated cheese, a large dollop of Guacamole (see page 309), Salsa Cruda (see page 308), and sour cream, if you like. A particularly delicious tostada to serve as an appetizer includes a thin layer of shredded cabbage on a crisp tortilla with lots of Alice's Ceviche (see page 298) on top. Garnish with Salsa Cruda and fresh cilantro leaves.

Quesadillas

Quesadillas are Mexican grilled cheese sandwiches—tasty and easy to make. They are great for lunches and appetizers; cut into wedges, quesadillas make wonderful bar snacks or finger food.

Jack or Cheddar are the most common cheeses used in quesadillas, but if you can find it, try *queso fresco,* the delicious fresh Mexican cheese found in Latino groceries. Other suitable cheeses include fontina, mozzarella, Swiss, Parmesan, fresh goat cheese, Gouda, Edam, and various smoked cheeses. In addition to cheese, other ingredients that can be added are diced ham and shredded grilled beef, rabbit, chicken, or pork. Pickled vegetables, jalapeños *en escabeche,* pickled carrots, onions, and olives, are often also added.

Vegetarian quesadillas can be made from fire-roasted peppers (see page 251), fried eggplant, fried or boiled potatoes, or other cooked vegetables such as zucchini, cauliflower, spinach, bitter greens, chopped turnips, or corn. Get the picture? Let the fridge and the pantry be your guide.

Salsa Cruda

This fresh salsa picante is great on all kinds of Mexican and Southwest dishes. It's also very tasty on poached fish or chicken, grilled pork chops or steak, with a glass of light ale like Albuquerque Brewing's Michael's Golden Ale or Santa Fe Pale Ale.

½ cup chopped fresh cilantro
1 cup finely chopped tomato
½ cup minced red or yellow onion
2 jalapeño chiles or other hot chiles, seeded, or 2 teaspoons crushed dried red chile

2 Anaheim or other mild green chiles, fire roasted and peeled (see page 251), or ½ cup chopped canned Ortega brand green chiles
¼ cup fresh lime or lemon juice
Salt to taste

Mix all the ingredients together in a serving bowl. Keeps 3–5 days refrigerated.

MAKES 2 CUPS.

Guacamole

Guacamole and freshly fried tortilla chips cry out for light Mexican-style lagers, such as Santa Cruz Brewing's Pacific Pils. Guacamole is a great topping on Gorditas, Tacos, Burritos, Tostadas, or Quesadillas. *

2 large avocados, peeled and seeded
½ cup Salsa Cruda (see page 308)

¼ cup chopped fresh cilantro
¼ cup finely chopped onion
Fresh lime juice and salt to taste

Mash the avocados to a coarse, lumpy texture. Stir in the salsa, cilantro, and onion. Add the lime juice and salt to taste.

MAKES 2 CUPS. *

Red Onions Pickled in Lime Juice

These zesty pickled onions are an essential part of a taco or gordita buffet. They also do wonders for sandwiches or grilled sausages. If you want to make up a Mexican plowman's lunch, try these onions with queso fresco, fresh Mexican cheese, or teleme jack, some pickled jalapeños (en escabeche), freshly fried tortilla chips, and a cold light lager like Rattlesnake Beer from Kershenstine Diamond in Missouri or Crazy Ed's Black Mountain Frog Light Pilsner from Arizona.

1 large red onion, thinly sliced
¼ cup fresh lime juice
1 tablespoon olive oil
½ teaspoon salt
2 tablespoons chopped fresh cilantro

1 teaspoon chopped fresh oregano or ½ teaspoon dried

Mix together all the ingredients, and let marinate at room temperature for at least 3 hours. Keeps 3–4 days covered in the refrigerator.

MAKES I CUP.

*See Index.

Chicken in Green Mole Nut Sauce

This unique Mexican sauce called mole (pronounced MO-lay) can be made up separately. Not only is it very tasty in the recipe that follows, but it is excellent spooned over grilled chicken, pork chops, or halibut. It is also makes a wonderful sauce for roast duck. The nuts serve as a thickener. Instead of using all three varieties, you can use ¾ cup of one type of nut, or any combination you choose.

We prepare this dish with cooked poultry—turkey, duck, or chicken—or pork; it is a nice way to use up leftovers. You will need 4 cups diced cooked meat. You can serve it over rice or with flour tortillas so that diners can make their own burritos.

A full, malty Dark Lager highlights mole's spicy, nutty flavors. Try Spoetzl's Shiner Bock or Coors Winterfest.

Green Mole Nut Sauce

4 tablespoons peanut oil
¼ cup almonds
¼ cup peanuts, unsalted
¼ cup walnuts
2 cloves garlic, chopped
6 mild green chiles, such as Anaheim or poblano, fire roasted (see page 251), peeled, and chopped or 8 ounces canned whole green chiles

4 tomatillos, coarsely chopped, canned or fresh and par-boiled
2 bunches cilantro, chopped (approximately 2 cups)
2 cups Rich Chicken Stock (see page 203)
2 limes or 1½ lemons
Salt and pepper

4 cups cubed cooked turkey, chicken, duck, or pork

To make green mole nut sauce: Heat the peanut oil in a heavy skillet over medium heat. Add the nuts and toast them until they develop a nutty aroma and are light brown, shaking the pan continually for about 5–7 minutes. Transfer the nuts to a food processor. Add the garlic, chiles, tomatillos, 1½ bunches of the cilantro, and the juice from 1 lime or lemon. Puree to form a thick sauce. Transfer the puree to a heavy, high-sided frying pan or Dutch oven, and gradually stir in the stock.

Add the cooked poultry or pork, and heat gently for 5 minutes. Do not boil the sauce as it will separate. Add the remaining lime or lemon juice and taste for salt and pepper. Serve garnished with the remaining ½ bunch cilantro.

SERVES 4–6.

Sonoran Lamb Stew (Birria)

Loni Kuhn, who teaches Southwestern cooking classes, gave us her version of this spicy Mexican lamb, or kid, stew, birria. *The earthy dish is simple to make: The meat doesn't even need to be browned, and, if you use dried Mexican chiles, it is not too spicy. Use a full-flavored Pale Ale in the stew and on the table: Boulder Extra Pale Ale from Colorado is a good one.*

Serve with O'Shea's Black Beans,* polenta, or fresh tortillas. Leftovers make superb fillings for Tacos* or Burritos.*

6 large dried red chiles, such as New Mexico, ancho, or California, or any combination	2 teaspoons dried oregano
	1 12-ounce bottle of beer or ale
1 small fresh chile, such as 1 jalapeño (optional)	5–6 pounds lean leg or shoulder of lamb, cut into 3-inch chunks
Pinch ground cloves	2 large onions, peeled and sliced
1 tablespoon whole cumin seed	
1 teaspoon ground cinnamon	12 cloves garlic, peeled

Tear up all the dried chiles and remove and discard the stems and seeds. Place the dried chiles in a bowl, cover with hot water, and soak for at least 5 minutes. Drain. In a food processor or blender mix together the soaked chiles, optional fresh chile, spices, oregano, and beer. Process until a smooth sauce forms. Mix the chile sauce with the lamb, onions, garlic, salt, and pepper. Marinate for 2 hours at room temperature.

Preheat the oven to 350° F. Place the mixture in a casserole or Dutch oven, cover and bake for 2–3 hours, until the meat is quite tender. Remove the meat, and boil the sauce to reduce it. Pour sauce over the meat before serving.

SERVES 6–8.

*See Index.

Lamb Shanks Braised in Beer and Cilantro

If you like the pungent Mexican herb cilantro, you'll love these braised lamb shanks. Some cilantro cooks along with the lamb, mellowing the fresh herb's powerful flavor. The remaining cilantro is added right at the end to give the dish a fresh herbal taste and bright green color. With this Southwestern dish, drink a light beer such as Rattlesnake Beer from Kershenstine Diamond Brewing of Missouri or Aspen Silver City Ale.

6 whole lamb shanks
(about 4 pounds)
Salt and pepper
¼ cup olive oil
1 rib celery, finely chopped
1 carrot, cut into ½-inch chunks
1 large onion, thinly sliced
4 medium leeks, cleaned and
thinly sliced (white parts
only)

2 bunches of cilantro
(approximately 2 cups)
3 garlic cloves, minced
1 teaspoon ground cumin
2 cups beer
Juice of 1 lemon

Preheat the oven to 350° F. Sprinkle the lamb with salt and pepper. Heat the olive oil in a large Dutch oven or high-sided skillet with a tight-fitting lid over high heat. Brown the shanks on all sides, for about 7 minutes total. Remove and reserve. Add the celery, carrot, onion, and about ⅔ of the leeks, cover the pot, and reduce the heat to medium. Cook for 10 minutes, or until the vegetables are soft.

Separate the stems from the leaves of the cilantro, and slice stems thinly. Add the cilantro stems, garlic, and cumin to the pot. Cook for 1 minute, then add the beer and lamb shanks. Bring to a boil. Cover and cook in the oven for 1 hour, or until the meat is tender.

Transfer the shanks to a heated platter and keep warm. Process the remaining leeks and all but ⅓ cup of the cilantro leaves until finely chopped in a food processor. Put them into the cooking pot over medium heat and cook, uncovered, 5–6 minutes. If the sauce is too watery, reduce it over high heat for 1 or 2 minutes. Add the lemon juice to the sauce, and pour over the lamb shanks. Garnish with the remaining cilantro leaves and serve over rice.

SERVES 4–6.

O'Shea's Black Beans

O'Shea's Mad Hatter is a San Francisco sports bar and restaurant that combines a bustling bar with over 30 beers on tap and hearty food that goes beautifully with full-flavored beers and ales.

This spicy black bean recipe is a great side dish or filling for Tacos,* Burritos,* or Quesadillas.* Serve with a hearty ale such as Boulder Red Ale.

1 pound dried black beans, soaked overnight in water to cover

¼ cup diced salt pork or bacon

½ cup diced onions

2 garlic cloves, minced

2 tablespoons ancho chile powder, or any good chile powder such as Gebhardt

4 tablespoons ground cumin

1 teaspoon ground cinnamon

½ teaspoon ground allspice

1 tablespoon chopped fresh oregano or 1 teaspoon dried

6 cups Rich Chicken Stock (see page 203)

1 12-ounce bottle lager

Salt to taste

Drain the beans and discard the soaking liquid. In a large heavy pot render the salt pork over medium heat. Add the onions and garlic, and cook until the onions are translucent, about 5 minutes. Add the chile powder, cumin, cinnamon, allspice, and oregano, and stir briefly. Add the beans, and stir to distribute the spices evenly. Pour in the broth and beer, bring to a boil, and reduce to a simmer. Cook until the beans are tender, but still hold their shape, about 1½–2 hours. Add salt to taste. (Note: Adding salt too early will toughen the beans and will necessitate a longer cooking time.)

SERVES 6–8.

*See Index.

Appendix I:
How Beer Is Made

Beer is basically fermented grain and water with hops added for flavor and preservative qualities. As opposed to the way other fermented beverages (wine and mead) are made, beer's main ingredient, barley, must undergo a complicated process of malting and mashing to convert the grain's natural starches to fermentable sugars.

Ingredients

Barley has been the primary ingredient in beer since the beginnings of brewing in the ancient Near East. Barley has definite advantages over other grains. It has a low gluten content and is therefore not suitable for bread-making or baking; it is easily malted; its starches convert quickly to sugars; its husk acts as a strainer during the final stages of brewing; it thrives in cooler climates.

Most American brewers use six-row barley (so named because of the arrangement of grains on the barley head), grown on the plains of Nebraska, Idaho, the Dakotas, Minnesota, and Wisconsin. Six-row barley provides high yields per acre and is thus cheaper to grow than other varieties, but has an elevated protein content and less flavor when compared with the other main variety, two-row.

Two-row barley grown in England, on the Continent, and in America is preferred by most European and many American craft brewers. Its lower protein content means that all-malt beers made from two-row barley remain clear and stable, and it is generally thought to provide richer malt flavors. Chill haze from the excessive proteins in six-row barley is often the rationale for adding adjuncts such as corn grits or rice to American beers, although cheaper cost of materials is also an important consideration.

Corn / Rice are commonly added as grits or flakes to American

Pilsner-style beers. These adjuncts, as they are called, are considerably less expensive than malted barley, and result in beers that are quite pale in color with very light flavor profiles.

Water is an essential part of brewing, and most brewing centers (Pilsen, Munich, Burton-on-Trent, Milwaukee) throughout history have been located near good water sources such as natural springs, rivers, and lakes. The chemical composition of the water has much to do with the beer style, and nowadays brewers often adjust the minerals and salts of water for brewing. Harder waters are said to be more suitable for high-hopped ales, softer waters for milder ales and lagers.

Hops (*Humulus lupulus*) provide the bitter flavors and floral aromas that create complexity and flavor interest in many beer styles. The bitterness that balances malt's inherent sweetness is derived from resins that differ from one variety of hops to another. Bittering varieties used in highly hopped ales and Stouts are Brewer's Gold, Bullion, Northern Brewer, and Galena. Other less bitter, but more aromatic varieties of hops are Fuggles, Hallertauer, Saaz, and Spalt, often used in lagers and milder ales. Some like Cascade, Cluster, Styrian Goldings, and Tettnanger can serve both purposes, and are found in lighter lagers and ales. The type and amount of hops used have a very strong influence on a beer's style and flavor.

Malting

Through malting, barley (and occasionally wheat and other grains) begins the process that converts its natural starches to the sugars that are necessary to nourish the growing plant. This is done by soaking or steeping the grains, and then germinating the seeds to start growth. At this point enzymes are developed, which begin the conversion of starch to sugars. Drying arrests the growth of the new green sprout, or chit, without harming the enzymes, and roasting develops the characteristic color and flavor of the finished malt. Malts range from standard or pale (the lightest and sweetest) through Munich, caramel or crystal, chocolate, and black patent, in ascending levels of color and flavor caused by caramelization of sugars during roasting. Roasted unmalted barley is often used in Stouts and Porters for flavor and color.

Mashing

Here ground malt is heated with water (mashed) to stimulate enzymatic activity and complete the development of the malt sugars that will ferment to create alcohol and carbon dioxide in the finished beer. Three basic mashing techniques are used, depending on local traditions and ingredients and the type of beer desired.

In the infusion mash, commonly used for ales, the grist or ground malt is heated with water and held at a single temperature throughout the mashing period. In the decoction mash, popular with lager-makers on the Continent and in the United States, a portion of the mash is heated separately and added back to the mash tun to raise its temperature and influence enzymatic action. In the double mash, created by American brewers who use adjuncts like rice and corn, these are heated separately, and then added to the barley mash.

The type of mash, its length of time, and the temperature have a very strong influence on the flavor, strength, and character of the resulting beer. The amount of extract, the presence or lack of unfermentable sugars or dextrins, and the body and flavors of the final beer are all largely created by mashing. The caloric and alcoholic content of beers is determined by the amount of water added at mashing along with the temperature and time of the processing: Light and Dry Beers, for example, are products of special mashing techniques.

Brewing

After mashing, the wort (pronounced *wurt*), or brewing liquid, is strained through the lauter tun, a large tank with a perforated bottom where the hot mash cools and drains. After the sweet wort is transferred into the brewing kettle, the remaining spent grain is sparged, or sprinkled, with hot water to wash off any remaining sugars. This is usually added to the sweet wort in the brew kettle, although in times past this thinner liquid became the basis for small beer or table beer, lower in alcohol and body than the regular brew.

Bittering or flavoring hops are now added to the kettle, and the wort is boiled for 1–2 hours to sterilize the beer, extract the hop flavors, boil off unwanted flavors, and to help clear and stabilize the brew. Aromatic or finishing hops are added towards the end of the boil to preserve their fragrant oils.

The wort is then strained and cooled, and the yeast added, or pitched, to begin the fermentation process. The type of yeast, ale or lager, top or bottom-fermenting, depends on tradition and the type of beer desired. Most breweries isolate their own specific strains of yeast for each type of beer made and take great care to preserve the purity of their yeast cultures.

Temperature and duration of fermentation depends on the type of beer being made. Typically, ales and other top-fermented beers such as Wheat Beer and *Altbier* ferment for a short time (3–5 days) at relatively warm temperatures (above 50° F.) before kegging or bottling. Bottom-fermented lagers ferment for a longer period, usually a week or so, at cool temperatures (under 50° F.), and then are lagered or stored at very low temperatures (about 32° F.) for at least a month, and often much longer.

Carbonation

The characteristic head or carbonation of beer is a natural by-product of fermentation. Carbon dioxide is formed along with the alcohol and is dissolved in the beer during brewing and aging. Ales sometimes receive an addition of sugar in the keg or bottle (this is called cask or bottle conditioning), but are generally less carbonated than lagers, especially if the ales are made in the English style. Lagers are often refreshed just before bottling with some sweet wort or freshly fermenting beer, a process called *kräusening*.

Most American mass-produced beers, however, are simply carbonated before being bottled, using CO_2 recovered from fermentation. The taste in America for sweet, fizzy, and cold drinks has much to do with the style of the national brew. It's not at all strange that most American Pilsners are low in hops, highly carbonated, and served icy cold.

Draft versus Bottles and Cans

Most commercial beers are filtered, pasteurized, and bottled or canned. Pasteurization is a controversial subject with beer lovers. Many feel that heating the beer, however briefly, to kill yeast, bacteria, and other microorganisms robs the beer of life. They feel that draft beer, usually unpasteurized before kegging and serving, is preferable, as the beer is still "alive" and is fresher than bottled or canned beer.

The question of freshness is the key here. Beer, unlike wine, definitely does not improve with age. If it is bottled unpasteurized and then shipped and stored in unrefrigerated conditions, deterioration is inevitable. Thus, most bottled or canned beers in the marketplace, whether domestic or imported, are pasteurized. And even pasteurized beers will be over the hill after a few months. Most beers are date-coded so that retailers will know when to rotate stock, but the problem for the consumer is that the codes vary with each brewer and are largely incomprehensible to the average shopper.

Some small brewers who do not pasteurize their beers—Baderbrau, for example, and Eureka—are printing expiration dates on their labels. The few large brewers like Coors that don't pasteurize require refrigerated shipment and storage, and rigorously police retailers' shelves to remove older brews.

The moral: Drink local beers as soon as possible after they have been brewed, if you can obtain that information. On draft, in the can, or in the bottle, ripeness is definitely not all when it comes to beer.

A note on cans versus bottles: Metal cans are lined with impervious materials so that the beer doesn't come in contact with metal—any "metallic" taste a drinker may find is probably imaginary. Many feel, however, that the carbonation level is higher in cans, and certainly the American habit of drinking directly from the can keeps the CO_2 higher than it would be if you poured the beer into a glass. But you'd get the same effect drinking from a bottle, so there isn't likely to be any real difference. The only quality factor is that very few, if any, fine beers end up in a can. The better beers of Europe and America are found either on draft or in a glass bottle. It's not so much the container that makes the difference, but what goes into the container. So if you are looking for top-quality beer, you should generally avoid the canned product.

APPENDIX II: WORLD BEER STYLES

SOURCES: Michael Jackson, *New World Guide to Beer;* Fred Eckhardt, *The Essentials of Beer Style*

Top-Fermented Ales

Ale (American)–Top fermented, pale to amber color, medium bodied, medium to high hops, medium to high alcohol. Example: Rainier Ale.

> *Cream Ale*–Top fermented or blend of ale/lager, pale color, light bodied, low hops, low to medium alcohol. Example: Genesee Cream Ale.

Ale (Canadian)–Top fermented, medium pale to deep amber, medium to full bodied, medium to high hops, medium to high alcohol. Example: Black Horse, Molson Ale.

Ale (British Isles/Ireland)–Most traditional brews in England, Wales, Scotland, and Ireland are made using top-fermented yeasts with plenty of hop and malt flavors. Types vary from region to region, especially after the work of CAMRA, the Campaign for Real Ale, which has revivified the brewing of authentic ales throughout Britain. Many American microbreweries specialize in British-style ales.

> *Barley Wine*–Top fermented in England and U.S., amber to dark color, very full bodied, very high hops to balance sweet malty character, fruity, estery aromas, very high alcohol (6–13 percent). Example: Anchor Old Foghorn Barley Wine.
>
> *Bitter*–Top fermented in England and U.S., amber color, medium to full body, medium to high hops, low carbonation, medium alcohol. Extra Special Bitter (E.S.B.) higher alcohol, more body. Example: Redhook ESB.
>
> *Brown Ale*–Top fermented in Britain/U.S., amber to dark color,

medium body, medium hops, low alcohol. Southern English style slightly sweet; Northern drier, hoppier. Some U.S. micros make high-hopped, bitter version.

India Pale Ale (IPA)–Top fermented, pale to amber color, originally strong, high-hopped ale brewed for shipment to India. Dry, high alcohol ale with powerful hop character. Example: Grant's India Pale Ale.

Mild Ale–Top fermented, amber to dark brown, medium to full bodied, low hops, low alcohol. Favorite with workers in Northern England.

Porter–Top fermented, dark brown, medium to full bodied, medium to high hops, moderately high alcohol. Rich, dark English ale originating in London in eighteenth century, recently revived by American microbreweries. Examples: Anchor Porter, Yuengling Porter, Samuel Smith Taddy Porter.

Scotch Ale–Top fermented, deep amber to dark brown color, low hops, very malty flavors, slightly sweet, can be quite strong. In Scotland alcohol ranked as Light, Wee Heavy, Heavy, Export, Strong, or in shillings (60/, 70/, 80/, 90/), ranging from 3 percent on the low side to 10 percent for the most powerful ales. Also a style of dark ale in France and Belgium. Examples: Grant's Scottish Ale, McKesson Edinburgh Ale, Pelforth Extra.

Stout–Top fermented, very dark to black color, high hops, strong roasted barley/burnt coffee flavors, full body, high alcohol.

Dry (Irish) Stout–Very dark, very high hops, distinct burnt barley flavors, creamy head, great depth of flavor and character. Example: Guinness.

Sweet Stout–Very dark, full-bodied stout sweetened with lactose (unfermentable milk sugar) before bottling. Sweet, black ale. Example: McKesson Stout.

Imperial Stout–Top fermented in Britain/U.S., dark amber to black, very strong stout originally brewed for shipment to Czarist Russia. Thick, deeply flavored, and high in alcohol (7–10½ percent). Examples: Samuel Smith Imperial Stout, Grant's Imperial Stout.

Alt(Bier)–Top-fermented, old-style German ale, copper to red-brown color, light to medium bodied, high hops, medium alcohol. Example: Düsseldorfer Alt, Pinkus Alt, Widmer Altbier.

Kolsch–Top fermented Altbier from Cologne, pale gold color, high hopped, tart with dry, winey flavors.

Bière de Garde–Top fermented in Northern France, Belgium, amber to dark color, very full bodied, complex and spicy flavors, made for aging. Example: Bière de Paris, St. Leonard.

Lambic–Top-fermented Belgian wheat ale using airborne wild yeasts. Often aged in wood or blended with fruits, syrup, young beers.

> *Faro*–Top-fermented Belgian ale (Lambic) made with wild yeasts, wheat malt. This is the sweetened variety, usually drunk young and fresh.
>
> *Framboise*–French word for raspberry, top-fermented Belgian ale (Lambic) blended with raspberries and refermented. Fruity and sometimes lightly sweet. Example: Lindemans.
>
> *Gueze*–Top fermented, Belgian blend of old Lambic with fresh to create second fermentation. Winey, low in hops, very fruity, complex.
>
> *Kriek*–Top fermented, old Lambic blended with cherries and refermented. Sharp, fruity, often slightly sweet. Example: Lindemans.

Saison–Top-fermented, Belgian summer specialty ale, sharp flavors, refreshing, slightly sour.

Trappist (Abbey) Ales–Top fermented, amber to dark brown color, spicy, estery aromas, can be quite strong with Double and Triple Malts ranging from 6–12 percent alcohol. Ales labeled Trappist must be made in specific monasteries in Belgium and the Netherlands, Abbey ales are made in a similar style. Example: Orval.

Wheat Beer/Weizenbier/Weissbier–Top fermented, pale color, lightly hopped, high carbonation, tart flavors. A class of beers using up to 50 percent wheat malt in addition to barley malt. Usually very light and refreshing. Often served with slice of lemon or a dash of fruit syrup. Example: Kemper Wheaten Ale, Widmer Weizen.

> *Berliner Weisse*–Wheat beer, top fermented in North Germany, very pale, often slightly cloudy, light bodied, highly carbonated, light hops with lactic (yogurt-like) sourness, low alcohol.
>
> *Weizen/Weissbier*–South German wheat beer with at least 50 percent wheat malt (*weizen* means wheat; *weiss* means white), tart, spicy flavors of cloves and applesauce.

Dunkelweizen–Dark version of Weizenbier, malty and complex flavors. Example: Sprecher Dunkel Weizen.

Hefe(weiss)–Top-fermented wheat beer in Germany/U.S., bottled unfiltered and still cloudy with yeast (*hefe*). Lightly hopped, slightly tart, with yeasty flavors, low alcohol. Example: Widmer Hefeweizen.

American Wheat Beer–Top fermented, gold to light amber color, light hops, high carbonation, fresh, tart beers without the spice and sour flavors of German counterparts. Refreshing and light summertime beers, excellent with lighter foods like fish and seafood. Example: Anchor Wheat Beer, August Schell Weizen.

Bottom-Fermented Lagers

Bock–Lager from Germany/U.S., amber to dark, full bodied, malty, slightly sweet, medium to high hops, high alcohol. Commercial U.S. bocks usually lighter in color, flavor, alcohol than German/U.S. microbrewery versions.

Dopplebock–Bottom fermented, amber to dark brown, full body, very malty, slightly sweet, very high alcohol (7.5 percent +). South German Spring specialty, names usually end in *-ator*. Example: Paulaner Salvator.

Eisbock–Very strong bock beer made by freezing brew to concentrate alcohol, sweet, malty and with quite a kick. Alcohol: 8–12 percent. Examples: EKU Kulminator, Samichlaus.

Maibock–Bottom fermented, pale color, Munich specialty brewed in spring, malty, full bodied, high alcohol, often slightly sweet. Example: Sprecher Maibock.

Märzen(bier)–Bottom fermented, amber color, Bock-type beer, malty and full, medium high alcohol. Traditionally brewed in March from last of winter's malt, stronger than usual to age over hot summer months. Often served at Oktoberfest.

Octoberfest–Similar to above. Amber lager, malty, strong. Example: Gartenbrau Oktoberfest.

Bremen-Hamburg–Bottom fermented in northern Germany, pale color, medium to full body, high hops. Drier version of Pilsner style. Example: Becks.

Dark (American)–Bottom fermented in U.S., amber to medium dark color, light body, light hops, low alcohol. Often simply standard American pale Pilsner with caramel syrup added for color. Example: Henry Weinhard Dark.

Dortmunder Export–Bottom fermented, pale to light amber, full bodied, medium hops, medium to high alcohol. In Germany/Continent less malty and drier than Munich-style lager; less hops, fuller than Pilsner. Example: Dortmunder Kronen Classic.

Dunkel–"Dark" in German, bottom fermented, deep amber to brown, usually refers to Munich style, full bodied, malty, low hops, slightly sweet. Example: Kemper Dunkel.

Export–Bottom fermented, pale, full bodied, medium hops, high alcohol. Dortmunder style, often used to denote premium/high alcohol pale beer on Continent.

Hell(es)–Bottom fermented, pale color (German *hell* means light), refers either to pale Munich lager, malty and slightly sweet or to Helles Bock, pale, malty, high in alcohol.

Light Beer–Bottom fermented, very pale, very light bodied, low hopped, mildly flavored American beer using very little malt and special yeasts to consume dextrins that contribute flavor and body in more substantial beers. Thin stuff, the equivalent of traditional English small beer.

Malt Liquor–Bottom fermented, pale color, low malt and hop character, very high alcohol. Thin, but strong American pale lager, usually advertising "More Bang for the Buck!" rather than flavor. Cheap and strong, generally of low quality. Some state laws require any beer above a certain alcohol to be labeled Malt Liquor, including Dopplebocks, Barley Wines, Stouts, and so on. Seems confusing, but one taste and you'll know the difference.

Pilsner–Bottom fermented, pale color, medium to full bodied, high hopped, intensely flavored lager originally from Pilsen in Czecho-slovakia. Example: Pilsner Urquell, Baderbrau.

American Pilsner–Bottom fermented, pale to very pale color, light bodied, low hops, low malt flavors, sometimes "corn" or grain flavors, often slightly sweet on palate. American imitation of original Pilsner style, but thin and watered down. The use of adjuncts (corn and rice) makes for an attenuated brew without the character and flavors of the original. Example: any standard American beer.

Continental Pilsner–European and American versions of the original Czech brew. Pale, moderately hoppy, crisp, dry flavors. Usually between true Pilsner and the American version in body and flavors. Also called the Continental lager style. Examples: Heineken, Carlsberg, August Schell Pilsner.

Rauchbier–Bottom fermented, amber color, unusual smoky flavor (*rauch* means smoked in German) comes from lightly roasting malt in smoke from wood or peat fires. Reminds some of single-malt Scotch "peat reek," others of home-smoked bacon.

Vienna–Bottom fermented, amber or "red" color, medium bodied, light hops, malty. Originally described Vienna's beer style made with malt roasted to characteristic amber color. Now used for any medium dark, mildly hopped lager. Examples: Ambier, Dos Equis.

APPENDIX III:
BREWING BEER AT HOME

Making your own beer is easy, can be fun, and yields delicious, full-bodied brews at very little cost. With a minimum investment in equipment, a little reading, and not much effort, the beginning home brewer can make Pale and Amber Ales, Porters and Stouts that are virtually indistinguishable from the commercial product. Lagers are a bit more complicated to achieve, but are well within the capabilities of more experienced brewers.

Many people's image of beer brewed at home is the old Prohibition "home brew," sour and gassy, with bottles prone to explode at odd times, and the brew itself often tasting as if it had been made in the bathtub (as it sometimes was). Modern home brewers are meticulous about sanitation, have access to the finest malt, hops, and yeast, and can reproduce virtually any beer style in the world.

Some beer hobbyists, if not to say fanatics, go so far as to grow their own barley and hops, and malt their own grain. Many of the more serious brewers mash grains, especially for full-bodied lagers. But most home brewers make very palatable beers from malt extract, either in syrup or dried form.

Malt extract is made by concentrating the sweet wort after mashing and is a product of the great malting houses of Europe, England, and America. It is sold to breweries and bakeries and to home brewers through a network of home brew shops and mail-order houses (see Appendix IV, Mail Order Sources). Malt extract comes in many colors and flavors, from pale to quite dark, hop-flavored or plain. Many home brewers using extracts add specialty malts such as crystal or caramel malt, chocolate malt, black patent malt, or unmalted roasted barley for more color and flavor.

Many varieties of hops are widely available in the home brew shops and by mail. Whole hops are preferred by many brewers, but they can oxidize and lose their flavor with time. Pelletized hops, looking just like rabbit food, are an excellent product, yielding much of the aroma and bitter resins of the fresh. Hop extract, hop-flavored malt extracts, and powdered hops are generally less esteemed, although they can produce palatable beers.

Most home brewers use commercial dry yeasts, ale or lager, from European or American yeast producers. More serious brewers seek out liquid cultures from labs, or even isolate and propagate yeasts from their own and from others' brews.

Noniodized table salt, gypsum, and other salts and minerals are often added to harden water, especially when brewing ales. Corn sugar is sometimes added to the brew and is used for priming to create CO_2 in the bottles. Corn sugar is preferable to cane or beet sugar as it doesn't contribute any winey flavors to the finished beer. All these ingredients are readily available at home brew shops or from mail order sources.

Equipment can range from a kettle, food-grade plastic trash can, and a carboy or five-gallon jug to an elaborate stainless steel and copper set-up that would make a small commercial brewer envious. And in fact, many of the serious home brewing hobbyists go professional after a while and start their own microbreweries.

We'll just describe here the basic equipment to make five-gallon batches of ale, along with suggestions about where to get more detailed information and elaborate equipment. You can do what most home brewers do, make some delicious and cheap ale now and then on your kitchen range, or you can go on to join the ranks of the true beer fanatics trying to reproduce Pilsner Urquell or Russian Imperial Stout in their own brewhouses.

Sanitation

Cleanliness is absolutely important in brewing beer, as there are microbes lurking about that could spoil the beer. Lack of sanitation is the main cause of unpalatable home brew, so be scrupulous about cleaning your equipment and bottles.

Chlorine is often used as a sterilant, and home brew shops sell packages with directions for use. Many brewers use a dilute solution of household chlorine bleach as a sterilant—a standard mix is 2 tablespoons in 5 gallons of water. Simply wash all your equipment before brewing in hot water, then soak in the bleach solution for 15 minutes to a half hour (the primary fermentor is a good container for this).

Sodium bisulfite or potassium metabisulphite in solution are also used by brewers for sterilization. These products are available at home brew and wine-making shops. Follow the directions on the package.

Equipment

To brew 5-gallon batches of beer you will need:

1. A brew pot with a 3-gallon capacity—stainless steel is preferred, but an enameled canning kettle works just fine.
2. A large stainless steel strainer or cheesecloth.
3. A 10-gallon primary fermentation vessel, a fancy name for a food-grade plastic trash can with lid or plastic sheeting.
4. A 5-gallon glass carboy (used for bottled water) or 5 single gallon jugs.
5. 60 or more cappable (no screw top) 12-ounce beer bottles.
6. A bottle capper and crown caps.
7. 6 feet of clear, ⅜-inch plastic siphon hose.
8. Optional, but helpful:
   A kitchen scale to measure ingredients.
   A kitchen thermometer to gauge wort temperature.
   A hydrometer to measure sugar in wort.
   Fermentation lock(s).
   A book or two on home brewing (see below).

This is a standard set-up for home brewing, and all the equipment listed should be easily available at a local home brewing shop or by mail order (see Appendix IV, Mail Order Sources). The equipment shouldn't cost more than about $75, and you may have some of the items in your kitchen already.

Books

One of the best all-around books for the beginning brewer is Byron Burch's *Brewing Quality Beers,* available from Great Fermentations of Santa Rosa, California (see Appendix IV, Mail Order Sources). Other excellent books for home brewers include *The Complete Joy of Home Brewing* by Charlie Papazian (Avon Books), and *Making Beer* by William Mares (Knopf). There are many books for more advanced brewers, available from home brew shops and mail order sources. The magazine *zymurgy* is published by the American Home Brewer's Association and is available through Brewer's Publications (see Mail Order Sources). It contains much information for advanced brewers and includes advertisements for home brew shops and mail order houses specializing in brewing supplies and equipment.

Lager

Making lager is much more complicated than making ale. You'll need a refrigerator fitted with a special thermostat to keep the fermenting temperature around 50° F., and generally more elaborate equipment than for ale. An excellent book on the subject is Greg Noonan's *Brewing Lager Beer,* available from Brewer's Publications (see Appendix IV, Mail Order Sources). Noonan's book also has a good section on mashing and making all-grain beers.

Cinque Zanni Brewers' Pale Ale

2 3½-pound cans light malt extract
½ teaspoon noniodized salt
1 teaspoon gypsum
2 ounces bittering or flavoring hops (Brewer's Gold, Bullion, Cluster, Cascade)

1 ounce aromatic or finishing hops (Fuggles, Cascade)
5 gallons water
1 14-gram package dried ale yeast
1 cup corn sugar for priming

Bring at least 3 gallons of water to a boil in the brew kettle. Turn off the heat, and stir in the malt extract, rinsing the cans with water to get all the syrup out. Stir thoroughly to dissolve all the malt in the water. Stir in the salt and gypsum. Turn the heat back on to high, and bring the wort to a rolling boil. When it begins to foam up, stir well, add half the flavoring hops, and reduce the heat slightly so the pot doesn't spill over. Cook the wort at a boil for 30 minutes.

Add the remaining flavoring hops and boil for another 30 minutes. Add the finishing hops and continue the boil for 5 more minutes.

Pour the hot wort carefully through a strainer or cheesecloth held over the top of the primary fermentor. If you only used 3 gallons of water in the kettle, you can now add 2 more gallons of previously boiled and cooled water to make up the batch and cool the wort. Be sure you leave plenty of room in the primary container for foaming; use a 10-gallon trash can for a 5-gallon batch.

Let the wort cool to about 80° F. or less. If you are using a hydrometer, take a reading at this time. For the recipe above, the starting specific gravity should be about 1.042–1.045.

Sprinkle the dried yeast on top of the cooled wort, and let it rehydrate for 10–15 minutes. Stir it in thoroughly, aerating the wort as you stir. This is called pitching the yeast and rousing the wort. Cover the primary container with a lid or tie plastic sheeting over the top, and store in a cool, dark place. Fermentation should take about 3–4 days.

When the foam has subsided, siphon the wort from the primary fermentor into a sterilized glass carboy, being careful to leave any sediment in the primary fermentor and to splash the beer as little as possible by keeping the end of the siphon tube near the bottom of the carboy. Fit the carboy with a fermentation lock, a device to let CO_2 escape but prevent air from entering, or cover the neck tightly with a plastic bag or plastic wrap and a rubber band.

Keep the carboy in a cool dark place for 3 more days and up to a week. You'll know when fermentation is over by the absence of bubbles in the beer and no positive pressure in the fermentation lock or plastic cover. For the recipe above, final specific gravity should be about 1.010–1.012.

Siphon the beer from the carboy back into the sterilized primary fermentor, and stir in 1 cup of corn sugar. (For sterilization, it is best to use a simple syrup of 2 parts sugar to 1 part water, boiled and cooled.) Siphon into sterilized bottles and cap.

Store the bottles in a cool dry place for at least a week. To serve home brewed beer: Uncap the bottle, and carefully pour out the contents in one continuous pour, leaving any yeast sediment behind in the bottle.

Taste the beer as described on page 17. If there is too much foam for your taste, the next time you brew decrease the amount of corn sugar added at priming. If you want more or less hop flavor or aroma, adjust the levels of bittering and finishing hops. If you want more malt flavor or color, try one of the recipes on the next page.

Nestor Marzipan's
O Death Where Is Thy Stingo Ale

1 3½-pound can light malt
  extract
1 3½-pound can amber or
  dark malt extract
½ teaspoon noniodized salt
1 teaspoon gypsum
1 pound ground crystal or
  caramel malt
2½ ounces bittering or flavoring hops (Northern Brewer,
  Bullion, Galena, Cascade)

2 ounces aromatic or finishing
  hops (Fuggles, Cascade,
  Northern Brewer, Styrian
  Goldings)
5 gallons water
1 14-gram package dried ale
  yeast
¾ cup corn sugar for priming

Follow the previous brewing directions, adding the crystal or caramel malt with the second addition of flavoring hops. Starting specific gravity: 1.045; final specific gravity: 1.010–1.012.

Byron Burch's Irish-Type Stout

5 pounds dry malt extract or
  6 pounds light malt extract
2 pounds amber or dark malt
  extract
½ teaspoon salt
2½ ounces bittering or flavoring hops (Northern Brewer,
  Bullion)

1 pound roasted unmalted
  barley, not crushed
½ ounce aromatic or finishing
  hops (Fuggles, Styrian
  Goldings)
1 14-gram package dried ale
  yeast
¾ cup corn sugar for priming

Follow the previous brewing directions, adding whole grains of roasted barley with the second addition of flavoring hops, and the aromatic hops for only the last 2 minutes of the boil. Starting specific gravity: 1.058; final specific gravity: 1.020.

APPENDIX IV: MAIL ORDER SOURCES

Beer

Beer and Wine Hobby
P.O. Box 3104
Wakefield, MA 01880
(800) 523-5423
Brewing supplies

The Celebrator Beer News
P.O. Box 375
Hayward, CA 94543
(510) 670-0121
FAX (510) 670-0639
West Coast Beer "BrewsPaper"
with up-to-date information about
microbreweries and brew pubs

F. H. Steinbart Company
234 S.E. 12th
Portland, OR 97214
(503) 232-8793
Brewing supplies

Great Fermentations of
Santa Rosa
Winemaking & Brewing Supplies
840 Piner Road, #14
Santa Rosa, CA 95403
(707) 544-2520
Byron Burch (author of Brewing
Quality Beers*), proprietor*

Institute for Brewing Studies/
Association of Brewers
P.O. Box 1679
Boulder, CO 80306
(303) 447-0816
FAX (303) 447-2825
zymurgy Magazine, The New
Brewer, Microbrewers Resource
Directory, *Brewer's Publications,*
The Great American Beer Festival

Sausages, Casings, Etc.

Aidells Sausage Company
1575 Minnesota Street
San Francisco, CA 94107
(415) 285-6660
Sausages, casings

Carlson Butcher Supply
50 Mendell Street #12
San Francisco, CA 94124
(415) 648-2601
Casings, equipment

Zingerman's
422 Detroit Street
Ann Arbor, MI 48104
(313) 663-3354
Sausages, spices, specialty products

Smoking Equipment

Cook'n Cajun Water Smokers
P.O. Box 3726
Shreveport, LA 71133
(318) 925-6933

Williams-Sonoma
P.O. Box 7456
San Francisco, CA 94120-7456
(415) 421-4242

Weber-Stephen Products
200 East Daniels Road
Palatine, IL 60067
(312) 934-5700

Specialty Items

Balducci's
424 Avenue of the Americas
New York, NY 10011
(212) 673-2600
Italian foods

Ginn Wall Co.
1016 Grant Avenue
San Francisco, CA 94133
(415) 982-6307
Asian foods

G. B. Ratto & Co.
821 Washington
Oakland, CA 94607
(800) 228-3515 (California)
(800) 325-3483 (U.S.)
Italian foods

Paprikas Weiss
1572 Second Avenue
New York, NY 10028
(212) 288-6117
Eastern European foods

Catfish Wholesale
P.O. Box 759
Abbeville, LA 70510
(318) 643-6700
Creole seafood

Louisiana Fish Fry Product
5267 Plonk Road
Baton Rouge, LA 70805
(504) 356-2905
Corn flour

BIBLIOGRAPHY

Abel, Bob. *The Beer Book*. London: Music Sales, 1981.

————. *The Book of Beer*. Chicago: Regnery, 1976.

Ade, George. *The Old Time Saloon*. New York: Ray Long & Richard Smith, 1931.

Anderson, Will. *The Beer Book*. Princeton, N.J.: Pyne Press, 1973.

————. *Beer USA*. New York: Morgan & Morgan, 1986.

————. *From Beer to Eternity*. Lexington, Mass.: Stephen Greene Press, 1987.

Arnold, John, and Frank Penman. *History of the Brewing Industry and Brewing Science in America*. Chicago: Master Brewers' Association, 1933.

Baron, Stanley. *Brewed in America: A History of Beer and Ale in the United States*. Boston: Little, Brown, 1962.

Batterberry, Michael and Ariane. *On the Town in New York: From 1776 to the Present*. New York: Scribners, 1973.

Bickerdyke, John. *The Curiosities of Ale and Beer*. London: Leadenhall Press, 1889.

Brown, John Hull. *Early American Beverages*. Rutland, Vt.: Charles E. Tuttle, 1966.

Carson, Gerald. *The Social History of Bourbon*. New York: Dodd Mead, 1963.

Cottone, Vincent. *Good Beer Guide: Breweries and Pubs of the Pacific Northwest*. Seattle: Homestead Books, 1986.

Darby, William, Paul Ghalioungui, and Louis Grivetti. *Food: The Gift of Osiris*. 2 vols. London: Academic Press, 1977.

de Talavera Berger, Frances, and John Custis. *Sumptuous Dining in Gaslight San Francisco*. New York: Doubleday, 1985.

Downard, William. *Dictionary of the History of the American Brewing and Distilling Industries*. Westport, Conn.: Greenwood Press, 1980.

Drummond, J. C., and Anne Wilbraham. *The Englishman's Food*. London: Jonathan Cape, 1959.

Eames, Alan. *A Beer Drinker's Companion*. Harvard, Mass.: Ayers Rock Press, 1986.

Earle, Alice Morse. *Home Life in Colonial Days*. New York: Macmillan, 1898. Reprint, 1957.

————. *Stage-Coach and Tavern Days*. New York: Benjamin Blom, 1900. Reprint, 1969.

Eckhardt, Fred. *The Essentials of Beer Style: A Catalog of Classic Beer Styles for Brewers and Beer Enthusiasts.* Portland, Oreg.: Fred Eckhardt Associates, 1989.

Edwords, Clarence. *Bohemian San Francisco.* San Francisco: Paul Elder, 1914.

Ehret, George. *Twenty-five Years of Brewing.* New York, 1891.

Erdoes, Richard. *Saloons of the Old West.* New York: Alfred A. Knopf, 1979.

Erickson, Jack. *Brewery Adventures in the Wild West.* Reston, Va.: Redbrick Press, 1991.

———. *Great Cooking with Beer.* Reston, Va.: Redbrick Press, 1989.

———. *Star Spangled Beer: A Guide to America's New Microbreweries and Brewpubs.* Reston, Va.: Redbrick Press, 1987.

Fahy, Carole. *Cooking with Beer.* New York: Drake Publishers, 1972.

Finch, Christopher. *Beer: A Connoisseur's Guide to the World's Best.* New York, Abbeville Press, 1989.

Gould, Judith, and Ruth Koretsky. *Brew Cuisine: Cooking with Beer.* Toronto: Summerhill Press, 1989.

Hackwood, Frederick. *Inns, Ales and Drinking Customs of Old England.* London: Bracken Books, 1985.

Harrison, Michael. *Beer Cookery.* London: Garden City Press, 1953.

Hillman, Howard. *The Gourmet Guide to Beer.* New York: Facts on File, 1987.

Hough, J. S., et al. *Malting and Brewing Science.* London: Chapman and Hall, 1971.

Jackson, Michael. *The New World Guide to Beer.* Philadelphia: Running Press, 1988.

———. *The Simon & Schuster Pocket Guide to Beer.* 3rd ed. New York: Simon & Schuster, 1991.

Jefferson, Thomas. *The Garden and Farm Books.* Golden, Colo.: Fulcrum, 1987.

Johnson, Steve. *On Tap: The Guide to U.S. Brewpubs.* Clemson, S.C.: WBR Publications, 1991.

Jones, Evan. *American Food: The Gastronomic Story.* 3rd ed. New York: Overlook Press, 1990.

Katz, Solomon. "Beer and the Origin of Cereal Grain Agriculture." *zymurgy,* Summer 1988, p. 22.

———. "Brewing an Ancient Beer." *Archaeology,* July/August 1991, p. 24.

King, Frank. *Beer Has a History.* London: Hutchinson Scientific and Technical Publications, n.d.

Klinkenborg, Verlyn. *The Last Fine Time.* New York: Alfred A. Knopf, 1991.

Lathrop, Elise. *Early American Inns and Taverns.* New York: McBride, 1926.

Lender, Mark, and James Martin. *Drinking in America: A History.* New York: Macmillan, 1982.

Mares, William. *Making Beer.* New York: Alfred A. Knopf, 1984.

Mathias, Peter. *The Brewing Industry in England, 1700–1830.* Cambridge: Cambridge University Press, 1959.

Mitchell, Joseph. *McSorley's Wonderful Saloon.* New York: Blue Ribbon Press, 1944.

Morris, Stephen. *The Great Beer Trek*. Lexington, Mass.: Stephen Greene Press, 1990.

Oldenburg, Ray. *The Great Good Place*. New York: Paragon House, 1989.

One Hundred Years of Brewing. New York: H. S. Rich, 1903. Reprint. New York: Arno Press, 1974.

Orton, Vrest. *The Homemade Beer Book*. Rutland, Vt.: Charles E. Tuttle, 1976.

————. *Proceedings of the Company of Amateur Brewers*. Privately printed. 1932.

Papazian, Charles. *The Complete Joy of Home Brewing*. New York: Avon Books, 1983.

Pasteur, Louis. *Studies on Fermentation*. London: Macmillan, 1879. Reprint. Millwood, N.Y.: Kraus Reprint, 1969.

Porter, John. *All About Beer*. New York: Doubleday, 1975.

Robertson, James. *The Connoisseur's Guide to Beer*. Aurora, Ill.: Caroline House, 1982.

Rohrbaugh, W. J. *The Alcoholic Republic: An American Tradition*. New York: Oxford University Press, 1979.

Russel, Maria, and Maxine Stromberg. *The Beer Makes It Better Cookbook*. New York: Simon & Schuster, 1971.

Thompson, Toby. *Saloon*. New York: Viking Press, 1976.

Waldo, Myra. *Beer and Good Food*. New York: Doubleday, 1958.

Wright, Richardson. *Grandfather Was Queer*. N.p. N.d.

Wykes, Alan. *Ale and Hearty: Gleanings from the History of Brews and Brewing*. London: Jupiter Books, 1975.

Yenne, Bill. *Beers of North America*. New York: W. H. Smith, 1986.

Yoder, Paton. *Taverns and Travellers: Inns of the Early Midwest*. Bloomington: Indiana University Press, 1969.

INDEX

Note: Page numbers in **boldface** refer to recipes.

Brooklyn Brewery (N.Y.), 230–31
Brown, Hull, 33
Brown Ale, 320–21
Brussels Sprouts with Bacon and Beer,
    211
Buffalo (N.Y.), 223–25
Buffalo Bill's (Hayward, Calif.), 150
Buffalo Chicken Wings, **225**
Burch, Byron, 328, 331
Burgers, **287–88**
Burritos, **306**
Busch, Adolphus, 68, 292
Buttermilk and Cauliflower Soup, **198**
Byron Burch's Irish-Type Stout, **331**

cabbage. *See also* sauerkraut
    and Leek Soup, **239**
    Peanut Slaw, **269**
    Red, Braised in Cider and Beer, **210**
    and Sauerkraut Braised in Dark
        Lager, **79–80**
    and sausage rolls (Edy's Beer Rocks),
        192–93
Caesar Dressing, Green Bean and Red
        Pepper Salad with, **114**
Cake
    Chocolate Porter, **131–32**
    Gingerbread Stout, **220**
    Spice, Kathy's Strong Ale, **61**
Calamari
    Fried, **244–45**
    Salad, California, **164**
California, 133–34
    brewing in, 134–46
        Altbiers and lagers in German tra-
            dition, 143–44
        microbreweries, 139–45
        Steam Beer, 136–39
California Ale, 16
California-style dishes, 142, 144,
        146–49
Campaign for Real Ale (CAMRA), 5,
        320
Camusi, Paul, 142
Canada, 20
Capital Brewery (Madison, Wis.),
        183–84
Caponata Sandwich, Tuna, **282**
carbonation, 136, 229–30, 318
carbon dioxide, 14–15, 17, 136, 318
Carrots and Leeks in Steam Beer,
        171–72
Catamount Brewing, 233
Cato's Tavern (N.Y.), 48

Cauliflower
    and Buttermilk Soup, **198**
    Curried, **214**
Cecchini, Maria, 207, 254
Celtic Ale, 109
Chase, A. W., 34
Chayote and Seafood Ragout Cajun
        Style, **276–77**
cheddar cheese
    and Ale Spread, **93**
    Corn Cakes, **54**
    Welsh Rarebit, **53**
cheese, 24–25. *See also* Blue Cheese;
        Brie; cheddar cheese; Parmesan
        cheese
    and Ale Spread, **93**
    and Beer Soup, Wisconsin, **196**
    Limburger and Raw Onion
        Sandwich, **286**
    Liptauer, **194–95**
Chestnut-Stuffed Quail with Sweet
        Stout Gravy, **54–55**
Chicago, 179–85, 188–91
Chicago Brewing Company, 189
chicken
    Breasts Stuffed with Eggplant,
        Shrimp, and Ham, **279**
    and Dumplings, **201–2**
    and Eggplant Soup, Balkan, **197**
    Greek Tavern, **201**
    in Green Mole Nut Sauce, **310–11**
    Liver, Good Chopped, **237**
    marinade for
        Bourbon Stout, **157**
        Chinese Hoisin, **157**
    Red Bell Peppers Stuffed with
        Seafood and, **278**
    Salad
        Smoked, with Orzo, **160**
        Szechuan, **161**
    with Sauerkraut and Peppers, Hun-
        garian (*Rakott Káposzta*), **204–5**
    Smoked, Brie, and Roasted Red
        Pepper Sandwich, **286**
    Stew, Boilermaker, **98–99**
    Stock, Rich, **203**
    Taco, **306**
    Torta, Mexican Grilled, **285**
    and Wild Rice Braised in Ale, **57–58**
    Wings
        Adobo, **301**
        Buffalo, **225**
Chick Peas, Chorizo, and Red Pepper
        Salad, Basque, **300**

Green Bean(s)
    and Chinese Noodles with Smoky
        Black Bean Sauce, Dry Fried,
        174
    and Red Pepper Salad with Caesar
        Dressing, **114**
Green Chili Beer, 297
Green Dragon Tavern (Boston), 41
Greens, Turnips and, **60–61**
Grossman, Ken, 142
Growlin' Gator Lager Beer, 267
Guacamole, **309**
Gueze, 322

Haffenreffer Brewery (Boston), 232
Hale, Mike, 104
Hale, Sarah, 33
Hale's Ale, 104
Hale's Pale Ale, 106
Halibut, Cucumber, and Avocado
        Salad, **299**
Ham
    Asparagus Wrapped in, in Mustard
        Vinaigrette, **271**
    Chicken Breasts Stuffed with
        Eggplant, Shrimp, and, **279**
    and Pepper Sauté, Hungarian
        (*Lescó*), **205**
    Steaks, Porter or Stout and Molasses
        Marinade for, **156**
Hamilton, Alexander, 43
Hare, Robert, 37–38
Hariot, Thomas, 32
Hart Brewing, 112
Hartung, Udo, 189
Harwood, Ralph, 37
Hash, Corned Beef or Pastrami, **259**
Hayward (Calif.), 149–50
head on beer, 15, 17–18
health, beer and, 31, 39–40
Hefeweizen (Hefeweiss), 110–11, 323
Helena (Mont.), 296
Hell(es), 324
Helles (Light) Lager, 107
Helm, Garith, 143–44
Hemings, John, 38–39
Herb(s)
    Croutons, **198**
    Summer, Lamb Chops with Whole
        Garlic Cloves and, **169**
Herring Salads, Marlene's Three, **71–73**
Higgins, Greg, 111
Higginson, Reverend, 31, 45
Hinds, Willy, 118–19

history of beer, 5–11. *See also specific
        topics*
Hoffman, Susanna, 305
Hoffman House (New York), 84
Holiday/Winter Ale, 16
home-brew clubs, 139
home brewing, 326–31
    books on, 328–29
    equipment for, 328
    recipes, **329–31**
    sanitation and, 327–28
Honey Beer Mustard, **99**
Hood River Brewing Company
        (Oreg.), 110
Hope Brewing (R.I.), 234
Hopland (Calif.), 138–39
hops, 8, 10–11, 14, 31, 141, 316–17, 326–27
    in early America, 35–36
    in the Northwest, 105, 107–9
Horseradish
    and Beer Mustard, **219**
    Cocktail Sauce, Creamy, **50–51**
    and Garlic Mashed Potatoes, **172**
    Vinaigrette
        Beet and Apple Salad with, **195**
        Cold Leeks in, **115**
Huber, John, 182
Huber, Joseph, 181
Huber Braumeister, 182
"Hymn to Ninkasi," 3, 9

Imperial Stout, 109, 321
    Stuffed Pork Loin in, **166–67**
Indian Queen Tavern (Philadelphia), 41
India Pale Ale, 15, 18, 109, 321
Institute for Brewing Studies, 20, 294
Italian neighborhoods, bar food in,
        225–26
Italian-style dishes
    Bollito Misto, **256–57**
    Broccoli Soup, **238**
    Caponata, **235–36**
    Chicken with Pasta, Anchovies, and
        Tomatoes, **255**
    Cotechino Sausage with White
        Beans, **258**
    Crostini, **236**
    Muffuletta, Fried Eggplant, **284**
    Pork Shoulder Braised in Bock, **207**
    Salsa Verde, **257**
    Sicilian Stuffed Peppers, **253**

Jackson, Michael, 12, 23, 189
Jamestown (Va.), 31, 45

Japan, 7
Japanese-style dishes, 247, 288
Jefferson, Thomas, 36, 38–39, 41
Jones, Evan and Judith, 300
Jones, William B. "Stoney," 228
Jones Brewing Company, 227–28
Joy of Cooking, The (Rombauer and
    Becker), 215, 217

Kalama (Wash.), 112
Katz, Solomon, 9
Kelly, Kathy, 61–62
Kemper Pilsner, 107
Kessler Brewing Company, 296
Killer Whale Stout, 150
Kirwan, Dorothy O'Connel, 88
Klinkenborg, Verlyn, 223–25
Koch, Jim, 232–33
kräusening, 229–30, 318
Kriek, 322
Kuhn, Loni, 101, 311

lager, 89, 323–25. *See also* Amber lager;
        Beer; *and specific brands of lagers*
    American, 16–17
    Batter
        for Fried Fish, Edy's, **246**
        for Fried Fish, Thin, **247**
        Tempura, **247**
    in California, 136–37, 143–45
    carbonation of, 14–15, 17
    and Cheese Soup, Wisconsin, **196**
    Clams or Mussels Steamed in, **252–53**
    Dressing, Warm Potato Salad with,
        76
    food matching and, 27
    home brewing, 329
    and Lemon Marinade for Fish or
        Chicken, **155**
    Maria's Pasta and Eggplant in, **254**
    in Midwest, 178
    Pork Shoulder Broiled in, **207**
    revolution, 63–70
    serving temperature for, 18
    yeast for, 10–11, 13, 64–66
lamb
    Burgers, **287–88**
    Chops with Whole Garlic Cloves
        and Summer Herbs, **169**
    with Leeks and Ale, Braised, **262**
    marinades for, **156–58**
    Shanks Braised in Beer and
        Cilantro, **312**
    Stew, Sonoran (*Birria*), **311**

Lambic, 322
Larkspur Landing (Calif.), 151–52
L'Avenue Restaurant (San Francisco),
    173, 212
laws, beer, 4, 34–35, 40, 105, 190, 232
Lear, Tobias, 38
Leek(s)
    Braised Lamb with Ale and, **262**
    and Cabbage Soup, **239**
    and Carrots in Steam Beer, **171–72**
    in Horseradish Vinaigrette, **115**
Lemon
    Beef Brisket with Spices and, **168–69**
    and Lager Marinade for Fish or
        Chicken, **155**
Lescó, **205**
Levinson, Marlene, 72, 235
light ale. *See also specific brands*
    Lobsters Boiled in, **51**
    Pheasant or Chicken and Wild Rice
        Braised in, **57–58**
light beer (lager), 5, 14, 16, 324. *See also*
        specific brands
    Sauce, Sole Stuffed with crab in,
        73–74
    Shrimp Boiled in Spices and, **273**
Lime Juice, Red Onions Pickled in, **309**
Lind Brewing (San Leandro, Calif.),
    142
Liptauer Cheese, **194–95**
Lobster(s), 45
    Boiled in Light Ale, **51**
    Rolls, **250**
Lone Star Brewing (San Antonio), 292
Long Island Brewing (N.Y.), 232
Lord Chesterfield Ale, 227
Los Angeles, 145–47, 172
Louisville (Ky.), 264–65
Lovett, Michael, 140
Lucas, Jimella, 112
lunch, saloon, 83–85, 89–90

macaroni, Broccoli Soup with, **238**
MacAuliffe, Jack, 139–41
McMenamin, Mike, 111
McSorley's Old Ale House, 86–90
Madison, James, 36, 39
Maerzen (Märzen), 17, 111, 323
Maibock, 14, 17, 323
mail order sources, 332–33
Main, Nancy, 112
malt, 8, 10, 326
    color and, 13
    in early America, 35–36

malt (*cont.*)
  in Midwest, 187
  in Northwest, 105, 107
malting, 316
Malt Liquor, 324
malt vinegar, 25
Manhattan Brewing Company (N.Y.),
  230
Mares, William, 328
Margaret's Onion Cheese Bread,
  199–200
Margaret's Potato Pizza, **117–18**
Marinade, 147, **155–59**
  Ale, for Steak or Lamb, **156**
  Bourbon Stout, **157**
  Chinese Hoisin, **157**
  Lemon and Lager, for Fish or
    Chicken, **155**
  Porter or Stout and Molasses, **156**
  Smoky Rauchbier, **158–59**
  Tandoori, **158**
Marinated Mussels, **251**
Marin Brewing (Larkspur Landing,
  Calif.), 151–52
Marlene's Three Herring Salads, **71–73**
Martin, Reid, 151
Marzipan, Nestor, 139, 331
mashing, 317
Massachusetts Bay Brewing Company,
  233
Massachusetts Bay Colony, 30, 34–35,
  44
Matt, F. X., 228–32
Matt's Light, 230
Matt's Premium, 230
Maytag, Fritz, 8, 137, 142
mead, 6
meat. *See* beef; Lamb; Pork; Sausage;
  Veal
Meat Loaf
  with Beer Gravy, Nancy's Spicy,
    260–61
  Sandwich, **286**
Mendocino Brewing Company
  (Hopland, Calif.), 140–41
Menger, William, 291
Merchant du Vin, 104
Mexican-style dishes, 293
  Burgers, **288**
  Burritos, **306**
  Chicken in Green Mole Nut Sauce,
    310–11
  Gorditas, **302–3**
  Grilled Chicken Torta, **285**

Mexican-style dishes (*cont.*)
  Guacamole, **309**
  Quesadillas, **308**
  Red Onions Pickled in Lime Juice,
    309
  Salsa Cruda, **308**
  Sonoran Lamb Stew (*Birria*), **311**
  Tacos, **305–6**
  Tamales with Chorizo and Sweet
    Potato Filling, **303–4**
  Tostadas, **307**
microbreweries, 20–22
  in Midwest, 139–45
  in Northeast, 226–34
  in Northwest, 104–12
  in South, 265–67
Micro-Brewery Convention (1989), 9
Middle Ages, 8, 24
Midwest, American
  brewing in, 177–78
    brew-pubs, 140, 149–50,
      188–91
    microbreweries, 183–86
  lager revolution in, 63–70
  recipes of, **192–220**
  taverns in, 187–88
Mild Ale, 14, 18, 112, 321
Millar, Bill, 142
Miller, Capt., 38–39
Miller, Frederick, 68
Miller, Margaret, 117–18, 199
millet, 7
Milwaukee, 65–67, 70, 185–88
Mirlitons and Seafood Ragout Cajun
  Style, **276–77**
Mitchell, Joseph, 87, 90
Modesto (Calif.), 143–44
Molasses and Porter or Stout
  Marinade, **156**
Mole Nut Sauce, Green, Chicken in,
  310–11
monasteries, 10
Monroe (Wis.), 180–83
Montana Beverages (Helena), 296
Morgan, Scotty, 144
Morris, Anthony, 36–38
Morrow, Dave, 144
Mother Fresh-Roasted, 88
Mountain Brewers (Vt.), 234
Muffuletta
  Fried Eggplant, **284**
  Salad, **270**
Mushrooms, Shiitake, and Asparagus
  in Sesame Dressing, **159**

Mussels
  Marinated, **251**
  Steamed in Beer, **252–53**
Mustard
  Beer and Horseradish, **219**
  Honey Beer, **99**
  Pork Chops in Beer with Onions
    and, **206**
  Vinaigrette, Asparagus Wrapped in
    Country Ham in, **271**
Mustard Greens, Turnips and, **60–61**

Nahcotta (Wash.), 112
Nancy's Spicy Meat Loaf with Beer
    Gravy, **260–61**
Near East, 7–8
Neptune's Nectar, 150
Nestor Marzipan's O Death Where Is
    Thy Stingo Ale, **331**
New Albion Ale, 140, 151
New Albion Brewery, 139–40
New Amsterdam, 34
New Amsterdam Ale, 231–32
New Amsterdam Amber Lager, 231
New England Brewing, 234
New Haven Brewing (Conn.), 234
New Orleans, 264–65, 280
New Orleans Hot Pot, **280–81**
New Ulm (Minn.), 178–79
New York City
  beer gardens in, 69
  breweries in, 230–31
  saloons in, 84, 86–90
  taverns in, 41, 48
Ninkasi (goddess), 3, 8–9
Ninkasi beer, 9
Noodles, Chinese, and Green Beans
    with Smoky Black Bean Sauce,
    Dry Fried, **174**
Noonan, Greg, 329
North Coast Brewing (Fort Bragg,
    Calif.), 141–42
Northeast, American, 221–62
  brewing in, 226–34
  recipes of, **235–62**
  taverns in, 222–26
Northwest, American, 103–32
  brewing in, 103–12
  recipes of, **113–32**
Nouhan, Joseph, 153
Nuts. *See specific names of nuts*

Oakes, Nancy, 212, 260
Oakland (Calif.), 150

oats, 7, 13
Octoberfest, 178, 323
Odell Brewing Company (Fort
    Collins, Colo.), 295–96
Ogelthorpe, Gen., 40
Oktoberfest, 17, 111
Old City Brewing (Austin), 293
Old Dominion Brewing (near
    Washington, D. C.), 266
Oldenberg Brewery (Fort Mitchell,
    Ohio), 266
Oldenburg, Ray, 70
Old Marlborough Brewing Company
    (Mass.), 233–34
Old New York Brewing Company
    (N.Y.), 231
Old Post Road Real Ale, 233–34
Olive Dressing, Muffuletta, **270**
Omelets, Hangtown Fry, **171**
Onion(s), 89–90
  and Beer Soup, **95**
  Braised in Porter, **60**
  Cheese Bread, Margaret's, **199–200**
  Pennsylvania Dutch Stuffed, **77**
  Pork Chops in Beer with Mustard
    and, **206**
  Raw, and Limburger Sandwich, **286**
  Red, Pickled in Lime Juice, **309**
  Rings, **248**
  Tavern Pickled, **94–95**
Orton, Vrest, 46
Orzo Salad
  Corn and Watercress, **160**
  Smoked Chicken, **160**
O'Shea's Black Beans, **313**
O'Shea's Mad Hatter (San Francisco),
    313
Owens, Bill, 150
Oxtail, Deviled, **101–2**
Oyster(s), 45
  and Fish Croquettes, **126–27**
  Fried, **242–43**
  in Garlic Bread Crumbs, Baked, **277**
  Hangtown Fry, **171**
  Loaf, **283**
  Pickled, **49**
  Po' Boy, **283**
  Steamed in Beer, **252–53**

Pabst, 67
Pabst, Frederick, 66, 68
Pabst Park (Milwaukee), 70
Pacific Coast Brewing, 150
Pacific Crest Ale, 112

ILLUSTRATION CREDITS

The photographs and illustrations reproduced in this book were provided with the permission and courtesy of the following:

Journal of the American Oriental Society: 3, 7 (top left, bottom left)
The Curiosities of Ale and Beer, Bickerdyke: 4, 8, 10 (all), 11 (all)
Academic Press, *Food: The Gift of Osiris,* Darby et al.: 6
New York Public Library Picture Collection: 7 (right), 40, 41, 68, 88, 89, 183, 223, 224, 225, 231 (left)
Anchor Brewing Co.: 9, 136, 137, 138, 140
Eldridge Pope Brewery: 24
Beer USA, Anderson: 30 (right), 34, 36 (left)
Saloons of the Old West, Erdoes: 30 (left), 134, 288
The Center of Alcohol Studies, Rutgers University: 35
100 Years of Brewing: 36 (right), 64 (all), 66, 67, 111, 178, 226, 231 (right)
Stagecoach and Tavern Days, Earle: 38 (left), 42, 48
The Historical Society of Pennsylvania: 38 (right)
Library of Congress: 69, 85 (right)
Missouri Historical Society: 68, 70 (right), 190 (both)
The Metropolitan Museum of Art, Bequest of Edward W. C. Arnold, 1954; The Edward W. C. Arnold Collection of New York Prints, Maps and Pictures. (54.90.166): 70 (left)
The Montana Historical Society: 82, 112, 290, 295
The Old Time Saloon, Ade (Omnigraphics, Inc.): 83 (both), 102, 152
The Book Club of California (Reproduced through the courtesy of the Book Club of California, copyright 1950, in *Bonanza Banquets.* All rights reserved. Reproduced by permission): 85 (left)
Henry E. Huntington Library and Art Gallery: 86, endpaper
Yakima Valley Museum and Historical Association: 109
California State Library: 135 (both)
Milwaukee County Historical Society: 177
Chicago Historical Society: 180, 181
State Historical Society of Wisconsin: 185
D. G. Yuengling & Son Brewery: 227
F. X. Matt Brewery: 229
Oldenberg Brewery: 266
Colorado Historical Society: 291
Spoetzl Brewery (Gambrinus Importing): 292 (both)

A Note About the Authors

Bruce Aidells was born and raised in California. He graduated from the University of California at Berkeley and holds a Ph.D. from the University of California at Santa Cruz. He is the chef and owner of the nationally known Aidells Sausage Company, and he teaches cooking. A founder of and formerly the chef at Poulet Restaurant and Charcuterie in Berkeley, he has also served as a restaurant consultant in the Bay Area. His articles have appeared in *Food & Wine* and *Bon Appétit*.

Denis Kelly was born in Brooklyn, New York, graduated from St. Mary's College in Moraga, California, and did graduate work at the Sorbonne in Paris and at Indiana University. Now living in Oakland, he teaches wine classes at the University of California Extension and throughout the Bay Area. He has written many articles on food and wine for such publications as *Wines & Spirits* and the Oakland *Tribune*.

Bruce Aidells and Denis Kelly are also the authors of *Hot Links & Country Flavors: Sausages in American Regional Cooking*, published in 1990, which was the first book in the Knopf Cooks American series and won the International Association of Cooking Professionals Award for Best Cookbook on a Single Subject that year.

A Note on the Type

The text of this book is set in Garamond. It is not a true copy of any of the designs of Claude Garamond (1480–1561), but an adaptation of his types, which set the European standard for two centuries. It probably owes as much to the designs of Jean Jannon, a Protestant printer working in Sedan in the early seventeenth century, who had worked with Garamond's romans earlier, in Paris, and who was denied their use because of the Catholic censorship. Jannon's matrices came into the possession of the Imprimerie Nationale, where they were thought to be by Garamond himself, and so described when the Imprimerie revived the type in 1900. This particular version is based on an adaptation by Morris Fuller Benton.

Printed and bound by Courier Book Companies, Westford, Massachusetts

Designed by Mia Vander Els and Barbara Balch

Knopf Cooks American

The series of cookbooks that celebrates the culinary heritage of America, telling different aspects of our story through recipes interspersed with historical lore, personal reflections, and the recollections of old-timers.

Already published:
Biscuits, Spoonbread, and Sweet Potato Pie by Bill Neal
Hot Links & Country Flavors by Bruce Aidells and Denis Kelly
Barbecued Ribs, Smoked Butts, and Other Great Feeds by Jeanne Voltz
We Called It Macaroni by Nancy Verde Barr
The West Coast Cook Book by Helen Evans Brown
Pleasures of the Good Earth by Edward Giobbi
The Brooklyn Cookbook by Lyn Stallworth and Rod Kennedy, Jr.
Dungeness Crabs and Blackberry Cobblers by Janie Hibler
Preserving Today by Jeanne Lesem
Blue Corn and Chocolate by Elisabeth Rozin
Real Beer & Good Eats by Bruce Aidells and Denis Kelly

"Our food tells us where we came from and who we are . . . "